## THE BRITISH HOLISTIC MEDICAL ASSOCIATION

# OVERCOMING DEPRESSION

## Dr Richard Gillett
MA MB BCh MRCPsych

SERIES EDITOR

## Dr Patrick C. Pietroni
MB BS FRCGP MRCP

DORLING KINDERSLEY · LONDON

To
Kathryn,
Arthur and
Alexander

**Senior editor** Jemima Dunne

**Art editor** Philip Lord

**Editor** James Allen

**Designer** Iona McGlashan

**Managing editor** Daphne Razazan

First published in Great Britain in 1987 by
Dorling Kindersley Publishers Limited
9 Henrietta Street, London WC2E 8PS

reprinted 1991

**British Library Cataloguing in Publication Data**

Gillett, Richard
 Overcoming depression.
 1. Depression, Mental
 I. Title
 616.85'2706    RC537

 ISBN 0-86318-223-2 Hardback
 ISBN 0-86318-161-9 Paperback

Printed and bound in Hong Kong

**NOTE**

In this book the masculine pronoun "he"
is generally used when referring to the
client or therapist. This is for convenience
and does not reflect a preference for
either sex.

# Contents

# ▪ Preface ▪

The British Holistic Medical Association was launched in 1983 to address a growing need amongst doctors, medical students, the practitioners of alternative, or complementary medicine and the public. This growing need was best expressed by H.R.H. the Prince of Wales when he spoke to the B.M.A. Conference in 1983. He suggested: *"Human nature is such that we are frequently prevented from seeing that what is taken for today's unorthodoxy is probably to be tomorrow's convention"*.

He went on to add: *"The whole imposing edifice of modern medicine, for all its breathtaking successes is like the celebrated Tower of Pisa, slightly off-balance"*.

"Balance" is a critical concept in "Holism". This new word is not synonymous with complementary or alternative and it must be stressed that the wholesale application of alternative medicine is not one of the aims of the British Holistic Medical Association. Nor is an unthinking and self-destructive criticism of orthodox medicine appropriate. Holism is about responding to the whole person in his or her environment. It involves actively encouraging a partnership between doctor and patient and this is especially true for depression.

Human unhappiness, malaise and a sense of hopelessness are the fertile soil for much dis-ease. The clinical label of depression can all too often be attached to situations and events that form part of everyday experience. The move away from medication of all sorts, especially the psychoactive drugs, is a clearly observable phenomenon in our culture. The best form of "alternative medicine" is to be able to listen. To listen to oneself and to others, be they immediate family, patients or clients. This book lays the groundwork for the medicine of the future – a true marriage between the best of scientific medicine and the most appropriate therapies for helping the person regain his or her physical, mental and spiritual well-being.

Dr Patrick C. Pietroni MB BS FRCGP MRCP
*Senior Lecturer in General Practice*
St. Mary's Hospital Medical School, London

# How to use this book

Whether you are prone to severe bouts of depression, or whether your life is more generally inhibited or unexciting, this book suggests possible ways to help you change the situation. There are some methods that I have not mentioned, and some I have only alluded to. This does not mean they do not work, but rather that I am willing to recommend only those ways I *know* can work from my own experience. This comes from three main sources. As a hospital psychiatrist I have treated people in the more severe states of depression. As a private psychiatrist and psychotherapist I have focused on people with more everyday problems, such as minor depressions and loss of spirit. Thirdly, and perhaps most important in providing me with the impetus to write this book, I have experienced periods of the blues, times of inhibition and years without much sparkle. I have a determined personal quest to live life as fully as possible; this has led me to try many different forms of therapy as a client, as well as to try out many approaches to the enjoyment of living.

Depression is such a wide subject, ranging from biochemistry to the antics of the life-force, that this book can take you in many different directions. You may prefer to take a broad overview or you may wish to find a specific route to treatment. If you want to find out what is currently happening to you, a relative, or a friend, then start by answering the "Are you depressed?" questionnaire in Part 1, which will place you on one of six levels of liveliness. If you are in a depressed state, turn to the flow charts at the beginning of Part 2 to find out the possible causes and influences in your situation. The answers will refer you to clarifying sections, from which you may be directed to a treatment in Part 3.

Whether you are referred to a specific treatment or not, it is worth reading the first section in Part 3 ("Choosing an appropriate therapy") to find out what kinds of treatment are likely to be suitable for you, given your own preferences, as well as the causes and severity of your depression. Whatever treatments you prefer, it is also a good idea to read the whole section on self-help which can be used on its own or in conjunction with other forms of treatment.

If, having answered the questionnaire in Part 1, you find yourself on one of the top two levels of liveliness, turn directly to the energy profile in Part 4. This will give you some indication of the aspects of your energy that are more or less developed, and where there is room for even greater vitality. Part 4 then continues with an ambitious programme for preventing depression and aiming for a more lively life.

# Part 1

# WHAT IS DEPRESSION?

# Introduction

Imagine yourself sitting down after a dull day at work or a tedious day at home. The sky is grey, a colour which reflects your mood. You turn on the television and sit down to watch the news, which is bad, followed by a programme which you have no interest in at all. Yet for some reason you continue to sit slumped in your chair, and you feel strangely tempted to stay there all evening. Perhaps you wake up the following morning with a vague sense of unfulfilment, and the thought of "another day" goes through your mind with a feeling of pointless inevitability.

I have not met anyone who has not at some time felt down or low. In those moments it seems as if your energy has just disappeared and you can't be bothered with anything. Even if you know that some favourite activity could lift you out of your low mood, you can't seem to find the motivation to start. The less you do and the more passively you allow the mood to possess you, the worse you feel. Perhaps you believe there isn't much to hope for or, if there is something, it's just not worth reaching. Somehow you don't even want to feel better. You don't want help and yet you would like to be delivered from the state of inertia. At any helpful suggestion you feel "What's the point?" You have lost your basic motivation and you feel that if your life ended without you having to do anything or feel any pain it would be convenient. The spirit of life has gone and it is hard to believe it will be back.

From such beginnings it is occasionally possible to spiral slowly downwards to the depths of depression where all seems black, where the world is hopeless, where you feel rotten to the core and a worthwhile future is impossible to imagine. In this state you have lost your sense of worth, your energy and your interest, and you are pervaded by a terrible sense of emptiness. You may feel like ending your life or you may be so depleted of energy that you cannot move your body or even speak. I have seen people totally mute and immobile, with faces haunted and blank, lost in depressive despair. Much more often I have seen other people experience times of low energy, or have myself experienced such times, when everything seemed blue.

Popularly, both states are described as depression, and clinically there is no distinct dividing line between feeling a bit low and being incapacitated in depressive immobility. Though the two states are enormously different, there is a continuum of intermediate states connecting them. This part of the book aims to define different energetic states and their characteristics beyond the established clinical terms. As a result, you should be able to identify your own state and some feelings and attitudes that accompany it.

# DIFFERENT ENERGETIC STATES

The whole spectrum of energetic states – from feeling fully alive to feeling hopelessly depressed – is divided in the chart (below) into six levels of liveliness. In clinical terminology only the more severe stages of depression are sub-divided, so I have included the clinical equivalents where applicable.

**CLINICAL TERMS USED TO DESCRIBE DEPRESSION**

*Reactive depression* means depression as a reaction to an external event. *Endogenous depression* means depression from within (i.e. caused by genetic or biochemical factors). These terms were based on the historical belief that milder depression was usually "reactive" to an outside situation, while severe depression was usually not related to external events. It is now realized that this is not necessarily true. So the two terms reactive depression and endogenous depression are now usually used only to denote the severity of depression – roughly equivalent to the categories used in this book, "grey" and "black". *Depressive psychosis* means a depression so severe that there is a loss of touch with reality. The person is crazy with depression. Such cases are extremely rare and usually seen only in psychiatric hospitals.

## ENERGETIC STATES AND THEIR CLINICAL EQUIVALENTS

In this chart, the spectrum of energetic states is divided into six levels of liveliness. These levels are used as categories throughout the book.

| Level of Liveliness | Energetic state | Common reply to question: "How do you feel?" | Clinical terms |
|---|---|---|---|
| GOLD | You feel good and fully alive. You are confident, creative and energetic | "Great" | Healthy |
| LOSS OF SPARKLE | You feel alright, but somehow life is not satisfying enough | "OK" | Healthy |
| BLUE | You have temporary episodes where you feel a bit low on energy | "Fed up" or "Depressed" | Healthy |
| GREY | You have a longer episode where you feel very down and lose confidence and self-respect. The world looks grey | "Depressed" | Reactive depression |
| BLACK | You feel utterly hopeless. Your thoughts are of self-blame and suicide. The future seems black | "Depressed" | Endogenous depression |
| WHITE | There is no future, only nothingness. You believe there is nothing inside you. You lose touch with reality | No reply | Depressive psychosis |

# HOW COMMON IS DEPRESSION?

According to the World Health Organization, something like 100 million people in the world are depressed at any one time. Figures on the incidence of depression over the last few decades seem to show that the incidence is rising alarmingly. In the 1930s the incidence of depression in many studies was found to be less than one in 1000, whereas now, studies of the prevalence of depression in society show incidences of between six and 25 per cent. The difference probably depends entirely on the definition of the word "depression", which has become more fashionable and is being used to describe far milder states than previously. If you include "loss of sparkle" as a category of depression, over 90 per cent of people are depressed. Perhaps it is, at the moment, more acceptable to say that 90 per cent of people are less lively than they could be, and of these, about 15 per cent have the quality of their lives seriously affected by periods of severe depression.

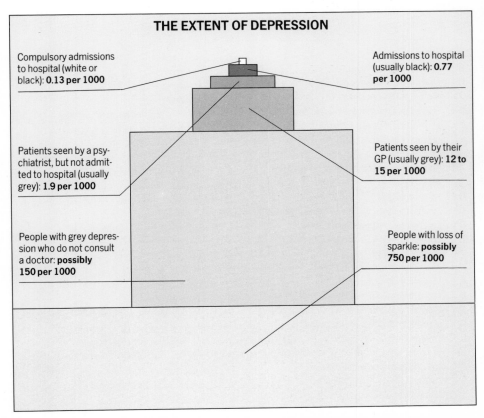

## THE EXTENT OF DEPRESSION

Compulsory admissions to hospital (white or black): **0.13 per 1000**

Admissions to hospital (usually black): **0.77 per 1000**

Patients seen by a psychiatrist, but not admitted to hospital (usually grey): **1.9 per 1000**

Patients seen by their GP (usually grey): **12 to 15 per 1000**

People with grey depression who do not consult a doctor: **possibly 150 per 1000**

People with loss of sparkle: **possibly 750 per 1000**

# Are you depressed?

Your place on the continuum of six levels of liveliness can be roughly determined by doing the questionnaire (below), then scoring it on page 15. For each question decide which of the statements A, B, C, D or E is most true for you at this moment and put a tick in the appropriate box. Don't spend too long deliberating on which gradation is more exactly applicable to you – answer the questionnaire as quickly as possible.

## QUESTIONNAIRE

### 1

A ☐ I am confident and decisive

B ☐ I am fairly confident and decisive

C ☐ I have less confidence than I could have and tend to put off decisions

D ☐ I have lost confidence and avoid decisions

E ☐ I have no confidence in myself and cannot make any decisions at all

### 2

A ☐ Though it has ups and downs, I thoroughly enjoy my life

B ☐ I quite enjoy life

C ☐ I do not enjoy my life as much as I could

D ☐ I am not enjoying my life any longer

E ☐ I do not enjoy my life at all and can hardly imagine doing so

### 3

A ☐ I value myself all the time

B ☐ I sometimes value myself

C ☐ I sometimes don't think much of myself

D ☐ I don't think much of myself at all

E ☐ I'm worthless

### 4

A ☐ I have love and respect for myself

B ☐ I like myself

C ☐ I am disappointed in myself

D ☐ I don't like myself at all

E ☐ I hate myself

### 5

A ☐ I am energetic and full of life

B ☐ I am fairly energetic

C ☐ I get more fatigued than I would like

D ☐ I get tired after any activity

E ☐ I am too tired to do anything

### 6

A ☐ I am curious and interested in what I do

B ☐ I am usually interested in what I do

C ☐ I am sometimes bored

D ☐ I've lost interest in things

E ☐ I couldn't care about anything at all

### 7

A ☐ I feel great

B ☐ I feel quite good

C ☐ I feel alright

D ☐ I feel depressed

E ☐ I feel miserable and desperate

### 8

A ☐ My feelings are varied and vivid

B ☐ My feelings are sometimes a bit bland

C ☐ My feelings are duller than usual

D ☐ I can hardly feel anything at all

E ☐ I feel totally empty

## 9

A ☐ Everything seems full of colour
B ☐ Everything sometimes seems a bit dull
C ☐ Everything usually seems a bit drab
D ☐ Everything seems grey
E ☐ Everything seems black

## 10

A ☐ In general, I love people
B ☐ In general, I like people
C ☐ I feel a bit distanced from other people
D ☐ I feel indifferent about others
E ☐ I don't care about anybody

## 11

A ☐ My sex life is full and deeply satisfying
B ☐ My sex life is quite good
C ☐ My sex life is less full than it could be
D ☐ I've gone off sex
E ☐ I have totally lost interest in sex

## 12

A ☐ My life is satisfying
B ☐ My life is fairly satisfying
C ☐ I keep feeling there could be more to life
D ☐ Nothing satisfies me any more
E ☐ Nothing will ever satisfy me

## 13

A ☐ I am motivated by an inner energy or excitement rather than by an idea of what I ought to be doing
B ☐ I often have to push myself and use my will to complete a task
C ☐ I often find it hard to get motivated
D ☐ I've lost my motivation
E ☐ I don't want to do anything at all

## 14

A ☐ Life's purpose is obvious to me or there's no need for me to know life's purpose
B ☐ I sometimes wonder "What's life's purpose?"
C ☐ I often wonder "What's life's purpose?"
D ☐ I see little point in living
E ☐ I see no point in living

## 15

A ☐ I feel I am a good person
B ☐ I feel I am quite a good person
C ☐ I am not a very good person
D ☐ I am a bad person
E ☐ I am a disgusting person

## 16

A ☐ I love life and don't want to leave it
B ☐ Occasionally the thought of not having to struggle any longer is a temptation
C ☐ Sometimes I have suicidal thoughts though I would never carry them out
D ☐ I have plans about committing suicide
E ☐ Death is the only answer and my family would be better off if I were dead

## 17

A ☐ I can concentrate on the task at hand
B ☐ I can usually concentrate well
C ☐ I have difficulty concentrating sometimes
D ☐ I can't concentrate any more
E ☐ My concentration is so bad that I cannot complete anything

## 18

A ☐ I am optimistic
B ☐ I am usually quite optimistic
C ☐ I am worried about the future
D ☐ The future is bad and I can't believe it will get better
E ☐ The future is utterly hopeless or I feel a catastrophe is coming soon

## 19

A ☐ I feel responsible for what I do but never guilty
B ☐ I sometimes feel guilty
C ☐ I can easily be made to feel guilty
D ☐ I feel guilty nearly all the time, even though I know this feeling is not rationally justified
E ☐ I feel wracked by guilt because I have done terrible wrongs

## 20

A ☐ I never deserve punishment for my mistakes
B ☐ I sometimes feel that life or God may punish me for what I think or do
C ☐ I feel I deserve to be punished
D ☐ I feel I am being punished or will be punished
E ☐ I know I am being punished or will be punished and I know I deserve it

## 21

A ☐ I cherish my body
B ☐ I take fairly good care of my body
C ☐ I don't care that much about my body
D ☐ I would like to harm my body
E ☐ I ought and deserve to die

## 22

A ☐ I am a success in my own eyes
B ☐ I am reasonably successful in my own eyes
C ☐ I sometimes think I'm a bit of a failure
D ☐ I feel I'm a failure
E ☐ I feel I'm a complete failure as a person

## 23

A ☐ I enjoy my work
B ☐ I quite enjoy my work
C ☐ I don't enjoy my work as much as I would like to
D ☐ I can't work as well as I used to
E ☐ I can't work at all

## 24

A ☐ I have initiative and never have trouble getting things started
B ☐ I usually have quite a bit of initiative
C ☐ I sometimes find it hard to get started at something
D ☐ It has become much harder to get things going
E ☐ I cannot initiate anything

## 25

A ☐ I feel I look good in my own way
B ☐ I feel I look OK
C ☐ I don't feel I look so good
D ☐ I feel more and more unattractive
E ☐ I feel I am ugly *or* I feel repulsive *or* I smell repulsive

## 26

A ☐ I feel healthy
B ☐ I feel fairly healthy
C ☐ I feel there could be something physically wrong with me
D ☐ I have become preoccupied with what may be physically wrong with me
E ☐ I am diseased. I have a serious physical illness. I know this despite investigations and medical advice to the contrary

## 27

A ☐ I sleep well (in terms of my own particular sleep patterns)
B ☐ I sleep fairly well
C ☐ I don't feel as refreshed by sleep as I would like
D ☐ I have been sleeping worse recently
E ☐ I awake very early in the morning and cannot get back to sleep

## 28

A ☐ I usually feel happy to wake up
B ☐ I usually feel OK when I wake up
C ☐ I often don't like waking up
D ☐ I am feeling much more down in the mornings
E ☐ I feel terrible in the mornings and feel a dread of the day to come

## 29

A ☐ I do not let other people's opinions make me judgemental about myself
B ☐ I sometimes let other people's opinions make me judgemental about myself
C ☐ I am easily affected by what I think others think about me
D ☐ I feel, perhaps irrationally, that people do not like me or are against me
E ☐ I believe people are disgusted by me *or* I believe people are plotting against me

## 30

A ☐ I have a good appetite and enjoy my food
B ☐ My appetite is fairly good
C ☐ I don't enjoy my food as much as I would like
D ☐ My appetite has got much worse *or* I can't stop eating though I don't enjoy the food
E ☐ I have no appetite at all

## 31

A ☐ My weight is stable and feels right for me
B ☐ I could do with gaining or losing a little weight
C ☐ I am too thin or too fat
D ☐ I have lost more than 2.3 kg (5 lb) without trying to diet *or* I have gained more than 4.5 kg (10 lb)
E ☐ I have lost more than 4.5 kg (10 lb) without trying to diet

## 32

A ☐ I move at a speed that is natural for me
B ☐ I sometimes move too fast or too slowly
C ☐ I often move too fast or too slowly
D ☐ I seem to have got slower than my usual speed
E ☐ I am much slower than usual and it's an effort to move at all

## 33

A ☐ Both I and the outside world feel real and present
B ☐ I sometimes feel a little distance between myself and the outside world

**C** ☐ I sometimes feel unreal or that the things around me are unreal

**D** ☐ I feel a distance and a sense of unreality with both myself and the outside world

**E** ☐ I feel I do not exist *or* I feel my brain is empty *or* I feel there is nothing inside me

### 34

Thinking about these questions has made me feel:

**A** ☐ Optimistic
**B** ☐ Nothing in particular
**C** ☐ Pessimistic
**D** ☐ Bad
**E** ☐ Awful

Work out your score according to the system below, and then refer to "What does your score mean?" to discover which level of liveliness you may be on.

#### How to score

| | | |
|---|---|---|
| Total number of **A** | ×4 = | |
| Total number of **B** | ×3 = | |
| Total number of **C** | ×2 = | |
| Total number of **D** | ×1 = | |
| Total number of **E** | ×0 = | |
| Total score= | | |

**What does your score mean?**

■ **126-136:** Write to me, care of the publisher, and tell me how you did it. Then throw away this book.

■ **110-126:** You are not depressed, though perhaps life could improve (see *Your energy profile*, page 191).

■ **70-110:** You have more or less lost your sparkle (see *Different levels of liveliness*, page 16).

■ **60-90:** If temporary, you may have the blues (see *Different levels of liveliness*, page 16).

■ **34-70:** You may be in a state of grey depression (see *Different levels of liveliness*, page 16).

■ **0-34:** You may be in a state of black depression (see *Different levels of liveliness*, page 16). Many people in black depression and all those in white depression would not have the energy or the interest to complete this questionnaire.

**The case of Mr. X.** The following story illustrates the depressed states (loss of sparkle to white depression), and the fact that they can be traversed by one person. This is an unusually extreme example, but it is based on a true case history.

Mr X tended to depend on others. He had a marriage in which nearly all the decisions were made by his wife. His work as a clerk was dull and he did not really enjoy his routine and well-organized life. He coped externally but had limited internal satisfaction. He had his good days occasionally and he had periods when he felt a little blue. There were no children and over the years he and his wife gradually became distant. He would come home from work, then watch television, read or do some household job; they would hardly talk. He had few friends. Life was dull but he did not complain.

His wife did. After 13 years she left him. Within two days he was in a grey depression. Quite suddenly he had lost his will to fight for anything, his wife and life included. He felt empty and miserable. He did not have much feeling about his wife leaving; rather he complained of a lack of feeling for anything. He felt worthless. He was interested in nothing and found he could not concentrate. Everything seemed grey and he did not wish to contemplate the future.

It was in this state that I first saw him. He had had thoughts of ending his life, and although it was clear that he was very angry with his wife for leaving him, he was too far depressed to be able to get in contact with such a feeling. His continuing deterioration served, whether consciously intended or not, to punish his wife with guilt. He was admitted to hospital and within twelve hours was in a state of black depression.

He felt hopeless and believed that there was no future and that he would never get better. The look on his face was one of blank apathy. He lost his appetite and woke up at about four

---

# DIFFERENT LEVELS OF LIVELINESS

The following flow chart lists some comparative characteristics of each level of liveliness. Having answered the questionnaire on page 12 to find out your own level, you may be able to identify with some of the characteristics and feelings described.

---

## ■ GOLD ■

Only a small percentage of people live out the potential colour, variety and creativity that is possible to them, given the limits of their talents and situations.

**Some characteristics** (though not at all times in all situations):
■ Confidence
■ A feeling of self-worth
■ Creativity
■ Love of self and others
■ Physical energy
■ Mental interest
■ Vivid emotions
■ Sexual energy
■ A sense of "aliveness"
■ The world appears bright and interesting
■ Clear and acute senses (vision, hearing, touch, taste and smell)
■ A capacity to wonder
■ Inquisitiveness
■ Full responsibility taken for life decisions and life course

**Advice:** stay here if you can. See *Keeping depression out of your life*, page 188.

## ■ LOSS OF SPARKLE ■

Few people manage to keep to the very high standards of gold. More frequently they cope externally and may be very successful, but life is a little muted, less vivid, more routine.

*Continued in next column*

---

*Continued from previous column*

**Some characteristics:**
■ Less inner confidence
■ The world appears less vivid
■ Life is not enjoyed to the full
■ Pressure and will-power are often required to keep going
■ Curiosity is diminished
■ Satisfaction and pleasure are limited, though there may be no awareness that there could be something more to life
■ Pleasure is limited
■ Some distance between self and others
■ Experiences tend to lack immediacy

**Advice:** see *Self-help*, page 121, and *Keeping depression out of your life*, page 188.

## ■ BLUE ■

Everyone gets the blues now and again. Temporary episodes of feeling down occur after unfortunate events or sometimes for no tangible reason. Popularly termed "depression", the episodes usually last only a few days, or even a few hours.

**Some characteristics:**
■ Feeling down
■ Feeling listless
■ Questioning the point of everything
■ Temporary loss of energy and motivation
■ Temporary loss of interest
■ Temporary loss of care about self or others

*Continued in next column*

o'clock every morning. He felt marginally better in the second half of the day, but no more hopeful. Everything appeared black to him: the world, the past, the present, the future, himself, other people. His wife leaving him had become only a small part of the global calamity he felt around him. He was in despair, yet too empty to be able to feel it. No understanding could change his black picture of life. He was put on anti-depressant drugs, which would take one or two

*Continued from previous column*

■ Considerable will-power may be needed to keep going
**Advice:** see *Self-help*, page 121.

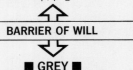

**BARRIER OF WILL**

### ■ GREY ■
**(Reactive depression)**
The first category which would clinically be termed "depressed". You may lose the will or interest to keep fighting, though you have not lost your sense of hope altogether.
**Some characteristics:**
■ Feeling down and empty
■ Lack of belief in self
■ Loss of energy, creativity and interest
■ Loss of concentration, forgetfulness
■ Loss of self-respect and confidence
■ Loss of feeling and libido
■ The world looks grey
■ Self-pity
**Advice:** see *Lifting depression*, page 118.

**BARRIER OF HOPE**

### ■ BLACK ■
**(Endogenous depression)**
A number of physical characteristics become prominent and there is a feeling of being taken over by an irresistible process of emptiness.
**Some characteristics:** characteristics of grey, plus:
■ Loss of appetite and/or weight
■ Tendency to wake early in the morning
■ Hopeless and suicidal thoughts

*Continued in next column*

*Continued from previous column*

■ Depression is worse in the mornings
■ Strong feelings of guilt, though with some realization that this is not wholly justified
■ The future seems black; indeed, it is difficult to contemplate a future at all
**Advice:** consult your doctor immediately. See *Physical treatments*, page 169.

### ■ WHITE ■
**(Depressive psychosis)**
Contact with reality is lost and awful delusions surround a core feeling of terrible stagnation. There is complete abdication of responsibility.
**Some characteristics:** characteristics of grey and black, plus:
■ Suicide appears the most positive action, perhaps including killing one's loved ones to save them from the terrible world
■ Physical neglect – you can no longer be bothered to eat or wash
■ "Retardation" – movements of the body become slower. This is accompanied by a slowing down of speech and in extreme states, muteness. "Agitation" may occur instead of retardation – wringing of the hands and pacing up and down in despair
■ Delusions: of smelling bad; of poverty and disease; of imminent catastrophe; of guilt (you believe you have done something for which you deserve to be punished); of paranoia (you believe others are plotting against you); or of nihilism (you believe your brain is empty or that you literally have no head or body)
**Advice:** consult your doctor immediately. See *Physical treatments*, page 169.

weeks to achieve their effect. Within another three days he had deteriorated to a state of white depression.

At this point he began to go beyond reason and reality. Starting with a belief that he might be physically ill, he became more certain, until he *knew* that his body was rotting inside and that he actually stank. The mark of psychosis was that he did not only feel that he stank as a symbolic expression: he believed that the stench could be perceived in the nostrils of the people he avoided. He believed with absolute certainty that a calamity would soon befall the world, though he did not specify what. It was clear to him that the only route was death; this seemed an apt punishment for the terrible things he had done in his life.

As he descended further into the depths of depression, his movement and speech became slower. Gradually the gaps between words grew until it took him a whole minute to utter a single sentence. At the same time his bodily movements began to look like exaggerated slow motion. Within two days he was completely mute, virtually immobile, and required total nursing care. He sat with slumped shoulders and drooped head, his face an empty mask, utterly voiceless, utterly still – with the exception of one response: an extremely slow, barely discernible shake of the head.

It was considered that the only possible treatment that might help was electro-convulsive therapy. But before the first treatment, Mr X had a small heart attack. Two days later he developed kidney failure and then pneumonia. Within ten days of going into hospital, he was dead.

It was discovered at the autopsy that he had suffered multiple thromboses, blood clots in both legs as well as in the coronary arteries of the heart. Both his kidneys were infected and his lungs were riddled with seemingly unresisted infection. It was as if his body had slowed down so much that the blood had begun to stagnate. His beliefs about rotting inside turned out to be a dreadful self-fulfilling prophecy.

Lest you should think that a moment of blueness or greyness could send you inextricably downwards, be assured that the case of Mr X was extraordinary. It is certainly the worst case that I have ever seen, and it is the only case I have seen where a depressed person has seemingly died from depression without committing suicide. Black depression and white depression are in fact rare and it is probable that only a minority of people are capable of moving down to those extremes.

The fact that Mr X descended from psychological reaction to morbid mental state to mental illness to physical illness illustrates the immense power of the human will. Used positively, such power can reverse the depressive process.

# Characteristics of depression

Common to all states of depression are five interrelated processes, or characteristics. These are: emptiness rather than sadness; loss of energy (which can affect every activity and feeling); sulking and self-pity (usually accompanied by loss of humour); giving up; and negative coloration (of the world, yourself, and of the future). The extent to which each characteristic is prevalent is variable in different people and cannot usually be predicted by the cause of the depression.

## EMPTINESS RATHER THAN SADNESS

You feel as if there is nothing of worth inside you. You may describe it as emptiness, or you may feel as if there is a barren wilderness within for which there are no words. An empty futility seems to permeate every activity and expression. In the rare extremes of white depression you may believe that your head is literally empty or that you have no body.

Although depression and sadness are popularly used as alternatives, they are different in quality. A sad event may be described colloquially as "depressing", and when someone is depressed it is certainly a sad sight to see. But the essence of depression is not sadness.

Sadness is active, depression is passive. Sadness is an appropriate emotion after a sad event. If someone near to you dies, it is natural to feel both sad and angry. Such feelings may shake you to the roots but, in the natural course of events, fully experienced grief is short-lived. Depression is a numbing of feeling or an absence of feeling. What might have been genuine sadness, that is, an emotion with energy and life, may be literally depressed, pushed down, leaving a lack of feeling characterized by low energy and inertia.

**Is this emptiness ever "normal"?**  Although emptiness is usually negative and unhelpful, sometimes the ability to numb yourself is an important and useful survival mechanism. For example, in the natural course of

## ARE YOU SAD OR ARE YOU DEPRESSED?

Since sadness and depression are often confused, the following table contrasts their characteristics, and may help you determine whether you are sad or depressed.

| Sad | Depressed |
| --- | --- |
| Periods of expression of feeling (crying, sobbing), which bring relief. | Crying is not "deep" and brings little relief. Often lose the ability to cry at all. |
| Feelings (especially emotional pain) are acute. Heartache. | Feelings are numbed. Pain is numbed. Feeling of dull lingering emptiness rather than acute pain. |
| The ability to laugh and experience other emotions is not lost. After feeling sadness, the ability to experience other feelings may even be heightened. | Loss of sense of humour. Loss of ability to experience any other feeling. |
| Sense of "movement" – feelings are experienced, "moved through", so that by the end you are ready for a new experience of life. | Sense of stagnant heaviness, of being stuck in a groove and unavailable to new experience. |
| No loss of self-respect. | Loss of self-respect. |
| No feeling of distance from self and others; in fact the expression of sadness may bring you closer. | Feeling of distance from self or others. |
| No loss of energy or motivation. | Loss of energy and motivation. |
| Usually short-lived when fully expressed. | Apart from moments of the blues, tends to last a long time and is self-perpetuating – the more your energy drops, the worse you feel about yourself, and the more you give up, the more your energy drops. |

grief there is often an initial period of numbness and disbelief – it is almost impossible to feel all at once the whole reality of the death of a person dear to you. This period of numbness is a kind of natural, temporary, depression. Within hours or days the full mixed flood of feelings of pain, anger, sadness and love may take over. It is when these feelings are not allowed to be experienced that the blank depression persists and becomes debilitating. Numbness can be a positive temporary measure but it is a costly long-term policy.

# LOSS OF ENERGY

The second hallmark of depression is loss of energy, a loss which permeates every aspect of the human being – feelings, body, mind and spirit.

**Loss of feeling and sensation**

Hand in hand with a sense of emptiness is an increasing inability to feel emotions. You look at your own child and no longer feel any tenderness. Someone at work deliberately provokes you and you feel emptiness instead of anger. The melody and harmony of the music you love loses its appeal.

The colours of your favourite scenes blend into greying monochrome. Singing birds mildly irritate. Flowers are odourless. In short, nothing turns you on any more. Your favourite food tastes as bland as unseasoned mashed potato. Taste is insipid, vision is vapid and desire is tepid. No matter what is happening, life feels almost overwhelmingly lifeless.

**Loss of body energy** Somehow it is hard to get moving, difficult to get up from a chair, difficult to get out of bed in the morning. Your body feels physically heavy and burdened, and may appear slumped and sagged. Your movements get slower and it takes longer to complete your usual everyday tasks. Going upstairs is exhausting. Minor chores become a major task. All pleasure in the movement of the body disappears as movement becomes more and more tiring and tiresome. The body feels debilitated, even ill, and there may be aches and pains – low back ache, "rheumaticky" joint pains, headaches and occasionally pain in the area of the cheek-bone.

Internally, your movements are slowed down, particularly bowel functions. Because glandular secretions are slowed, your mouth feels dry. Because your intestines slow down, you may experience bouts of indigestion and constipation. Sometimes constipation becomes a preoccupation and may lead on to hypochondriacal notions that the cause is a major physical illness like cancer.

Just as emotional expression and bodily excretion slow down together, similarly impressions of sensation and intake of food are slowed together. You lose your appetite for both life and food. Initially, common sense may force you to eat but in more severe depression you cannot be bothered and may lose a lot of weight. The lack of food intake then contributes physically to the already debilitating loss of energy.

In very severe depression, bodily motion may cease altogether, the person sitting in languid immobility, quite unable to initiate the smallest movement, even of the mouth in order to talk. Although this is very rare, it serves to emphasize the direction in which untreated depression travels: towards immobilization.

**Loss of mental interest** Interest in work, hobbies and conversation dwindles. At work it becomes impossible to innovate. You find that jobs are done mechanically with the least possible amount of thought. Decisions become slower and procrastination longer. In severe depression, your capacity for any creativity of thought is virtually non-existent and decisions are simply not made at all. This creates a secondary anxiety because, at the back of your mind, you know that unmade decisions are piling up, or that a job is not being done. At work this may lead to you being sacked. At home it may mean that your family is not being cared for properly. The loss of interest pertains to all activities. Fascinating hobbies become dull and pointless. It is difficult to focus on a book or newspaper because there is no eagerness to know – this results in a complete lack of concentration. As you try to read, your mind simply goes blank, or else it wanders through the various tasks you have not done, or, perhaps, depressive negative thoughts intrude, such as "I'm a terrible mother", "I don't deserve any better than this", "Everything is pointless anyway". Preoccupation with depressive thoughts contributes to increasing forgetfulness. You forget names and instructions which you would normally find easy to remember. Thus your performance declines further and your grounds for depressive thoughts seem to grow.

**Loss of spirit and hope**

Depressed people seem to lose the strength of their life-force: it is as if they hang on by a few threads of habit. Their spirit dwindles and shrinks so that it seems deeply buried within an immobile mask.

Somehow the belief in life, the belief in goodness and the belief in positive possibilities get lost. They are replaced by a belief in badness and doom – you are bad, others are bad, the world is bad, the future is bad. It is as if an all-enveloping black cloud descends and permeates every aspect of existence, discolouring everything grey and black.

Past, present and future are reinterpreted in black. History is darkened by selectively remembering mistakes and magnifying them. A tiny misdemeanour, for instance, being unkind to a brother or sister in a far distant childhood, is seen as a major crime and as evidence that your assessment of yourself as unworthy, guilty and bad is wholly justified. The belief in present hopelessness is reinforced by a declining performance due to declining activity – the less you do, the worse you feel, the less you do. Future doom seems a logical conclusion from an extrapolation of this downward trend.

It is as if the gate to the inner spirit is blocked by a warped censor which selectively, and with some finesse, discards the positive and encourages the negative. Most positive input, positive feelings from others, positive interest, exciting sensation are dulled, while negative thought is allowed through, even magnified to fill in the empty spaces. Output of any kind is censored and diminished – thoughts, feelings, bodily movement all have very limited expression. It seems as if the spirit is cut off from its own body and cut off from the world, and it is difficult for a spirit in isolation to maintain hope.

# SULKING AND SELF-PITY

It is difficult to tell the difference between sulking and mild depression. Both occur when something happens that you do not approve of, but which you do not speak about directly. Both can occur when something happens, or someone does something, that annoys you. You do not mention your anger or annoyance, but sulk and become moody, so that the "black cloud" that surrounds you serves to punish the perpetrator of the annoying act.

A friend of mine gave his wife a pair of ear-rings which he had especially made. Knowing her to be rather careless, he asked her to take extra care with them, and then, within 24 hours, she had lost one. Of course he was angry, but since on the rational surface it was an unfortunate accident, he confined himself to saying "It's a pity" and then sulked for a week. He was miserable, while she felt punished by the distance his sulk created.

**Seeing yourself as a victim**

When you are sulking, you do not see yourself as someone handing out punishment. It seems that you have been hard done by, that you are a victim of another's action or a victim of circumstance or a victim of life – certainly, anyway, a victim. As a victim you feel sorry for yourself, you feel that life is unfair or that you have been treated unjustly. Perhaps you have been treated unjustly: but when self-pity becomes depressive it also becomes self-perpetuating and stops you from taking positive action. Instead of dealing with the unjust situation or expressing your own feelings of frustration, you focus on yourself and how badly you have been treated. Since this feeling takes the place of positive action, your situation remains unchanged, which seems to give you further reason for self-pity. It is tempting to hold on to the self-pity, since, so long as you remain a victim, you are less responsible – you are tempted to swap the serious burden of responsibility for the heavy yet empty burden of depression. Some depressions start as intransigent sulks which grow like mushrooms, feeding on the debris of dismal self-pity rather than the light of reality and action.

**Avoiding humour**

In order to continue sulking or feeling sorry for yourself, it is essential to avoid humour at all costs. When a sulking child laughs, the sulk cracks with the smile. Humour and depression can hardly co-exist; when you laugh at yourself or your situation, self-pity is impossible. However, when you are depressed it is very hard to laugh at anything; you feel sour and wonder how you ever could have found your favourite jokes funny; the only humour left to you becomes bitterly ironic, morbid or sarcastic. Although it is true that *all* feelings are damped down in depression, somehow the loss of fun and laughter is central. You can regain your ability to be angry but still remain depressed. You cannot regain your capacity for fun and laughter without your depression lifting.

# GIVING UP

The process of deepening depression involves a gradual abdication of responsibility. Someone in white depression, out of touch with reality and requiring total nursing care, will have reached a stage where responsibility, even for the most basic needs, will have to be taken over by others.

Those people who tend to look to an outside authority for decisions and fulfilment of needs have a greater tendency to become depressed (see *"Dependent" personality*, page 98). Since other people and outward circumstances are seen as responsible for what happens to them, when things go wrong it seems there is nothing much that can be done.

The more you believe in an external authority as the basis for your decisions, rather than in your own authority, the more prone you are to guilt. Guilt and responsibility are opposites: a responsible person who has made a mistake may greatly regret the mistake, but will then take action to rectify it, or if it cannot be rectified, will learn from the mistake before moving on to the next part of life; a very guilty person who has made a mistake becomes so preoccupied with self-punishing feelings that no action is taken to rectify the mistake, and the inactivity fuels the guilt even further.

The process of giving up in deepening depression involves the relinquishing of: the desire for maximum satisfaction; the will to fight; hope for the future; and, ultimately, the ability to discern reality. But the vast majority of people give up what they give up without noticing what they are doing. People with loss of sparkle forget or do not know that more is available. People in grey depression feel so little want or will that it feels as if they are in the power of an alien process that has numbed all desire to change for the better. People in black depression have lost all belief that change is possible, and this is then supported by the physical evidence of loss of appetite and early morning waking, and by a physical feeling of debility. At this stage it feels as if there is a physical process outside one's control, and to some extent this is true. People in white depression have got to a stage where they are convinced that giving up is the only intelligent thing to do.

# NEGATIVE COLORATION

With a feeling of emptiness, loss of energy and a sub-conscious wish to give up, it is hardly surprising that the view of the world and the self becomes tainted.

It is difficult to understand just how powerful the force of darkening is. Initially it is a reversible process – you can see that your view is dimmed and even laugh about it. But there comes a stage, as depression deepens to grey and especially black, where it is as if you have put on grey-tinted or black-tinted spectacles but cease to realize that you are wearing them. Everything then gets coloured – past, present, future. So do feelings, the body, the self, others, the world, God. Yet at the same time the coloration appears completely real.

I remember giving a phone number to a man in a state of grey depression. He asked me to repeat one digit of the number and then was quite distraught that he had needed a single number repeated. He saw this as clear evidence of his worsening concentration, proof that he was on the downward path. When I told him that I had on many occasions asked for a number to be repeated, he was totally unimpressed. He either took my statement to be a polite therapeutic manoeuvre or else considered it irrelevant since it was not directly connected with him. Either way, the negative coloration of events, by means which seemed to him to be completely logical, distorted his momentary lapse of concentration (or perhaps my poor enunciation) out of all proportion. He had lost his sense of perspective and, even though he was an intelligent man, he could not see the distortion. When I tried to help him see the negative exaggeration, he could see what I meant intellectually, but he knew all the while that his view remained right – I had been witness, in his opinion, to a clear example of his inexorable deterioration. This was further evidence, he believed, that things were getting worse. The colour of the future was confirmed as black.

## COLOUR OF THE FUTURE

If you ask someone about the future the coloration is often clear. The awful thing about it is that it is easy to create a self-fulfilling prophecy. If the future seems hopeless and therefore you do nothing, the future does indeed become hopeless. This is the power of negative thought. Negative thought feeds on inactivity, while positive thought, just as powerful, grows and thrives on activity.

| Mood | Future |
|---|---|
| GOLD | Bright and exciting |
| LOSS OF SPARKLE | Could be brighter |
| BLUE | Temporarily dull |
| GREY | Grey |
| BLACK | Black |
| WHITE | No future, death |

# Depression and related states

Anxiety, mania, suicide and attempted suicide are often associated with depression. This chapter clarifies where these conditions overlap with depression, and in what aspects they differ. Some depressed people attempt or commit suicide, though most attempted suicides and some suicides are carried out by people who are not depressed. A few depressed people have periods of extremely high energy called mania, and most people who have periods of mania also have depressive periods. Many depressed people also become anxious.

## ANXIOUS OR DEPRESSED?

At base, anxiety and depression are very different, but since they often occur together the picture can sometimes be confusing. Under stress, you can respond by fighting or running away (anxiety), or alternatively, you can fail to respond at all, play dead, or give yourself up to fate (depression).

**Healthy anxiety**　Healthy anxiety is based on the fight or flight reaction. If a lion is stalking you with intent to eat, nonchalance is a poor aid to longevity, whereas a healthy surge of anxiety prepares you either to do battle or to run with adrenalin boosted speed. Thus the feeling of fear is accompanied by faster breathing to improve the oxygenation of your blood, faster heartbeat to improve the circulation, a shunting of the blood away from the extremities and from the guts to the muscles where it's needed, and an energization of the muscles which tremble with anticipation. At the same time you sweat and if the lion is very hungry and you are unarmed, you may be scared enough to lose control of your bowels.

**Morbid anxiety**　Morbid anxiety is the same but without the lion. You have a feeling of continuous apprehension or of attacks of panic for no obvious external reason. Prolonged faster breathing may cause faintness, dizziness and a feeling of being choked or

# THE CHARACTERISTICS OF ANXIETY AND DEPRESSION

From the tables (below) comparing depression with anxiety, it does not seem too hard to tell them apart. Yet they often occur together, because it is depressing to be anxious and, more commonly, it is anxiety-provoking to be depressed. If, for example, you are primarily depressed and through lack of concentration and indecisiveness your working efficiency is reduced, you could be at risk of losing your job. This thought may be enough to spark off an attack of anxiety with the physical symptoms of uneasy anticipation, perhaps somewhat muted by the depressive loss of energy. Many depressions are disguised like this by secondary anxiety, which is based on an understandable fear of the results of the depression.

## DIFFERENCES

| Anxiety | Depression |
|---|---|
| Feeling of fear, apprehension | Feeling of emptiness, misery |
| Speeding up of thoughts (leading to loss of creativity) | Slowing down of thoughts (leading to loss of creativity) |
| Speeding up of intestines, leading to diarrhoea | Slowing down of intestines, leading to constipation |
| Speeding up or jerkiness of bodily movement | Slowing down of bodily movement |
| Body tense and rigid | Body slumped |
| Tendency to look for outside causes rather than to blame self | Guilt, unworthiness, self-blame and self-deprecation |
| Sleep generally poor. If anything, tendency to feel worse in the evenings | Early morning waking and tendency to feel worse in the mornings |
| Over-interested in results (may result in poorer performance) | Loss of interest and ambition (may result in poorer performance) |
| Sexual difficulty through tension and over-concern about performance | Loss of libido – little or no interest in sex |
| Frightened but not hopeless | Loss of hope |
| May fear death but do not want it | Suicidal thoughts are sometimes present |

## SIMILARITIES

| Anxiety | Depression |
|---|---|
| Hypochondriasis – often the fear of illness is based on a real physical symptom related to the anxiety (e.g. palpitations) | Hypochondriasis – often the fear of illness is based on a real physical symptom related to the depression (e.g. constipation) |
| Fatigue – related to over-use of nervous energy and physical energy (muscular tension) | Fatigue – related to lack of energy |
| Loss of appetite (or over-eating for comfort) | Loss of appetite (in milder depression there is sometimes an increase in appetite) |
| Sleep disturbances (especially difficulty in getting to sleep) | Sleep disturbances (especially early morning waking) |
| Difficulty in concentration (related to unproductive speed of thought) | Difficulty in concentration (related to slowness of mind) |
| Headaches and aches and pains | Headaches and aches and pains |

smothered; all these feelings then add to your anxiety. The faster heartbeat may cause palpitations – a thumping of the heart which may further your fear. The shunting of the blood from the extremities makes you look pale, while the shunting of the blood from the guts makes you feel sick. The tense trembling of your muscles has no release in action. You may sweat and you may have diarrhoea.

These symptoms are obviously quite different from depressive symptoms but there are some which overlap. As anxiety produces so many physical symptoms, it is easy to start to believe that the physical symptoms denote a serious organic disease. It is difficult to eat, sleep, concentrate or have good sex in a state of fear, just as it is in a state of depressed energy. The continuous unproductive activity of the anxious body is tiring, while the unrelieved muscular tension may cause aches and pains, including headaches.

In black depression, some people experience extreme anxiety accompanied by agitated movements – shifting of the feet, pacing up and down, wringing of the hands – known as "agitated depression". Such people are in a curious mixed state of blankness and terror. They are incapable of acting productively and need to be taken care of.

# MANIC DEPRESSION

Mania is a state of heightened energy and euphoria. It is in almost every way the opposite of depression. You feel good about yourself and good about the outside world. You feel that you are superbly intelligent, healthy and beautiful. Your thoughts move with such rapidity that you fly from subject to subject with bubbling enthusiasm. To an observer these flights of ideas are difficult to follow and it becomes exhausting being with someone who talks so much. Your body, too, becomes hyperactive, requiring only small amounts of sleep, and busy with everything: cleaning the house at five o'clock in the morning, writing poetry during breakfast, talking, pacing up and down – incessant activity. Perception is heightened – colours, smells and sounds are vivid and exciting. You feel so euphoric you find it hard to understand why your friends cannot stick around you for very long.

A step higher than the feeling of euphoria takes you to a state of delusion. You become grandiose – you may believe you have invented new things and can understand things beyond others' capacities. I remember one man telling me that he was the fourth most intelligent man in the world – he was absolutely convinced of this. He did not know who the

## THE OPPOSITE CHARACTERISTICS OF MANIA AND DEPRESSION

| Mania | Depression |
|---|---|
| Increased energy | Loss of energy |
| Feel good, high, exhilarated | Feel down, low, empty |
| Think yourself a wonderful person | Think yourself a terrible person |
| Think fast | Think slowly |
| Voluble | Reticent |
| Perception and sensation heightened | Perception and sensation dull |
| Activities increased | Activities decreased |
| In severe cases, grandiose delusions, e.g. believing you are a king | In severe cases, "nihilistic" delusions, i.e. believing you have no substance within |

first three were. A young woman who felt all-powerful told me that she could alter the flight paths of planes by thinking "left" or "right". You may believe you are extremely rich and may indeed be so enthusiastically convincing that you succeed in buying a Rolls Royce or two. In extreme states you may believe you are a saint or Jesus Christ.

The connection between mania and depression is that most people who become manic have depressive phases also (see the "Comparative mood swings" graph, overleaf), while a small minority of people who become severely depressed have manic phases. Manic depression is uncommon. Something like one in 200 people are affected at some time in their lives, and some of those who are affected have only one or a few episodes. Mania by itself is rarer, and manic episodes are rarer than depressive episodes in someone prone to both.

**Characteristics common to depression and mania**

● Loss of sleep (though the manic person is unworried about it).
● Mood and energy out of touch with actual outside events. Depression and mania may both be ways of avoiding feeling a painful reality.
● In more severe states, it becomes impossible to keep a job or hold any responsibility.
● In very severe states, loss of touch with reality.

**"CYCLOTHYMIC" PERSONALITY**

This term refers to a character trait of swinging mood from mild states of depression to mild states of elation (see the "Comparative mood swings" graph, overleaf), the swings not necessarily relating to outside events. Everybody has changes

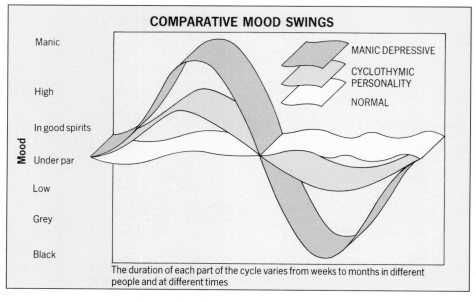

**COMPARATIVE MOOD SWINGS**

MANIC DEPRESSIVE

CYCLOTHYMIC PERSONALITY

NORMAL

Mood: Manic / High / In good spirits / Under par / Low / Grey / Black

The duration of each part of the cycle varies from weeks to months in different people and at different times

in mood which seem to be unrelated to obvious external events. They may be related to unseen internal changes, to natural biorhythms, or to configurations in the heavens. The "cyclothymic" personality is not a distinct clinical syndrome but someone who has larger mood swings than usual. Such people are slightly more likely to be predisposed to depression, mania and manic depression.

# SUICIDE AND ATTEMPTED SUICIDE

In grey, black and especially white depression suicide seems a frighteningly logical conclusion. It is possible to feel so bad that the prospect of death promises relief. It is possible to consider oneself such a bad person that death seems a suitable punishment. It is possible to believe that one is so rotten and diseased inside that death must be imminent anyway. And it is possible to believe that the future is so black, that death is the most positive answer.

Suicidal thoughts and intentions intensify as you grow more depressed, although it becomes harder to carry out the act because energy and initiative are so low. This is why suicide sometimes occurs when someone seems to be getting better. In the depths of depression, they may decide to die and as the depression seems to lift they regain enough initiative to carry out the act (see the graphs, opposite).

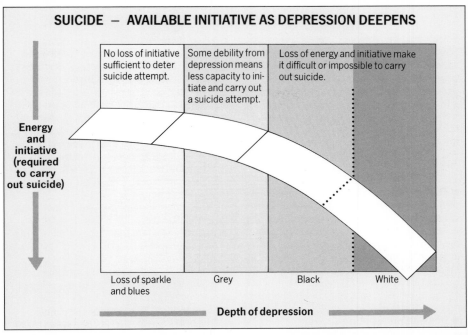

## SUICIDE — AVAILABLE INITIATIVE AS DEPRESSION DEEPENS

No loss of initiative sufficient to deter suicide attempt.

Some debility from depression means less capacity to initiate and carry out a suicide attempt.

Loss of energy and initiative make it difficult or impossible to carry out suicide.

**Energy and initiative (required to carry out suicide)**

Loss of sparkle and blues

Grey

Black

White

**Depth of depression**

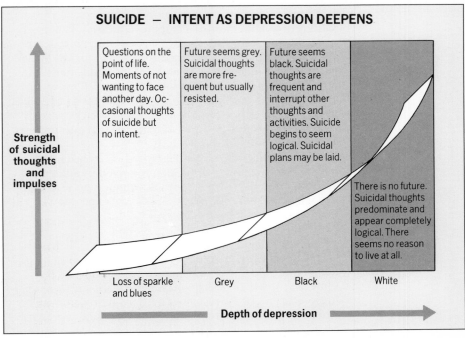

## SUICIDE — INTENT AS DEPRESSION DEEPENS

Questions on the point of life. Moments of not wanting to face another day. Occasional thoughts of suicide but no intent.

Future seems grey. Suicidal thoughts are more frequent but usually resisted.

Future seems black. Suicidal thoughts are frequent and interrupt other thoughts and activities. Suicide begins to seem logical. Suicidal plans may be laid.

There is no future. Suicidal thoughts predominate and appear completely logical. There seems no reason to live at all.

**Strength of suicidal thoughts and impulses**

Loss of sparkle and blues

Grey

Black

White

**Depth of depression**

## SUICIDE DANGER SIGNALS AND SITUATIONS

Suicide is more common in spring and autumn in both the northern and the southern hemispheres. It is more common in cities than in the country, and it is more common where there has been a family history of suicide. If you have a friend who could be suicidal, listed here are some of the important danger signs. Combinations of these factors increase the danger; there are people to whom all seven pertain. If you or someone you know is or may be suicidal, please seek professional advice. Your GP should be able to help.

■ **The person hints or gives direct warning of a wish to die or an intention to commit suicide** They may be direct signs, or you may notice that he or she is "preparing for death" by, for example, making a will, tidying up belongings, giving things away, or stockpiling medicine. Such warnings should not be discounted lightly as threats or cries for help. Even if they are threats or cries for help, the result may be death.

■ **Depression** Especially:
□ On the upswing from a severe depression

□ When there is guilt or self-accusation
□ When there are feelings of unworthiness
□ When there is a strong sense of emptiness.

■ **Alcoholism and drug abuse** Especially:
□ Just after an alcoholic or drug addict has finished a relationship or been left by a partner.

■ **Previous suicide attempts** Statistically, suicide is a hundred times more likely amongst those who have already tried to commit suicide than in the general population. Especially:
□ When the previous attempt was premeditated or when precautions were taken in order to avoid discovery
□ When violent methods were used, e.g. firearms, lacerations, corrosive poisons.

■ **Recent bereavement** Especially:
□ After a loss of a spouse
□ When a mother loses her only son.

■ **Loneliness and isolation** Especially:
□ In old men particularly when there is also unemployment or physical illness.

■ **"Dependent" personality** Especially:
□ After the loss of the person or situation which provided support.

Most people who commit suicide are depressed. People who have been clinically depressed (grey, black or white depression) have a much higher chance of dying by suicide. Such people usually give warnings of their intent and often these warnings are communicated to many people. *Warnings of suicidal thoughts and suicidal intent should always be taken seriously.* Studies on people who have been seen by psychiatrists for depression (grey or black) suggest that over ten per cent eventually kill themselves.

In most industrialized countries, suicide is one of the ten most frequent causes of death among university students, and, after traffic accidents, the most common cause of death in young men. Between 50 and 75 per cent of people who kill themselves are clinically depressed.

**"ATTEMPTED SUICIDE"** "Attempted suicide" is not usually associated with depression. The phrase is in inverted commas because most "attempted suicides" are not actual attempts at suicide. But some are. Although perhaps 60 per cent claim they intended to die, this may be the result of a need to save face – it can be embarrassing coming round from an overdose and even more embarrassing if you took it for any other reason than to die.

Whereas actual suicide is much more common in the elderly and more common in men than in women, "attempted suicide" is most common in the young, often between the ages of 20 and 24, and is more common in women than in men. "Attempted suicide" is 15 to 30 times more common than suicide. Frequently it is carried out impulsively and not uncommonly under the influence of alcohol.

By far the most common method is poisoning, usually with an overdose of drugs, often those that are more frequently prescribed. Twenty years ago barbiturate sleeping tablets were the commonest drugs taken, but now benzodiazepine sleeping tablets (such as Mogadon), tranquillizers (such as valium) and anti-depressants are used much more often. Most adults take drugs prescribed by their GP. Unfortunately, teenagers tend to use aspirin and paracetamol without realizing how dangerous these drugs are. Aspirin is highly toxic in overdose and paracetamol can cause fatal liver damage. Some gestures end in tragedy.

**Probable motives for "attempted suicide"**

There are several common motives for "attempted suicide"; often there is a combination of the following:

- To have a break from unbearable stress.
- A cry for help. A plea to be heard or to be taken seriously. Most often occurs with teenagers who are living in difficult family situations.
- An expression of aggression sometimes designed to make another person feel guilty. Most often occurs after a row between husband and wife or girlfriend and boyfriend. Sometimes the overdose is actually taken in front of the partner. Nearly all attempts at suicide contain a strong element of aggression as well as punishment of self or, especially, others. Spite is quite often a large part of the motive.
- Russian roulette – a testing out of fate.
- A real and definite attempt to die.

Only a minority of people who "attempt suicide" are depressed, but they are the ones most likely to want to die and therefore the most likely to premeditate the attempt and to take precautions to avoid discovery. They are also the most likely to take a higher dose. However, because of ignorance of the required dose to kill, mistakes are made both ways – people dying who did not really think they wanted to, and people not dying who thought they wanted to. Any talk of suicide, let alone attempt, is potentially dangerous. If you are at all worried about yourself or someone else who may be contemplating suicide, please seek professional advice. Again, your GP should be able to help. (See also *Living with a depressive*, page 142.)

# Part 2

# WHY DEPRESSED?

## THE MANY WAYS DOWN

# Introduction

Many centuries ago a teacher called Nasrudin was walking down the street when he was approached by a scholar who asked, "What is fate?"

"An endless succession of intertwined events, each influencing the other," Nasrudin replied.

"That is hardly a satisfactory answer", the scholar said, "I believe in cause and effect."

"Very well," said Nasrudin, "look at that." He pointed to a procession which, conveniently for the purposes of education, happened to be passing at the time. "That man is being taken to be hanged. Is that because someone gave him a silver piece and enabled him to buy the knife with which he committed the murder; or because someone saw him do it; or because nobody stopped him?"

In true science there is no such thing as a cause that can be proved: there are only associations between events which can be noted and from which theories can be made. However, scientists, doctors, and all those in the field of mental health, being human, have a tendency to be less dispassionate than they may pretend. People like to have a cause, and people like to fight for a cause. So it is in the field of depression; many people like to believe that the cause is (primarily) physical *or* psychological *or* behavioural.

## THE COMPLEXITY OF CAUSE

Let's take Mr. P, a 43 year-old-man who is depressed. Is he depressed because:
- His father and his grandfather were both people who had episodes of depression
- He has just lost his job where he had been for fifteen years
- He has always been a rather needy and dependent kind of person
- He has just stopped taking amphetamines
- He has had an argument with his wife but is suppressing his anger and directing it inwards against himself
- He feels himself becoming more alienated from, or never felt part of, society
- According to his mother he suffered a lack of oxygen just before his birth
- His parents had little emotional contact with him in his early childhood
- His biogenic amines are depleted in the lateral hypothalamus and medial forebrain bundles of his brain
- He is anaemic
- He has been taking a drug called reserpine
- It has been raining for the tenth day in succession?

While it may need only one of these reasons to make Mr. P depressed, they could all be true at the same time. The same factors, however, may have absolutely no depressive effect on another person, who, for constitutional or other reasons, may be more immune.

**THEORIES ON DEPRESSION**

Classically there are three major groups of theories on depression – psychodynamic, behavioural and physical – defined as follows:

**Psychodynamic theories**

Events in early life may have an effect on emotional development. Lack of parental love, for example, may result in diminished self-esteem in adulthood and therefore a diminished capacity to deal with stress without experiencing a crisis in self-esteem (depression).

**Behavioural theories**

A person is conditioned into an unconstructive response, such as depression, because this has been rewarded or at least not punished in the past. The most positive response of a child in an inescapably bad situation, such as having unloving parents, may be passivity. Future stress may be handled with the same habitual passivity (depression).

**Physical theories**

A person is born with a predisposition towards depression, and/or changes within the brain diminish transmission of nervous impulses causing diminished excitability (depression).

**LEVELS OF CAUSATION**

There is no contradiction whatsoever between these theories – they merely deal with different levels of causation: the feeling level, the behavioural level, and the level of physical mechanism. In the sections on childhood causes of depression (see *Past history and personality*, page 90) for example, you will find no separation between behavioural and psychodynamic theories. In fact, they overlap and complement each other. If anyone tries to tell you that the cause of depression *is* physical (e.g. biochemical) or that the cause *is* psychodynamic (e.g. motivation limited by parental influences in early childhood) ask them if they have ever flown to a holiday resort. If the answer is "Yes", then ask: "Was the cause of your particular flight the fact that you wanted to go on holiday, or the fact that the thrust of the jets combined with the aerodynamic structure of the aeroplane was sufficient to create a lift greater than the weight of the fully loaded aeroplane at take-off speed?"

**SEVERITY AND CAUSE**

There is no exact relationship between the severity of depression and the types of causes. However, it is likely that with milder depression (loss of sparkle, blue and blue-grey), the present situation (current stress or current boredom) is often of much greater importance than past influences. Everybody is probably susceptible to these types of depression, which are far more common. With more severe depression (darker grey, black and white), predisposition, either hereditary, or from early family influence, tends to play a much greater part. Those prone to more severe depression form a small minority of the total population of depressives, though they are the ones seen by doctors and psychiatrists. It

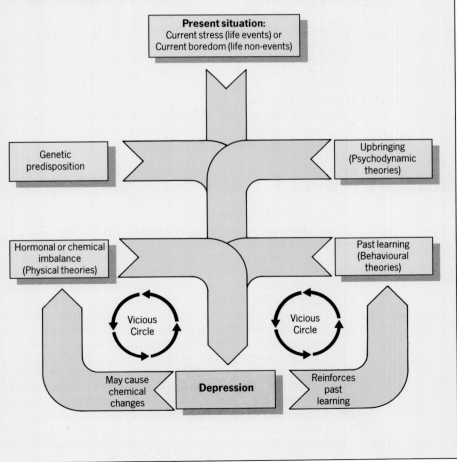

## POSSIBLE CAUSES OF SUSCEPTIBILITY TO DEPRESSION

Stress may change body chemistry; changes in body chemistry may make you more susceptible to stress. Chemical changes may lead to depression; depression may lead to chemical changes. It may take a combination of many different influences to cross a threshold of significant depression, and different people have different breaking points.

**Present situation:**
Current stress (life events) or
Current boredom (life non-events)

Genetic predisposition

Upbringing
(Psychodynamic theories)

Hormonal or chemical imbalance
(Physical theories)

Past learning
(Behavioural theories)

Vicious Circle

Vicious Circle

May cause chemical changes

**Depression**

Reinforces past learning

is probable that most people cannot descend to these levels of depression even with severe stress. For the people who have enough predisposing factors and who can descend to these levels, current stress may act only as a precipitant to severe depression. If, for instance, you were moving house, you might find the whole affair tiresome and mildly depressing. But if you were heavily predisposed towards severe depression, perhaps through hereditary influence, the same move could precipitate a black depression out of all proportion to the immediate stress.

**FINDING THE CAUSE OF YOUR DEPRESSION**

The main causes of or influences on depression are described in this part of the book. They are divided into the following four main categories:
- **LIFE EVENTS** Immediate stress from events such as birth, illness, overwork and loss may precipitate depression.
- **LIFE NON-EVENTS** Stagnation and boredom may lead to chronic depression.
- **PAST HISTORY** Upbringing and (early) life experiences, which may be affected by social culture, may create a personality more predisposed towards depression. There may be a genetic predisposition.
- **PHYSICAL FACTORS** Various drugs, hormonal changes or infections may lead to depression. Other illnesses may either cause or mimic depression.

# POSSIBLE CAUSES CHARTS

If you are depressed and wish to find out which sections are relevant to you, go through all four charts of causes since there may be several different influences in your case. Each chart consists of a series of questions to which you answer YES or NO. Each answer of YES or NO then leads on to either another question or to a diagnosis of a causative influence. The fact that you may find several influences does not necessarily relate to the severity of your depression, which may be influenced by such unknowables as innate predisposition and susceptibility. All the influences in the charts need to be seen as possibilities. For example, you may have had parents who were over-critical, and this could be an important predisposing factor towards depression, but this influence could have been counteracted by warm support from a loving aunt who lived next door. The chart on physical factors is important because many illnesses may either cause or mimic depression, and it is worthwhile excluding possible physical causes that may be easily treated.

# 1 □ LIFE EVENTS

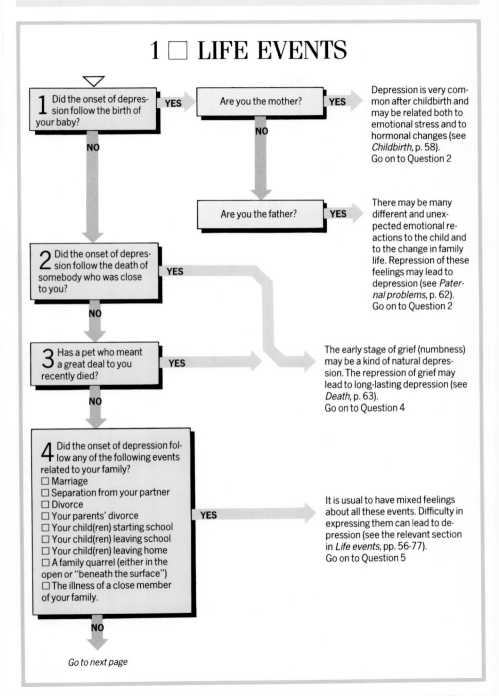

**1** Did the onset of depression follow the birth of your baby?

**YES** → Are you the mother?

**YES** → Depression is very common after childbirth and may be related both to emotional stress and to hormonal changes (see *Childbirth*, p. 58).
Go on to Question 2

**NO** ↓

Are you the father? **YES** → There may be many different and unexpected emotional reactions to the child and to the change in family life. Repression of these feelings may lead to depression (see *Paternal problems*, p. 62).
Go on to Question 2

**1** — **NO** ↓

**2** Did the onset of depression follow the death of somebody who was close to you?

**YES** →

**NO** ↓

**3** Has a pet who meant a great deal to you recently died?

**YES** → The early stage of grief (numbness) may be a kind of natural depression. The repression of grief may lead to long-lasting depression (see *Death*, p. 63).
Go on to Question 4

**NO** ↓

**4** Did the onset of depression follow any of the following events related to your family?
□ Marriage
□ Separation from your partner
□ Divorce
□ Your parents' divorce
□ Your child(ren) starting school
□ Your child(ren) leaving school
□ Your child(ren) leaving home
□ A family quarrel (either in the open or "beneath the surface")
□ The illness of a close member of your family.

**YES** → It is usual to have mixed feelings about all these events. Difficulty in expressing them can lead to depression (see the relevant section in *Life events*, pp. 56-77).
Go on to Question 5

**NO** ↓

*Go to next page*

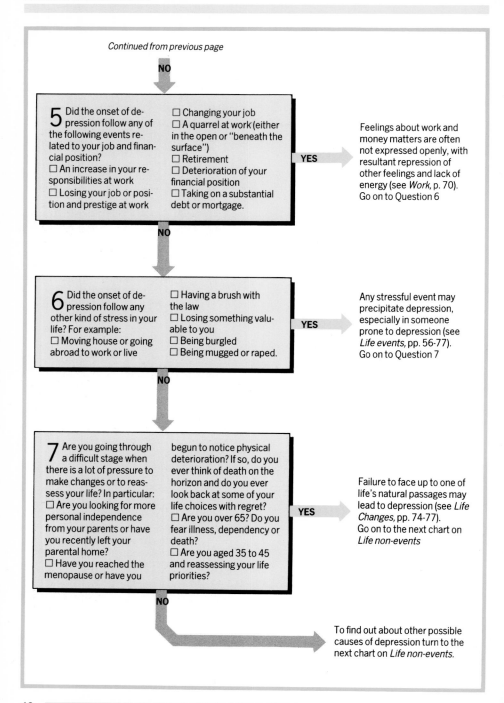

*Continued from previous page*

**NO**

**5** Did the onset of depression follow any of the following events related to your job and financial position?
☐ An increase in your responsibilities at work
☐ Losing your job or position and prestige at work
☐ Changing your job
☐ A quarrel at work (either in the open or "beneath the surface")
☐ Retirement
☐ Deterioration of your financial position
☐ Taking on a substantial debt or mortgage.

**YES** ▶ Feelings about work and money matters are often not expressed openly, with resultant repression of other feelings and lack of energy (see *Work,* p. 70). Go on to Question 6

**NO**

**6** Did the onset of depression follow any other kind of stress in your life? For example:
☐ Moving house or going abroad to work or live
☐ Having a brush with the law
☐ Losing something valuable to you
☐ Being burgled
☐ Being mugged or raped.

**YES** ▶ Any stressful event may precipitate depression, especially in someone prone to depression (see *Life events,* pp. 56-77). Go on to Question 7

**NO**

**7** Are you going through a difficult stage when there is a lot of pressure to make changes or to reassess your life? In particular:
☐ Are you looking for more personal independence from your parents or have you recently left your parental home?
☐ Have you reached the menopause or have you begun to notice physical deterioration? If so, do you ever think of death on the horizon and do you ever look back at some of your life choices with regret?
☐ Are you over 65? Do you fear illness, dependency or death?
☐ Are you aged 35 to 45 and reassessing your life priorities?

**YES** ▶ Failure to face up to one of life's natural passages may lead to depression (see *Life Changes,* pp. 74-77). Go on to the next chart on *Life non-events*

**NO**

To find out about other possible causes of depression turn to the next chart on *Life non-events.*

# 2 □ LIFE NON-EVENTS

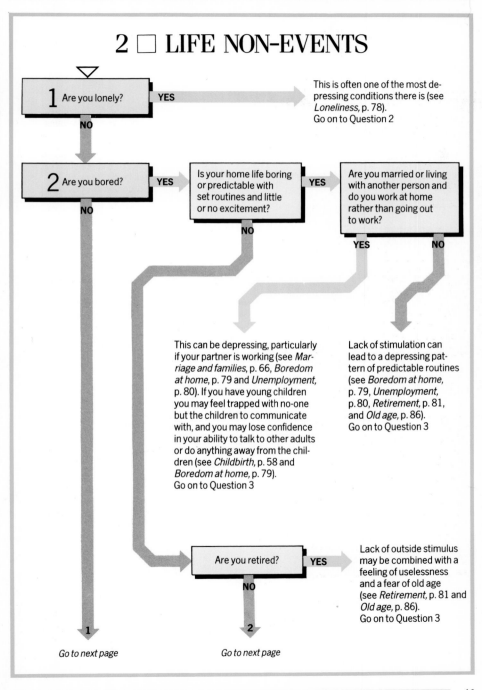

**1** Are you lonely? — **YES** → This is often one of the most depressing conditions there is (see *Loneliness*, p. 78).
Go on to Question 2

**NO**

**2** Are you bored? — **YES** → Is your home life boring or predictable with set routines and little or no excitement? — **YES** → Are you married or living with another person and do you work at home rather than going out to work?

**NO**

**YES** / **NO**

This can be depressing, particularly if your partner is working (see *Marriage and families*, p. 66, *Boredom at home*, p. 79 and *Unemployment*, p. 80). If you have young children you may feel trapped with no-one but the children to communicate with, and you may lose confidence in your ability to talk to other adults or do anything away from the children (see *Childbirth*, p. 58 and *Boredom at home*, p. 79).
Go on to Question 3

Lack of stimulation can lead to a depressing pattern of predictable routines (see *Boredom at home*, p. 79, *Unemployment*, p. 80, *Retirement*, p. 81, and *Old age*, p. 86).
Go on to Question 3

Are you retired? — **YES** → Lack of outside stimulus may be combined with a feeling of uselessness and a fear of old age (see *Retirement*, p. 81 and *Old age*, p. 86).
Go on to Question 3

**NO**

1
*Go to next page*

2
*Go to next page*

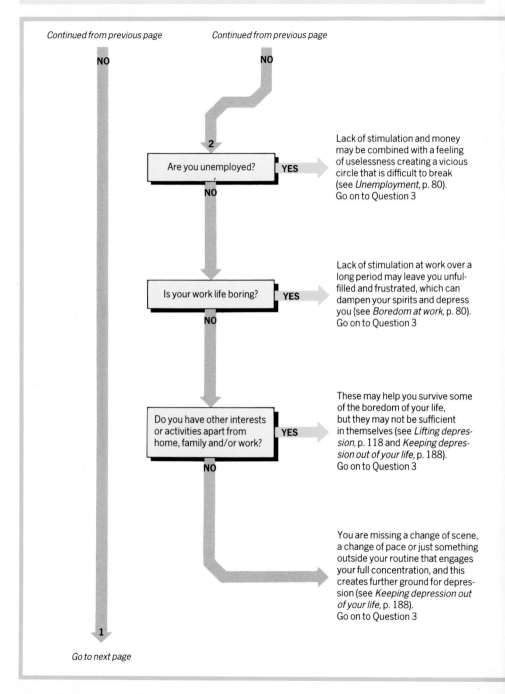

*Continued from previous page*   *Continued from previous page*

NO          NO

**2**

Are you unemployed?   **YES**   Lack of stimulation and money may be combined with a feeling of uselessness creating a vicious circle that is difficult to break (see *Unemployment,* p. 80). Go on to Question 3

NO

Is your work life boring?   **YES**   Lack of stimulation at work over a long period may leave you unfulfilled and frustrated, which can dampen your spirits and depress you (see *Boredom at work,* p. 80). Go on to Question 3

NO

Do you have other interests or activities apart from home, family and/or work?   **YES**   These may help you survive some of the boredom of your life, but they may not be sufficient in themselves (see *Lifting depression,* p. 118 and *Keeping depression out of your life,* p. 188). Go on to Question 3

NO

You are missing a change of scene, a change of pace or just something outside your routine that engages your full concentration, and this creates further ground for depression (see *Keeping depression out of your life,* p. 188). Go on to Question 3

**1**

*Go to next page*

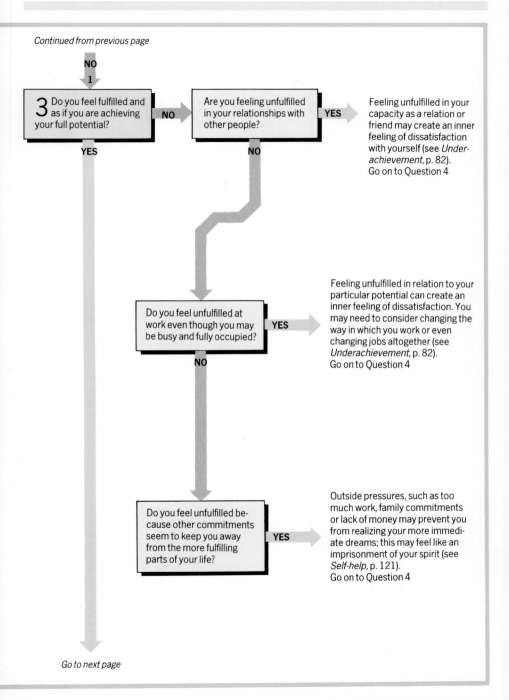

*Continued from previous page*

**NO**
**1**

**3** Do you feel fulfilled and as if you are achieving your full potential?

**NO** →

Are you feeling unfulfilled in your relationships with other people?

**YES** →

Feeling unfulfilled in your capacity as a relation or friend may create an inner feeling of dissatisfaction with yourself (see *Under-achievement*, p. 82).
Go on to Question 4

**YES** (below Q3)

**NO** (below relationships box)

Do you feel unfulfilled at work even though you may be busy and fully occupied?

**YES** →

Feeling unfulfilled in relation to your particular potential can create an inner feeling of dissatisfaction. You may need to consider changing the way in which you work or even changing jobs altogether (see *Underachievement*, p. 82).
Go on to Question 4

**NO**

Do you feel unfulfilled because other commitments seem to keep you away from the more fulfilling parts of your life?

**YES** →

Outside pressures, such as too much work, family commitments or lack of money may prevent you from realizing your more immediate dreams; this may feel like an imprisonment of your spirit (see *Self-help*, p. 121).
Go on to Question 4

*Go to next page*

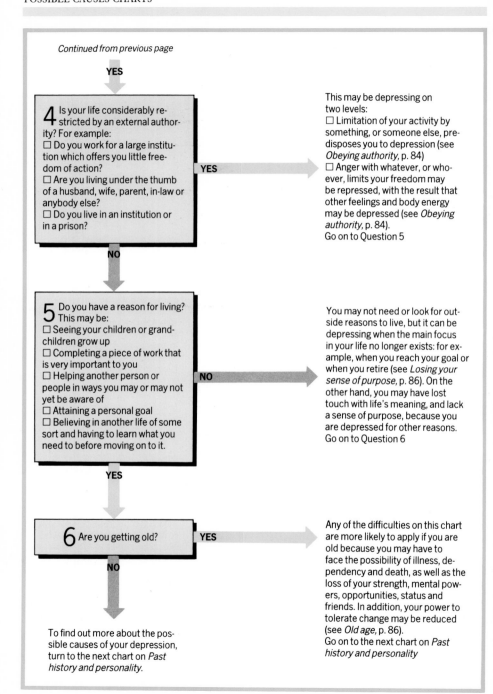

*Continued from previous page*

**YES**

**4** Is your life considerably restricted by an external authority? For example:
☐ Do you work for a large institution which offers you little freedom of action?
☐ Are you living under the thumb of a husband, wife, parent, in-law or anybody else?
☐ Do you live in an institution or in a prison?

**YES** →

This may be depressing on two levels:
☐ Limitation of your activity by something, or someone else, predisposes you to depression (see *Obeying authority*, p. 84)
☐ Anger with whatever, or whoever, limits your freedom may be repressed, with the result that other feelings and body energy may be depressed (see *Obeying authority*, p. 84).
Go on to Question 5

**NO**

**5** Do you have a reason for living? This may be:
☐ Seeing your children or grandchildren grow up
☐ Completing a piece of work that is very important to you
☐ Helping another person or people in ways you may or may not yet be aware of
☐ Attaining a personal goal
☐ Believing in another life of some sort and having to learn what you need to before moving on to it.

**NO** →

You may not need or look for outside reasons to live, but it can be depressing when the main focus in your life no longer exists: for example, when you reach your goal or when you retire (see *Losing your sense of purpose*, p. 86). On the other hand, you may have lost touch with life's meaning, and lack a sense of purpose, because you are depressed for other reasons.
Go on to Question 6

**YES**

**6** Are you getting old?

**YES** →

Any of the difficulties on this chart are more likely to apply if you are old because you may have to face the possibility of illness, dependency and death, as well as the loss of your strength, mental powers, opportunities, status and friends. In addition, your power to tolerate change may be reduced (see *Old age*, p. 86).
Go on to the next chart on *Past history and personality*

**NO**

To find out more about the possible causes of your depression, turn to the next chart on *Past history and personality*.

# 3 ☐ PAST HISTORY AND PERSONALITY

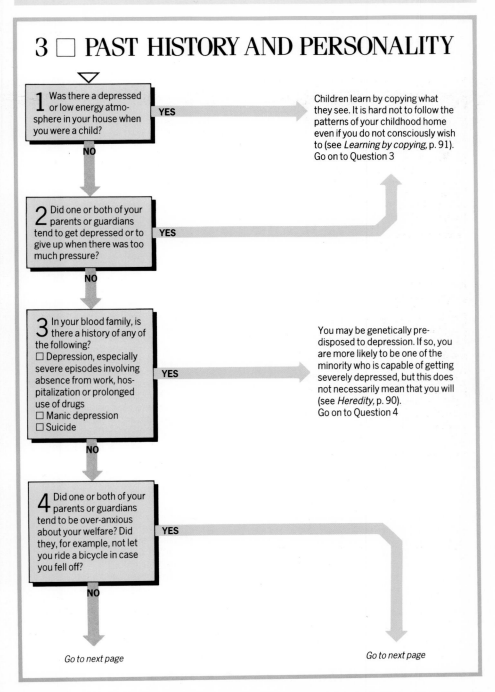

**1** Was there a depressed or low energy atmosphere in your house when you were a child?

**YES** → Children learn by copying what they see. It is hard not to follow the patterns of your childhood home even if you do not consciously wish to (see *Learning by copying,* p. 91). Go on to Question 3

**NO** ↓

**2** Did one or both of your parents or guardians tend to get depressed or to give up when there was too much pressure?

**YES**

**NO** ↓

**3** In your blood family, is there a history of any of the following?
☐ Depression, especially severe episodes involving absence from work, hospitalization or prolonged use of drugs
☐ Manic depression
☐ Suicide

**YES** → You may be genetically pre-disposed to depression. If so, you are more likely to be one of the minority who is capable of getting severely depressed, but this does not necessarily mean that you will (see *Heredity,* p. 90). Go on to Question 4

**NO** ↓

**4** Did one or both of your parents or guardians tend to be over-anxious about your welfare? Did they, for example, not let you ride a bicycle in case you fell off?

**YES**

**NO** ↓

*Go to next page*

*Go to next page*

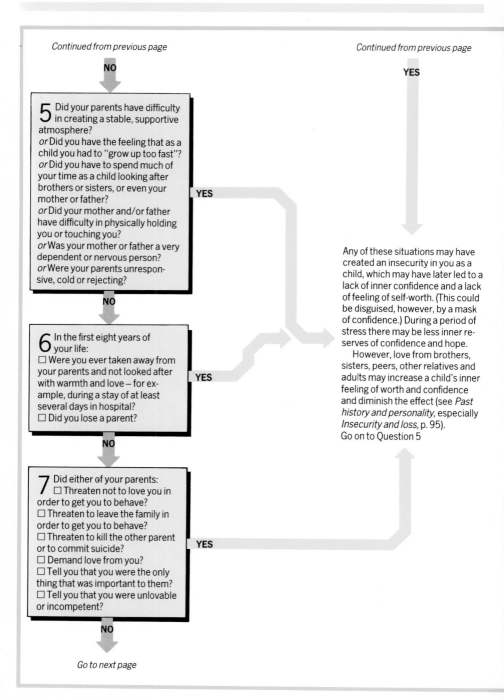

*Continued from previous page*

**NO**

**5** Did your parents have difficulty in creating a stable, supportive atmosphere?
*or* Did you have the feeling that as a child you had to "grow up too fast"?
*or* Did you have to spend much of your time as a child looking after brothers or sisters, or even your mother or father?
*or* Did your mother and/or father have difficulty in physically holding you or touching you?
*or* Was your mother or father a very dependent or nervous person?
*or* Were your parents unresponsive, cold or rejecting?

**YES**

**NO**

**6** In the first eight years of your life:
☐ Were you ever taken away from your parents and not looked after with warmth and love – for example, during a stay of at least several days in hospital?
☐ Did you lose a parent?

**YES**

**NO**

**7** Did either of your parents:
☐ Threaten not to love you in order to get you to behave?
☐ Threaten to leave the family in order to get you to behave?
☐ Threaten to kill the other parent or to commit suicide?
☐ Demand love from you?
☐ Tell you that you were the only thing that was important to them?
☐ Tell you that you were unlovable or incompetent?

**YES**

**NO**

*Go to next page*

*Continued from previous page*

**YES**

Any of these situations may have created an insecurity in you as a child, which may have later led to a lack of inner confidence and a lack of feeling of self-worth. (This could be disguised, however, by a mask of confidence.) During a period of stress there may be less inner reserves of confidence and hope.
However, love from brothers, sisters, peers, other relatives and adults may increase a child's inner feeling of worth and confidence and diminish the effect (see *Past history and personality,* especially *Insecurity and loss,* p. 95).
Go on to Question 5

*Continued from previous page*

**NO**

**8** Do you have three or more of the following tendencies or traits?
□ You tend to get entangled in relationships in such a way that you become dependent
□ You have a tendency to collapse and let someone take care of you
□ You feel you are a loser
□ You often don't try because you fear failure
□ You avoid work as much as possible
□ You have a feeling that people owe you something or that the world owes you a living
□ You tend to eat or drink excessively when things get difficult.

**YES** ▶ You may have a "dependent" personality and tend to rely, especially during periods of stress, on the strength of others rather than yourself. If there is no-one to support you, you may get depressed (see *Personality*, p. 98).
Go on to Question 9

**NO**

**9** Do you have three or more of the following tendencies or traits?
□ You are excessively conscientious
□ Your standards are very high
□ You are often worried about what the neighbours might say, or what other people might think
□ It is very important to you to feel "in" with your peers
□ You dislike disobeying rules
□ The approval of those senior to you is important
□ It is very important to you not to make a mistake
□ It is very important to you to be seen as good.

**YES** ▶ You may have a "good behaviour" personality, which means that what other people think of you may be more important than your own enjoyment of life. Such dependence on an external source of approval is accompanied by an inner (sometimes unconscious) sense of inferiority. When the act fails or if you realize that the mask never creates true happiness, a period of depression may follow (see *Personality*, p. 98).
Go on to Question 10

**NO**

**10** Do you have two or more of the following traits?
□ You feel that it is a sign of strength to avoid showing your feelings
□ You feel it is wrong to show aggression
□ Passion or too much physical contact makes you feel uncomfortable
□ You disapprove of too great a show of emotions (by yourself or others)
□ You like to be cool and calm, or aloof.

**YES** ▶ You may have a "controlled" personality. You may not be predisposed to severe depression, but your capacity for enjoyment is limited by your control. This is especially true when you have a strong feeling inside you which you control (repress). Dissatisfaction and loss of sparkle are likely (see *Personality*, p. 98).
Go on to Question 11

**NO**

*Go to next page*

47

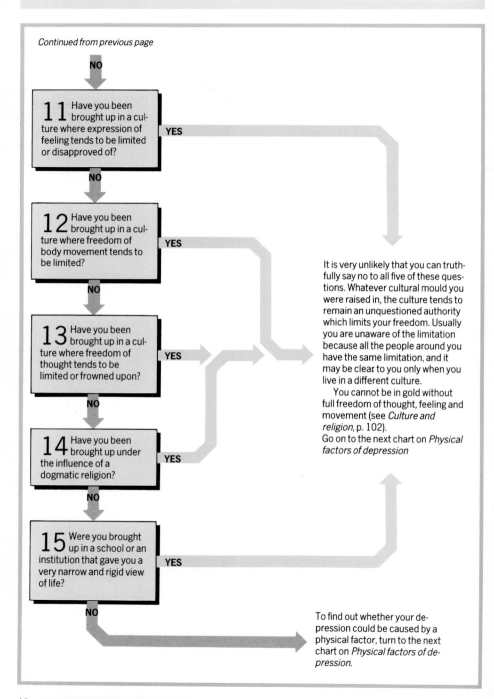

Continued from previous page

NO

**11** Have you been brought up in a culture where expression of feeling tends to be limited or disapproved of?

YES

NO

**12** Have you been brought up in a culture where freedom of body movement tends to be limited?

YES

NO

**13** Have you been brought up in a culture where freedom of thought tends to be limited or frowned upon?

YES

NO

**14** Have you been brought up under the influence of a dogmatic religion?

YES

NO

**15** Were you brought up in a school or an institution that gave you a very narrow and rigid view of life?

YES

NO

It is very unlikely that you can truthfully say no to all five of these questions. Whatever cultural mould you were raised in, the culture tends to remain an unquestioned authority which limits your freedom. Usually you are unaware of the limitation because all the people around you have the same limitation, and it may be clear to you only when you live in a different culture.

You cannot be in gold without full freedom of thought, feeling and movement (see *Culture and religion*, p. 102).
Go on to the next chart on *Physical factors of depression*

To find out whether your depression could be caused by a physical factor, turn to the next chart on *Physical factors of depression*.

# 4 ☐ PHYSICAL FACTORS OF DEPRESSION

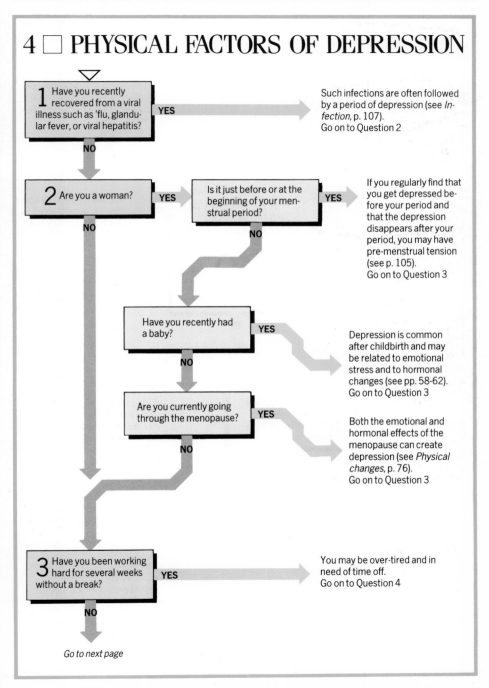

**1** Have you recently recovered from a viral illness such as 'flu, glandular fever, or viral hepatitis?

**YES** → Such infections are often followed by a period of depression (see *Infection*, p. 107).
Go on to Question 2

**NO**

**2** Are you a woman?

**YES** → Is it just before or at the beginning of your menstrual period?

**YES** → If you regularly find that you get depressed before your period and that the depression disappears after your period, you may have pre-menstrual tension (see p. 105).
Go on to Question 3

**NO**

Have you recently had a baby?

**YES** → Depression is common after childbirth and may be related to emotional stress and to hormonal changes (see pp. 58-62).
Go on to Question 3

**NO**

Are you currently going through the menopause?

**YES** → Both the emotional and hormonal effects of the menopause can create depression (see *Physical changes*, p. 76).
Go on to Question 3

**NO**

**3** Have you been working hard for several weeks without a break?

**YES** → You may be over-tired and in need of time off.
Go on to Question 4

**NO**

*Go to next page*

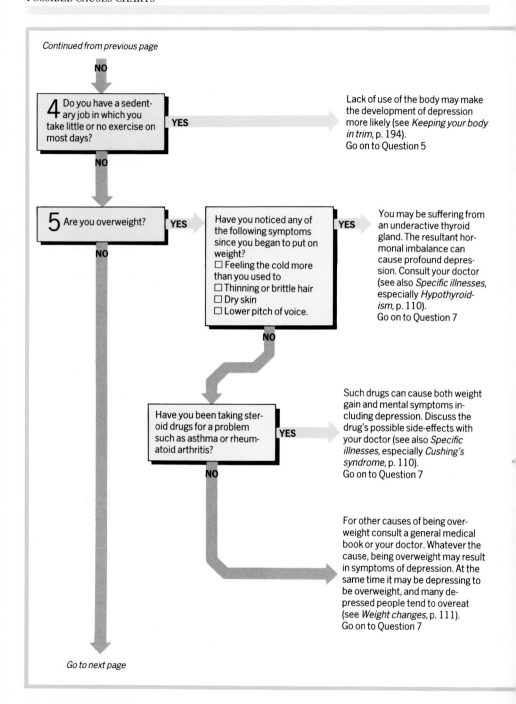

*Continued from previous page*

**NO**

**4** Do you have a sedentary job in which you take little or no exercise on most days?

**YES** → Lack of use of the body may make the development of depression more likely (see *Keeping your body in trim*, p. 194).
Go on to Question 5

**NO**

**5** Are you overweight?

**YES** → Have you noticed any of the following symptoms since you began to put on weight?
☐ Feeling the cold more than you used to
☐ Thinning or brittle hair
☐ Dry skin
☐ Lower pitch of voice.

**YES** → You may be suffering from an underactive thyroid gland. The resultant hormonal imbalance can cause profound depression. Consult your doctor (see also *Specific illnesses*, especially *Hypothyroidism*, p. 110).
Go on to Question 7

**NO**

**NO**

Have you been taking steroid drugs for a problem such as asthma or rheumatoid arthritis?

**YES** → Such drugs can cause both weight gain and mental symptoms including depression. Discuss the drug's possible side-effects with your doctor (see also *Specific illnesses*, especially *Cushing's syndrome*, p. 110).
Go on to Question 7

**NO**

For other causes of being overweight consult a general medical book or your doctor. Whatever the cause, being overweight may result in symptoms of depression. At the same time it may be depressing to be overweight, and many depressed people tend to overeat (see *Weight changes*, p. 111).
Go on to Question 7

*Go to next page*

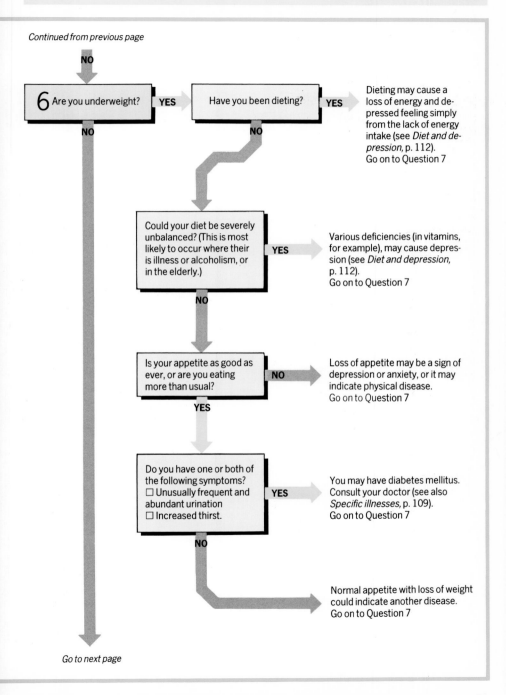

*Continued from previous page*

**NO**

**6** Are you underweight?  **YES** → Have you been dieting?  **YES** → Dieting may cause a loss of energy and depressed feeling simply from the lack of energy intake (see *Diet and depression,* p. 112). Go on to Question 7

**NO**

**NO**

Could your diet be severely unbalanced? (This is most likely to occur where their is illness or alcoholism, or in the elderly.)  **YES** → Various deficiencies (in vitamins, for example), may cause depression (see *Diet and depression,* p. 112). Go on to Question 7

**NO**

Is your appetite as good as ever, or are you eating more than usual?  **NO** → Loss of appetite may be a sign of depression or anxiety, or it may indicate physical disease. Go on to Question 7

**YES**

Do you have one or both of the following symptoms?
☐ Unusually frequent and abundant urination
☐ Increased thirst.  **YES** → You may have diabetes mellitus. Consult your doctor (see also *Specific illnesses,* p. 109). Go on to Question 7

**NO**

Normal appetite with loss of weight could indicate another disease. Go on to Question 7

*Go to next page*

*Continued from previous page*

**NO**

**7** Do you have any of the following obvious physical symptoms?
☐ Is your temperature 38°C (100°F) or above?
☐ Do you have bleeding from any part of your body or *have you noticed blood or blackness in your phlegm, vomit, urine or faeces?*
☐ *Do you have obvious swelling in the ankles, your face, or any other part of your body when there has been no physical injury to cause it?*
☐ Have you experienced vomiting, diarrhoea or *increasing difficulty in swallowing?*
☐ *Have you had any unusual discharges from the skin, nose, mouth, anus or genitals?*
☐ *Has your urine become consistently much darker or your faeces consistently much lighter?*
☐ *Have you recently had a period or periods of unconsciousness?*
☐ *Is passing urine painful?*
☐ *Have you had headaches associated with nausea or vomiting?*

☐ Do you have a rash or has *your skin gone yellow?*
☐ *Have you had recurrent attacks of abdominal pain?*
☐ *Have you noticed the onset of unusual weakness in one part of your body, or difficulty in speaking properly or in balancing?*
☐ *Have you seen or heard things that nobody else can see or hear?*
☐ *Have you been so confused that you do not know the time of day (within an hour or two), the day of the week or where you are?*
☐ Has your eyesight become worse recently?
☐ *Have you recently experienced pain in the chest which gets worse with exercise or worse with breathing deeply or coughing?*
☐ *Have you been hoarse for more than two weeks?*
☐ *Have you had a persistent cough for more than four weeks?*
☐ *Do you get short of breath at rest or do you find yourself much more breathless on exercise than before?*
☐ Do you have any other unexplained physical symptom?

**YES**

Any one of these symptoms or conditions indicates that it is possible that you have some organic disease which may or may not be serious. You should consult your doctor if you are not sure. If you have any of the symptoms *in italics* and have not yet consulted a doctor, it is wise to do so.

Any physical disease may cause loss of appetite and energy. Thus any physical disease may be physically depressing, apart from the possible depressing mental effect of your life being changed by being ill (see *Severe illness*, p. 107).
Go on to Question 8

**NO**

*Go to next page*

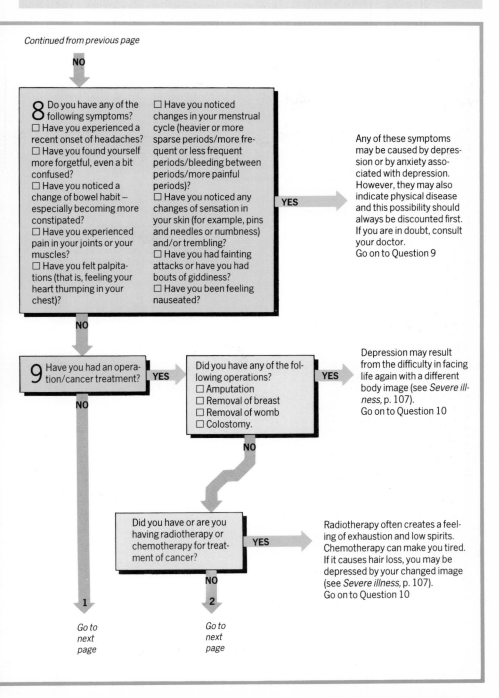

Continued from previous page

**NO**

**8** Do you have any of the following symptoms?
☐ Have you experienced a recent onset of headaches?
☐ Have you found yourself more forgetful, even a bit confused?
☐ Have you noticed a change of bowel habit – especially becoming more constipated?
☐ Have you experienced pain in your joints or your muscles?
☐ Have you felt palpitations (that is, feeling your heart thumping in your chest)?

☐ Have you noticed changes in your menstrual cycle (heavier or more sparse periods/more frequent or less frequent periods/bleeding between periods/more painful periods)?
☐ Have you noticed any changes of sensation in your skin (for example, pins and needles or numbness) and/or trembling?
☐ Have you had fainting attacks or have you had bouts of giddiness?
☐ Have you been feeling nauseated?

**YES** →

Any of these symptoms may be caused by depression or by anxiety associated with depression. However, they may also indicate physical disease and this possibility should always be discounted first. If you are in doubt, consult your doctor.
Go on to Question 9

**NO**

**9** Have you had an operation/cancer treatment? **YES** →

Did you have any of the following operations?
☐ Amputation
☐ Removal of breast
☐ Removal of womb
☐ Colostomy.

**YES** →

Depression may result from the difficulty in facing life again with a different body image (see *Severe illness,* p. 107).
Go on to Question 10

**NO**

Did you have or are you having radiotherapy or chemotherapy for treatment of cancer? **YES** →

Radiotherapy often creates a feeling of exhaustion and low spirits. Chemotherapy can make you tired. If it causes hair loss, you may be depressed by your changed image (see *Severe illness,* p. 107).
Go on to Question 10

**NO**

**NO**

**1**
Go to next page

**2**
Go to next page

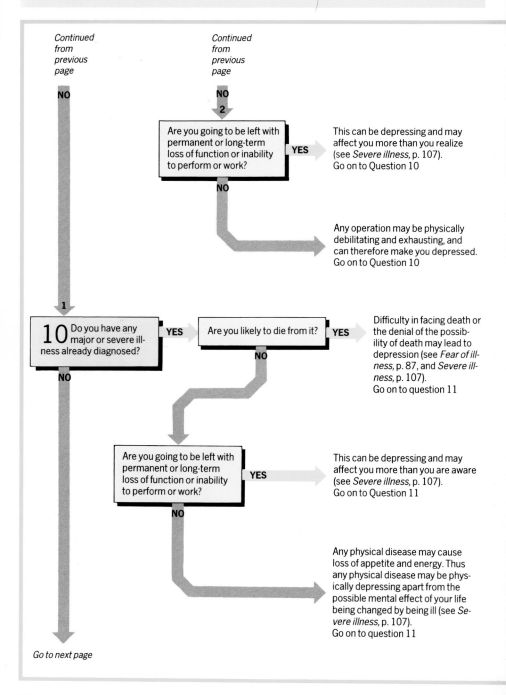

Continued
from
previous
page

NO

Continued
from
previous
page

NO
2

Are you going to be left with permanent or long-term loss of function or inability to perform or work? **YES**

This can be depressing and may affect you more than you realize (see *Severe illness*, p. 107). Go on to Question 10

NO

Any operation may be physically debilitating and exhausting, and can therefore make you depressed. Go on to Question 10

1

**10** Do you have any major or severe illness already diagnosed? **YES**

Are you likely to die from it? **YES**

Difficulty in facing death or the denial of the possibility of death may lead to depression (see *Fear of illness*, p. 87, and *Severe illness*, p. 107). Go on to question 11

NO

NO

Are you going to be left with permanent or long-term loss of function or inability to perform or work? **YES**

This can be depressing and may affect you more than you are aware (see *Severe illness*, p. 107). Go on to Question 11

NO

Any physical disease may cause loss of appetite and energy. Thus any physical disease may be physically depressing apart from the possible mental effect of your life being changed by being ill (see *Severe illness*, p. 107). Go on to question 11

Go to next page

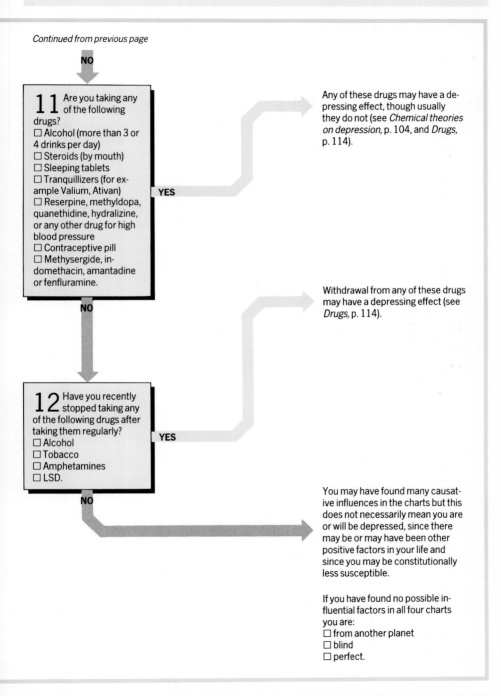

*Continued from previous page*

**NO**

**11** Are you taking any of the following drugs?
☐ Alcohol (more than 3 or 4 drinks per day)
☐ Steroids (by mouth)
☐ Sleeping tablets
☐ Tranquillizers (for example Valium, Ativan)
☐ Reserpine, methyldopa, quanethidine, hydralizine, or any other drug for high blood pressure
☐ Contraceptive pill
☐ Methysergide, indomethacin, amantadine or fenfluramine.

**YES**

Any of these drugs may have a depressing effect, though usually they do not (see *Chemical theories on depression*, p. 104, and *Drugs*, p. 114).

**NO**

Withdrawal from any of these drugs may have a depressing effect (see *Drugs*, p. 114).

**12** Have you recently stopped taking any of the following drugs after taking them regularly?
☐ Alcohol
☐ Tobacco
☐ Amphetamines
☐ LSD.

**YES**

**NO**

You may have found many causative influences in the charts but this does not necessarily mean you are or will be depressed, since there may be or may have been other positive factors in your life and since you may be constitutionally less susceptible.

If you have found no possible influential factors in all four charts you are:
☐ from another planet
☐ blind
☐ perfect.

# Life events

The major events that occur in your life create strong feelings within you. If these feelings are unacceptable for personal, family or cultural reasons, you are likely to repress them. For instance, if someone dies, in many cultures it is not acceptable to grieve openly, or to wail, sob and rage. Repression of such feeling in itself does not sound like too great a problem – except for one thing: it is generally not possible to repress one specific feeling without repressing feeling and energy in general. The commonest causative factor in loss of sparkle and blue-grey depression is quite simply the withholding of unacceptable feelings. In other words, repression leads to depression. This is illustrated by the case histories (opposite).

## THE COST OF REPRESSION

In a healthy response to a life event, thoughts and feelings should be in tune and unblocked. The event creates feelings which direct the flow of thoughts; and thoughts of the event, thoughts of the past leading up to the event, thoughts of the future leading away from the event, all affect the inner feeling. Such a flow, if uncensored, may lead to a creative expression which has a positive effect on either the life of the person or on the event affecting his or her life. An expression of feeling may stop somebody from hurting you further; but even if you cannot stop them (for instance, if they have "hurt" you by dying), your vital expression can free your energy and spirit.

Unfortunately, inner feeling and gut reactions are often disapproved of and censored. In many western cultures there is a strong tradition that gut feeling and animal reaction *should* be repressed for the common good. For instance, aggression should be repressed so that no-one gets hurt.

On the face of it, this seems reasonable. The problem is that the cost of the repression is not usually put into the equation. By repressing a feeling you imprison your life force, resulting in a minimum sentence of loss of sparkle. Repression creates depression.

The alternative is often depicted as an explosion of uncontrollable animal impulse, leading to chaos, anarchy, hurt and destruction. If you were to put this view to any respectable chimpanzee, and even the most respectable chimpanzees do not repress their feelings, he would not understand what you were talking about. The chimpanzee record on destruction is better than the human one, chimpanzees enjoy a high degree of social order and they do not repress their feelings. In the case history (below) Mrs B did not repress her feeling, but she did channel it so that only the plates were damaged (and even

## CASE HISTORIES

Mrs. A found out that her husband was having an affair. Usually, the natural reaction to such a revelation would be anger, as well as feelings of hurt, jealousy and sadness. But while Mrs. A had no difficulty in feeling and expressing the hurt, she could not bring herself to be overtly angry, and was in fact so successful at hiding aggressive impulses that she did not even realize that she was angry. There were many reasons for this: she was brought up by a mother who never asserted herself and by a father who was often drunk and violent – thus she learnt non-assertion from her mother and was taught only the negative side of aggression by her father; secondly, her background dictated that women were not supposed to be angry or aggressive – accommodating, yes – assertive, no – angry, never; thirdly, she was afraid that if she were to be angry, her husband would leave her (because she would be breaking the unwritten rules of their particular marriage contract which, unconsciously but specifically, stipulated that he was the only one allowed to get angry). So she did not get angry, which took a considerable, though unconscious, effort of repression. Occasionally an angry thought would break through to the surface: she would imagine, for a moment, catching her husband and his lover in the act and . . . the shutters would come down and she would force the thought to the back of her mind. Since this whole process was fairly automatic, she was unaware of the cost of inhibiting her reaction and unaware that there was even a relationship between the shutting out of the anger and the shutting out of other feelings. She was only aware of beginning to feel low, empty and depressed. It was as if all her energy had been used up in battening down her strong

feelings. The strong wall that she created to withstand the strong feelings now served to imprison her, and although she could communicate rationally, she lost the ability to communicate with vitality.

As she became more depressed she found one small consolation: her husband became aware of her state and began to feel guilty; he had to suffer her slow punishment of him. So in wreaking a round-about revenge she found she could gain from continuing the depressive process – but nowhere near as much as she was losing. Her explanation to herself was, "Of course it is natural to be depressed by your husband having an affair" – but it is not natural.

Mrs. B was in a similar situation. She was, quite simply, furious. At first she said nothing and then, later, at a moment of her own choosing and with brazen impoliteness, she unleashed all the angry force of a wounded animal. Her husband tried to stop her by saying soothing words, and then by shouting back; but nothing would stop her, and in the end he listened and was moved. They both felt relieved, she from having let go of her feelings, and he from not having to endure another moment of guilt-provoking silence. The directness of expression gave them a quality of human contact which they had not experienced in years (a quality which, incidentally, made his affair seem to him a little tawdry by comparison). They even laughed together as they cleared up the shards of broken plates.

This is not to say that all the bad feeling was over: it would take time for the wounds to heal. The pain rocked the marriage and could have ended it. But though there were many different feelings during a time of turmoil, she was never depressed at all.

then, she probably picked out the ones she didn't like). For channelling of feeling, as opposed to repression, see *Creative expression*, page 207.

The effect of repression of feeling varies from a mundane sulk to the sometimes terrible depression of unexpressed grief. Whatever the event, the important factor in this cause of depression is the blocking of gut reaction and hence the cutting off of the very seat of vitality.

# CHILDBIRTH

Depression is very common in a mother after the birth of her child. Some mothers notice depression only at this time and at no other time in their lives. The reasons why depression is so much more common soon after giving birth are both complex and conjectural, but can be conveniently divided into two groups: physical stress and emotional/psychological stress (see opposite and page 60). Depression after childbirth generally takes one of three forms: maternity blues, post-natal depression, or post-natal psychosis.

**Maternity blues**  These usually start two or three days after birth. You may quite suddenly get weepy and irritable, and then just as suddenly, you are out of them. They are very common and do not usually lead on to any longer-lasting depression.

**Post-natal depression**  This occurs after about 10 per cent of births. It may start soon after birth or it may start after an initial few weeks of happiness and high spirits. It is a common experience to feel more emotionally vulnerable for four to six weeks after giving birth – you feel more open and sensitive to everything. This period of greater openness is often remembered with pleasure, but sometimes, after four to six weeks, the physical and emotional demands of looking after a child twenty-four hours a day begin to get a mother down, and you may feel grey and exhausted for many months or even a year or more. A minority of mothers will go into a more severe depressive process which occasionally lasts years.

**Post-natal psychosis**  This is very rare. It usually starts soon after birth with quite a sudden change of personality. Sometimes the symptoms are similar to those of black or white depression and sometimes they are more like those of mania or other psychotic conditions. Often there is a strong element of suspicion and paranoia – you might, for instance, be convinced that someone is poisoning your baby. One woman with white post-natal

## DEPRESSION AFTER CHILDBIRTH

| Severity | Common clinical terms | Frequency | Timing | Treatment |
|---|---|---|---|---|
| Blue depression (see page 16) | Maternity blues | 50% | Usually starts on the 2nd or 3rd day after childbirth and lasts only a few days | Understanding |
| Grey or dark grey depression (see page 17) | Post-natal depression | 10% | Starts within first three months after childbirth and may last months or even years | Professional advice |
| Black or white depression (see page 17) | Post-natal psychosis or Puerperal psychosis | 0.3% | Usually starts soon after childbirth | Urgent hospitalization |

depression tried to drown her children in the bath, sincerely believing that she and they would be better off. Her only interest was to die. Another woman I saw was frantic and screaming: she was convinced that she was the Virgin Mary.

**PHYSICAL STRESS**

During pregnancy another being growing inside you puts a strain on all your body systems – you are eating, digesting, breathing, excreting and pumping your blood for two.

The birth itself is physically exhausting, especially if labour is long. Muscles, ligaments and skin are stretched, sometimes torn, and there is a loss of blood.

**Hormonal changes**

A hormone is a chemical messenger in the body which, in very small quantities, can regulate the activity of particular parts of the body. Hormone levels begin to change within a day of conception, which is probably how some women know they have conceived long before a pregnancy test is possible. Levels of progesterone (one of seven intricately related female hormones so far discovered) rise during pregnancy 15 to 30 times higher than the highest level in non-pregnant women (see graph, overleaf). Such changes may have a considerable effect on your mental state, but the exact relationship between hormone level and mental state is not well understood, and is certainly very variable in different women. It is quite likely that the maternity blues which can start so suddenly, after about two days, are related to drastic change in hormone levels immediately after birth. Hormonal changes may well be a major factor in some of the post-natal psychoses – especially when the psychosis occurs only after each childbirth and at no other time.

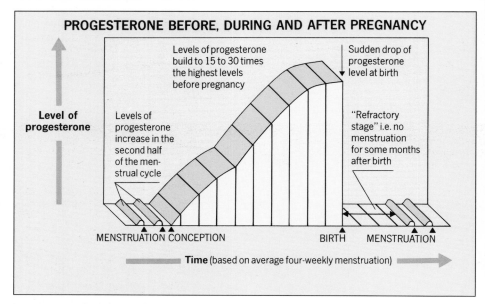

## PROGESTERONE BEFORE, DURING AND AFTER PREGNANCY

**Level of progesterone**

Levels of progesterone increase in the second half of the menstrual cycle

Levels of progesterone build to 15 to 30 times the highest levels before pregnancy

Sudden drop of progesterone level at birth

"Refractory stage" i.e. no menstruation for some months after birth

MENSTRUATION CONCEPTION      BIRTH    MENSTRUATION

**Time** (based on average four-weekly menstruation)

| | |
|---|---|
| **EMOTIONAL/ PSYCHOLOGICAL STRESS** | Birth may be an emotionally stressful time, and any stress may precipitate a depression, particularly in somebody who is already predisposed to depression. Stress may also affect hormonal levels which may have a secondary effect on mood. In addition to the general stresses, there are many specific feelings that may arise at or around the time of childbirth. |
| **Stress during pregnancy** | A special relationship may develop between you and the baby as it grows inside you. Your pregnancy may become an expression of hope and commitment between you and your partner. But as every pregnant woman knows, the process has its costs: the baby makes you big, and sometimes sick; the baby may give you varicose veins, stretch marks, pigmentation, gas, piles, heartburn, and unwanted hair. The baby can make you uncomfortable and interferes with your freedom to move and eat as you wish. Your life patterns are interrupted. It is quite natural to have feelings of resentment about these things at times. Although such feelings may start as being very small compared to those of love and hope, they may grow and begin to obscure the "good" feelings if they are not expressed (see *Express the feeling*, page 122 and *Creative expression*, page 207). |
| **Stress during labour** | Childbirth can be a time of intimacy, excitement, wonder and openness. It can also be a time of fear and pain, sometimes in a place that is forbidding and lacking in warmth. There may |

## CASE HISTORY

A couple with two daughters consulted me because of a loss of sparkle in their marriage and their lives generally. There were many reasons for this: one of them related to the birth of their first daughter six years earlier. The labour had been very long and the baby finally had to be delivered by forceps. The parents were angry that at no point had they been consulted about the decision. Before the forceps were used the father was asked if he would mind leaving the room temporarily, and was given no indication that he would not be there for the birth. When he was called back in, the baby had been born and had already been taken away into another room.

Six years later, when consulting me, he felt the full fury about the doctor's deception, the precious moments he had been deprived of, and later, his own lack of courage: after all, the doctor could not have forced him to leave the room. In expressing his feelings he picked up a chair and smashed it on the floor, shouting "How dare you! . . . It was my daughter!" A perfectly rational and intelligent man, he simply not realized how furious he was. For six years he had repressed the feeling. After expressing himself, he felt freer and more confident for a while, though he would need to keep on expressing himself in other situations to maintain his feeling of freedom (see *Creative expression*, page 207).

The mother, too, was angry about her husband not being there at the delivery. But what made her more angry was feeling that she had been completely ignored as a person, and that there had been no consultation about decisions concerning her body or consideration for her feelings. At the time all this was irrelevant compared to the celebration and joy of the birth, but later a chronic, underlying, repressed resentment persisted. She remained somewhat subdued and certainly lacking in sparkle, until one day, when she was walking in a wood thinking about the delivery, she started hacking down ferns imagining each fern to be a doctor. This gave her some feeling of liberation, but it also gave her a more balanced view so that she could see more clearly her own responsibility in not, for example, demanding consultation on decisions before the delivery. Both parents realize that they were partly responsible for allowing what happened, although it is difficult not to hand over authority in times of stress, fear and pain.

be all kinds of left-over feelings, which are usually repressed. First of all, the birth hurts you – it is quite natural for some women to be angry about this. Secondly, you may resent the way your delivery was handled. Unfortunately, the case history above is not an isolated example. I have heard of so many similar and worse cases that it sometimes makes me feel ashamed of my profession as a doctor. The resentment is usually related to lack of consultation on decisions. Medical interventions are sometimes carried out (for instance, routine episiotomies, injections to speed up the birth of the placenta) without any explanation of side-effects. If the side-effects occur, the natural reaction is anger, but this is often repressed, with the explanation that the doctor knows what is best. It is this attitude of the patient handing over authority to the doctor and the doctor taking assumed authority over another's life that may lead to later feelings of resentment. Some women have told me they felt like a nonentity, going through a process that was designed by the hospital to maximize speed and efficiency. Others have told me that it felt like being taken over by machines and fingers. The residue of resentment may go very deep and is usually repressed, with a resultant depression of spirits in general.

At other times, medical interventions are clearly necessary and hospital staff act with sensitivity and kindness. But some mothers have strong feelings about having to have an obstetric intervention. With a caesarean birth, for example, a mother may feel inadequate or abnormal because she couldn't give birth through the proper channels. Such feelings may also be repressed, or they may, quite unfairly, be converted into resentment against the doctor or hospital.

**Stress after the baby is born**

This can be a time full of wonder and joy. Emotionally, you are likely to be very vulnerable for several weeks – more open to happiness, more likely to feel tearful or experience any other feeling. It can be a time full of love and promise.

On the other hand, your whole life is turned upside down. Every routine is disrupted and your life simply isn't your own any more. It is hard to anticipate quite how much your freedom will be curtailed. Meals, sleep, television programmes, telephone conversations – all aspects of your life will be interrupted and you cannot avoid attending to the demands of the totally dependent being. Added to this are the repetitive routines of feeding, changing nappies, comforting and cleaning. You are likely, at times, to have some feelings of resentment about the way your life has changed. For many mothers, there may be moments when you feel like hitting or shaking your child. The problem is not that these resentful feelings exist – if the expression of them is channelled away from the child, they present no difficulty – but that it is often culturally not acceptable either to be angry in general or, more especially, to have "negative feelings" about your child. Ironically, the pressure to be a "good mother" (which, unfortunately, is interpreted as a requirement to repress resentful feelings) can end up contributing to the creation of a mother who is depressed and lacking in warmth. For expression of "negative feeling", see *Creative expression*, page 207.

**PATERNAL PROBLEMS**

As a father, the period after the birth of your child is much easier since your life is usually far less disrupted, both physically and emotionally. But some fathers, especially those who cherish exactitude, will be frustrated by changes in routine. There are times when you have been woken up yet again in the middle of the night and wonder whether it can possibly all be worth it. You may also find yourself jealous: suddenly your partner is devoting most of her attention to the baby and giving little to you; this feeling is usually stronger if the baby is a boy. You may find yourself resenting the baby that you wanted and you cannot quite understand why: sometimes this turns out to be because it is difficult to see the baby receiving more care than you had as a baby or child. This sounds strange since usually you cannot consciously remember that far back, but somehow for both mother and father the birth may bring back the earliest memories; generally these are not exact memories of events but emotive memories – a sense of the feeling that was around you. If you lived in an uncaring atmosphere when you were tiny, seeing your own vulnerable little baby before you may bring back old pain.

All these feelings, including jealousy and anger, are common and natural. They require only to be handled creatively (see *Creative expression*, page 207). Unfortunately, what is more likely to happen is that you judge the feelings you have and therefore do everything you can to repress them. The result then becomes the opposite of what you want, for your own good feeling and love for your child are repressed too.

# DEATH

When you experience the death of someone close to you, or when you have lost somebody who has gone away or whom you have left, it is natural to grieve. In fact, a process of mourning is necessary in order for you to come to terms with the loss and adjust yourself to a life without the dead person.

**GRIEF**  Grieving openly is an acutely painful process which is not usually encouraged in western cultures. Even when people believe that grieving and openly demonstrating your feelings are good for you, their fear of the sheer power of the feeling of grief often makes them try to stop you or calm you down. The commonest alternative to grief is the prolonged numbness of depression which, unfortunately, can last years. Although the expression of grief differs in different individuals, there is a pattern to grief that is fairly common, consisting of three basic stages: numbness, despair and detachment.

**Numbness**  It is hard to believe that it really has happened. Even if the death was expected, for instance after a long illness, it is difficult to accept that a loved one has gone. There may be a feeling of unreality as if the things around you, and even your own body, seem to be not totally there, distanced and lifeless. All feelings may be numbed, and if this stage is prolonged, it can lead to longer-term depression. Normally the numbness lasts only a few hours or a few days.

**Despair**   Typically, there are waves of strong feeling, perhaps every 20 minutes or every hour, in which you may feel intense sorrow, intense anger and intense love. In some cultures it is acceptable to wail at the funeral, which provides a way to release the feeling of sorrow and rage combined. You may feel the pain as an ache in your chest and you may physically feel the emptiness in your stomach. If you resist the expression of the strong feelings within you, this usually requires a tensing of the body, which you may experience as a tightness in the throat, a choking sensation, or a stiff neck. If you do not find a way of expressing the anger, you may find yourself hostile and irritable towards others or perhaps aloof and withdrawn.

You may feel guilty, believing that in some way you were responsible for the death: perhaps you did not call the doctor early enough or perhaps you had just had a row. Or else you think: "If only, if only" – "If only I had told him I loved him" or "If only I had been there when she died", for example.

It is common to identify and be preoccupied with the image of the dead person, sometimes to such an extent that you wonder about your own sanity. It is very common to imagine that you see or hear the dead person alive again: perhaps you see the back of a head in a crowd and for a moment you are sure he is still alive; perhaps you see her face before you. You may identify so much with the dead person that your face seems to look like his in the mirror; or you may even experience symptoms that you know she had in her last illness.

It is hard to be interested in anything new. You may feel restless and pace up and down, wringing your hands and sighing. You are preoccupied with the past and the future seems far away.

If these feelings are worked through, allowed to be felt and at times expressed, this painful process usually lasts a few weeks or a few months, though it can last longer.

**Detachment**   There comes a point in the state of despair when it is time to begin to emancipate yourself from the ties to the person who has gone. This is not to say that you forget the person – the detachment is not cold – but that you can say in your heart "Goodbye". At this time you begin to be available again to new relationships and to adjust to an environment that is different without your old friend.

**GRIEF AND DEPRESSION**   Because grief is painful there are many mechanisms designed to avoid it: some people drink, others have psychosomatic reactions like asthma or rheumatoid arthritis, others become overactive and deny any feeling of loss. Many people become depressed.

The stage of numbness is a kind of natural depression. Although this normally lasts only a few hours or a few days, it may persist for years. There are many cases of people beginning to grieve ten or even twenty years after the death of someone close to them – the cost of that delay is at the minimum a loss of sparkle during those years, since the wall built around the grief imprisons the freedom of all feelings.

**Repressing anger**  Many people have difficulty with being angry and think that it is unfair to be angry with the dead person (since it was not really his fault) and dangerous to be angry with God or life. Such anger directed at the deceased and life is quite natural, but the taboo may be so strong that the feeling is not even realized. Sometimes the anger is directed against the hospital or doctor. More often the anger is simply repressed, with the inevitable repression of all other feelings.

**Guilt and self-blame**  You may find yourself so preoccupied with guilt and self-blame that this becomes a self-perpetuating process; the bad feeling affecting your confidence, your diminished confidence affecting your performance and your poor performance making you feel worse about yourself, and justifying your self-castigation.

If you have had severe depression in the past or are prone to severe depressive reactions, the stress of the grief may precipitate a black depression, in which the preoccupation is hardly with the lost person at all, but with the blackness and hopelessness of self.

**The extent of grief**  The extent and difficulty of grieving is related to how much interaction you had with the dead person. (This may be the case even if the interaction was hostile and hateful.) Losing a spouse is usually extremely difficult; though you may be prepared to go through the despair of your loss, you are still faced with having to build a different life. When a parent loses a young child, the grief may be the hardest of all to bear.

Grief will be involved in any loss, not only the death of a close person. For some, the closest being is a cat or a dog and the loss of this dear friend may cause great pain – though there may be shame and reluctance to admit to the strength of the feeling. You can grieve over the loss of an opportunity, over the loss of a country and culture on emigration, or over the loss of part of your body (see *Loss as a result of illness*, page 107). Whatever the loss, depression may beset some of those who will not or cannot allow themselves to feel their grief, but can often be averted by allowing the feelings to surface (see *Dealing with the life event*, page 121).

# MARRIAGE AND FAMILIES

Depression is about twice as common in women as it is in men. There are probably many reasons for this (see *Child-birth*, page 58), and some of them are connected with marriage. Recent research points out that married women are more likely than married men to feel unhappy; to have feelings of inadequacy; to have difficulty in sleeping; to feel apathetic or inert and to behave in a passive way; to have bouts of depression, and to have symptoms of mental ill-health in general. Unmarried women, on the contrary, tend to have better mental and physical health than both unmarried men and married women.

Men, on the other hand, tend to have better mental health when married than when not married. Unmarried men in the United States have a suicide rate twice as high as married men. Men who lose their wives are usually more prone to depression than women who lose their husbands, and men tend to remarry as soon as possible. Though it may not seem like it on the surface, the man may be more dependent than the woman, even though he may not play an obviously dependent role. He is more likely to get depressed when the marriage is over or when his conventional role as sole or main bread-winner is upturned. He may feel inadequate and helpless if he realizes that his spouse can and does manage well without him.

**Conventional roles**

Either partner is likely to get depressed if his or her role within the marriage is subordinate. For some women, particularly those who do not go out to work, marriage can lead to self-subordination, dependency and a lack of stimulation. There may be a feeling of being trapped by children. The woman who maintains a position of submission must necessarily repress her reactions and spirit, and marriages built on a pattern of superiority and inferiority often create boredom and disappointment.

Although conventional roles have been upturned to a certain extent, a married woman is still more susceptible to depression. One of the reasons for this is that emotional change lags at least a generation behind intellectual change. Although intellectually most people realize that women and men are both equal and different, cultural traditions take decades to die. An intellectually "liberated" couple may easily drop back into roles they learned from their parents without even noticing that they are doing so. Secondly, a woman's greater freedom of choice has its own pressures and problems. A woman can choose whether to pursue her own

career, with or without having children. She may take on the
dual role of working woman and mother/housewife, thus
subjecting herself to considerable pressure, both physical and
emotional. She may feel that she is fulfilling neither role to the
best of her ability. She may feel guilty that she is not caring
enough for her children, and she may resent the fact that her
husband doesn't help more than he does. A woman who does
stay at home to care for her children may feel pressure from
her peers to get a job.

**Social expectations**

Social expectations of marriage are coloured by idealized
romantic fiction of couples "living happily ever after", and it
is often a shock to both partners to discover just how hard
they have to work at marriage to make it a success. Compromise, mutual trust and sharing are essential for it to flourish.
When one partner has a different expectation to the other,
there is conflict which can only be cleared with communication and understanding. Lack of proper communication between partners is always a source of unhappiness. If you
cannot communicate, all your fears, worries and resentments
are repressed, leading to inevitable loss of sparkle and lack of
energy. However, in the closeness of a relationship it is often
difficult to see things in perspective (see *Talking to somebody*,
page 124).

**MARITAL
QUARRELS**

Battles between husband and wife often lead to depression.
Compare, for example, the ways Mrs. A and Mrs. B react to
infidelity (see page 57). Often, however, the precipitating
events seem much smaller – such as leaving clothes on the
floor yet again. In a situation of equality between husband
and wife, such issues can often be dealt with, without the
need to repress response (see *Dealing with the life event*, page
121). Unfortunately many marriages are not equal. One partner often takes a subservient role. If a marriage is based on
traditional perceptions, the woman may repress her response
in order to fit in with the man who, they may both consciously
or unconsciously believe, is meant to know better. If this
happens over a period of years she is left with a chronic
resentment of the man to whom she has handed over power.
This may be expressed by retaliatory measures such as bitter
nagging, getting the children on her side against him, doing
things behind his back and so on, but the indirect retaliation
does nothing to lift her spirits. Often the man does not want to
see what is happening, because he is comfortable in his
position and would prefer to pretend that everything is going
well rather than feel inadequate. If the woman has the clarity
to point out what is happening and how she feels, he calls her

"irrational". If she allows herself to be stopped by that label, then she is back in her old depressed position – and so it goes on, sometimes for years. And if after years, she or he has had enough, the ending can be bitter indeed – years of old resentment pouring out like the infection from a wound. Meanwhile, the years of chronic resentment have been years of limited life and depressed spirits. This is true for both wife and husband, because the atmosphere permeates the home (see *Therapy for couples*, page 161).

**FAMILY QUARRELS**

Quarrels between husband and wife or between parents and children can create an atmosphere that is tense or depressed. There may be many reasons for the quarrels. A husband may strongly resent the fact that his mother-in-law has come to live with his family, or a wife may hate spending every Christmas with her husband's family; both may repress the anger, in an attempt to avoid hurting their spouse's feelings. Children of unstable marriages may become depressed when they see their parents fighting – they bottle everything up rather than risk adding to the fraught atmosphere.

Some families, in an attempt to stop the quarrelling, repress all emotional reactions. When you walk into such a household, you can *feel* the repression in the atmosphere, and it seems that it would be a relief if someone would say what they really felt. But within your own family, it is usually much harder to see what is happening. You may have had the experience of bitter battles in the past leading nowhere, and decided it was a better policy to keep quiet. Eventually the quietness becomes a way of life, and you hardly even notice the feelings you have underneath. Although many families survive in this depressed fashion, the quality of life is inevitably lowered.

For quarrels between parents and children, see *Achieving independence*, page 74, and *Therapy for families*, page 162.

**SEPARATION AND DIVORCE**

When your marriage, or indeed any relationship, has broken down, you may find separation preferable to keeping up appearances. But the separation itself is hardly ever easy. You may feel anything from relief to grief, and often both at the same time. When there has not been very much interaction between you, when your relationship really has become nothing more than a formality, and particularly if the recent period has been full of stress, it may just be a relief to get away from each other. But when you have been very involved with each other, whether in love or hate, the loss of your partner is often hard to bear. You may need to grieve (see *Grief*, page 63) and if you do not, you may risk becoming depressed.

Separation and divorce are particularly hard to tolerate in those of a dependent nature (see *"Dependent" personality*, page 98). If you are more or less dependent, you tend to rely on your partner to supply you with incentive, and your valuation of yourself tends to depend on your partner's valuation of you. It is as if your investment is made outside yourself rather than in the development of your own capacities – so when the outside support goes, you collapse: you have lost incentive and self-value and may become depressed.

Whether you are dependent or not, it is very difficult to be alone after years of being together. Your previous life has been set in various patterns which are now mostly upset and in disarray; it is easy to feel disorientated and confused. There are so many disrupting and isolating influences that it can be hard to maintain hope. It is often a time when you need to talk to someone (see *Talking to somebody*, page 124).

If you have children, you have to bear the pain of their disappointment as well as your own loss of seeing them every day. Yet if your marriage is truly ended, if you do not involve the children in your battles and even, for their sakes, tend to stress positive aspects of your old partner in front of the children, the children will probably be happier in two harmonious homes than in one divided one.

**CHANGES IN YOUR CHILDREN**
In the natural progression of events, your children start life wholly dependent on you and gradually grow to achieve full adult independence. It is not unusual for a parent to find this transition difficult. It is hard to see yourself being needed less and less, and finally not at all, especially if your career has been your children.

**Starting school**
For most mothers, the children starting at school is a blessed relief from the strain of 24-hour care, but for some, especially those who rely on their children for a sense of meaning in their lives, the children going to school is felt as a loss so strong that depression may result from the suppression of these feelings. Mothers who rely on their children for a sense of purpose tend to be more dependent people, with a susceptibility to depression when outside sources of support become less available. (See also *"Dependent" personality*, page 98.)

**Independence**
When children become teenagers they often need to test out their strength and feel their independence. As the verbal mastery of the expression of feeling is at its beginning, this burgeoning independence is often expressed as a recalcitrant silence, which can be difficult to live with day after day. Some parents react by repressing their reactions and energy.

**Leaving home**  The most difficult stage for a parent to come to terms with is the children leaving home, which is a major life change for the whole family. After 16 or 20 years of living with somebody, caring for them and watching them grow, it is a wrench when they finally must go. This may be the most intimate relationship you have ever had and it is perfectly natural to need to grieve over the loss.

One mother I know was both sad and furious that her favourite daughter was leaving. She knew better than to try to stop her daughter, so she took care to express her feeling when her daughter was not around: "I don't want you to go! . . . You are so much of my life . . . I wish I could stop you . . . but I love you, and I don't want to stand in your way!" This expression of grief, shouted with anger and cried with sorrow, was the opposite of depression, freeing her to be genuinely available for her daughter and supportive of her freedom without causing guilt or bad feeling. She had been helped by finding somebody to encourage her feeling.

If you do not grieve (and it is hard to go through feelings of grief on your own), you may depress your feelings, or else be tempted to try to stop your child from leaving, rather than facing the pain of your loss.

When the children have gone, your marriage may suddenly look very different. Both parents may have related far more to the children than to each other. If this is so, you may realize with a shock that you have become near strangers to each other. A mother whose career has been her home and children is faced with a feeling of redundancy and has to reassess her whole career as well as her marriage. Naturally, it is tempting to repress all these feelings of loss and the fear of change, but when they are faced, beyond the uncertainty lies the possibility of a new, exciting and, in many ways, freer life (see *Dealing with the life event*, page 121).

# WORK

Since most people spend a large portion of their lives at work, and since it usually provides a sense of meaning in life, problems related to work are a common cause of depression. The problems mentioned below may also pertain to voluntary work or work on committees.

**INCREASING PRESSURE**  When you start a new job, or if you are given more responsibility at work, you may relish the new challenge. As you go on up the ladder, however, there may come a point where the extra responsibility puts too much pressure on you. This is more likely if you are exceptionally conscientious, finding it hard to delegate to anyone, in which case you are faced with an increasing work-load. You may find that this eventually becomes insurmountable.

If you are over-conscientious, you probably tend to over-value others' opinions of yourself. Your strong ideals to be worthy, superior, good, strong and, most of all, to make no mistakes, are quite impossible to attain. But at the same time there is often an irrational feeling that these impossible goals have to be reached for fear of disapproval by peers or super-iors. In this position, the response is often to build a mask so that the underlying insecurity and lack of self-esteem (hence over-reliance on the esteem of others) are well hidden behind a coping and conforming image. At a low level of responsibil-ity you may be able to keep up the image, but as responsibility increases and pressure mounts, the image may crack. For the person governed by external approval, a cracked image is intolerable. It may be followed by severe self-recrimination and feelings of complete inferiority – the precursors of what may become a grey or black depressive collapse.

Sometimes, taking on a large debt or mortgage may create a pressure to succeed financially that cannot be tolerated. One of the factors that makes it so difficult to change a job that is too taxing is the financial responsibility you have already taken on, and the standard of living you have come to expect. For help with trying to overcome problems related to increas-ing responsibility, read the self-help section, pages 121 to 144, particularly *Changing the situation at work*, page 127.

**LOSS OF POSITION**
When you lose your job, your position or prestige at work, or when your financial position deteriorates, you are faced with the feeling of failure. I have never met anyone who finds failure easy, but some can tolerate it better than others.

First of all, you may have been right and only lose your position because of the stupidity of others or through a neces-sity beyond your control. If so, you are going to feel angry, and this feeling may be repressed. On the other hand you may feel angry with "them" because you are unwilling to see your own responsibility in your failure.

For those with a greater need of others' approval, failure can be harder to take because of the loss of image (see *Increas-ing pressure*, opposite). For others with a depressive tendency, another failure hits an old chord within which rings with sombre tone: "Here we go again, this proves that I'm no good and never will be. I might as well give up now. I'm a useless person. There's nothing inside me of value. I am a failure – and this finally proves it."

Quite apart from the feeling of failure, you may also be aware of the loss of the pleasures and perks of your old position, the loss of workmates, and the loss of a whole working society and culture which you miss. You may find that you miss these aspects of work far more than you ever imagined you would. For the long-term effects of a less fulfilling position, a loss of prestige, losing your job or retiring, see *Life non-events: Boredom at work*, page 80; *Unemployment*, page 80; and *Retirement*, page 81.

**DISAGREEMENT AT WORK**

You may have experienced moments of aggravation at work, or in any situation, to which at the time and in the circumstances you thought you could not respond. Perhaps the wisest and most economical action in terms of the stability of your position seemed to be to keep your mouth shut – but how false this economy can be. Withholding your feeling has a long term personal cost, which is easy to forget if you are more focused on your work place than yourself.

**Mind and body in opposition**

Let us suppose you are in a meeting and someone says something with which you disagree strongly and which makes you angry, or at least irritated. Perhaps it is not politically wise to say anything at that moment so you hold your tongue. Electrical recordings of tension levels within muscles show that you can, in fact, literally hold your tongue by tensing the muscles in your tongue when you do not speak a thought that you want to speak (that is, the thought remains "on the tip of your tongue"). Similarly, when you "keep your mouth shut", you actually tense the jaw muscles that close your mouth, even though you may not be conscious of doing so. If you are angry, a natural expression of your anger is to punch with your fists or to kick with your legs; therefore when you stop your anger, involuntarily and sometimes imperceptibly, your level of muscular tension rises in both arms and legs – perhaps you feel your hands clench into fists or perhaps you just feel quite inexplicably tired (see *"Good behaviour" personality*, page 99).

Often your emotional attention stays directed to what you would like to have said but didn't . . . "I think you are mistaken" . . . "But don't you think, Mr. C that" . . . "Mr. C, I'm getting angry" . . . "Mr. C, shut up!" Or perhaps directed to what you would like to do – for instance, wave your arms in remonstration, shake him, or stuff his papers down his throat. Involuntarily it seems you are preoccupied with your intended response both in mind and in body, your mind rehearsing replies, your body tensing against actually speaking them or moving. The next speaker may be exciting and his data clear and relevant, but your creativity of thought has been lost like a needle stuck on a single groove of a record: the needle and its minute vibrations are your thought processes, and the groove is maintained by consistent, though often unrecognized, muscle tension. The amount of work done in keeping the muscles tense may be equivalent to carrying around two heavy suitcases, but the tiredness is unlike the rather pleasant tiredness you may feel after exercise: it is a tiredness without satisfaction which depletes you into a kind of morose weariness. At the same time your mind is fixed on a negative thought; that is, what you did not say, and so the anger begins to turn inwards against yourself: "What a fool, I should have said . . . I'm useless at meetings" etc. Thus, in the space of a few hours, you have the beginnings of the first symptoms of depression: tiredness, loss of energy, negative thinking, self-deprecation and loss of creativity.

The process is not the same for everyone. "Dependent" personalities (see page 98) do not tense their muscles so much, but appear to be able to block a reaction before it has time to reach the level of the organs of action, the muscles. While these reactions to difficulties with other people often arise in a work environment, they can just as well be the result of disagreement with anyone, be it your obstructive neighbour or your son's unhelpful physics teacher. To learn how to use these kind of feelings in a constructive way, see *Creative expression*, page 207.

# MOVING HOUSE

Moving is invariably a time of stress. Whatever the reasons for the move, such as a marital problem or a change of job, which may cause depression in themselves, the upheaval involved may cause physical tiredness and emotional strain. Selling a house may take months, during which you have to put up with strangers traipsing through your private life, and there may be weeks of uncertainty while financial transactions succeed or fail.

A house is almost always a home, invested with feelings and memories. Part of you will always be there. You may even have built it or part of it yourself. However much bigger and better or more exciting the new house may be, there is inevitably a feeling of loss about what you are leaving behind. Unless you are moving locally, you will be leaving familiar faces and places, probably good friends, and you will be facing the unknown where you may initially feel isolated and lonely.

**Changing cultures** If you are moving abroad, or even, sometimes, to a different part of the country, you may be hit by culture shock. There may be language difficulties – even in your own country. You may find shopping more of a problem than you could have imagined – goods and shops have different names, people may not understand your accent, and they may be hostile to new faces. It is difficult not to feel alienated, isolated and lonely. Rather than risk making a mistake, you may be tempted to withdraw. Perhaps you decide not to buy something that you want because you do not want to go to the trouble of explaining it in a language you are not fluent in, which might make you look foolish – that little moment of denial can be one tiny step towards depression.

Many people find changing cultures far more difficult than they expected, and some very capable people break down or get depressed. The hardest thing is that the differences between you and your new environment are at one and the same time subtle and far-reaching. Your hosts may not be consciously aware of which reaction, choice of words or facial expression was "wrong", but it will be very clear that you are different, and however polite, accommodating and welcoming they may be, the fact that you are an outsider is usually unavoidably present. So it is that many "aliens" club together for company – this way, they can avoid some of the feeling of isolation. However, it is still necessary to take the awkward steps to understanding and bridging the gap, especially if you are to be in a different environment for some time and want to get the most out of it. Many immigrants to new societies refuse to assimilate themselves and to learn the language, with the result that they inevitably become alienated even from their own children, who in turn have the pressure of having to span two cultures.

# LIFE CHANGES

There are particular periods in your life, when changes are faster, more far-reaching and often more stressful than at other times. It is difficult to put exact ages on these times of change because people vary greatly in their timing of the stages of life, as well as in how much difficulty they have with each stage. Any stage that is only partly negotiated, or avoided, can lead to a period of depression.

**ACHIEVING**
**INDEPENDENCE**
**Age 12 to 40**

Children start life as almost totally dependent on their parents and must, for their own personal fulfilment, break away to form their own lives in their own way. But the period of breaking away, usually in adolescence, though it can be at any time between the ages of 12 and 40, is often fraught with conflict. You want to be independent, but you still may want your parents' love, and perhaps their house, food and financial support for your education too. As you test out your new strength, your parents may take it very personally and get hurt or cut off their feeling for you. That can be confusing because then you feel guilty and start doubting yourself, and yet you are angry with them for stopping you. You do not want to hurt them, but you feel you have to go ahead and do what you want and need to do. The turmoil can be intense. The conflict with your parents may obscure another conflict – the question of whether you really dare be independent with all the responsibility that entails. It is one thing to be angry with those whom you see stopping you and quite another to find yourself in the world with no one to blame. Freedom may be frightening when you are not used to it.

For the parent, it is a difficult task to achieve a balance between protecting the interests of your child and allowing your child to make the necessary exploration and mistakes which initiate adulthood.

**Parental influence**  Adolescence is not a time of turmoil for everyone: some break away gradually, and for some the conflict comes much later. Even when you have left your parental home and live your own way, you may nevertheless remain partially imprisoned in the parental mould in that, quite unconsciously, you only allow yourself to think, feel and even act in the manner your parents did.

Since a child's most basic method of learning is to imitate its parents, it is impossible to avoid this trap altogether. Whoever your parents were, you will inevitably have grown up with hundreds of hidden rules about behaviour and a whole belief system about the world and others. Some people will, at some time between 20 and 40, sort out which of these codes and understandings they wish to keep. But you may find that as you mature in this way, your different way of thinking will clash with your parents' nearly every time you meet them, and this may create open battles and ill feeling. On the other hand, if you give in to your parents' way of thinking, you may become depressed from having repressed your own response. Some will never challenge the codes of their parents and thereby choose a safer but more restricted life, lacking in sparkle. Others will develop their own independent lives and may sometimes find, to their pleasure, that their parents can still listen and learn. (See also *Unconscious Limitations*, page 211.)

**THE HALF-WAY STAGE**
**Age 35 to 45**

Usually somewhere between 35 and 45 it hits you that half your life is probably over. Up to now you may have been able to coast along, not too worried about the future and with scarcely a thought about your own mortality. But at the half-way stage you begin to realize that time is not infinite and that you can no longer afford the luxury of a fantasy of success. If you are going to be successful it is time for serious action.

If these thoughts occur to you earlier and you can take action, it may save you from bitter disappointment later on, perhaps at around 40 to 45. These can be wonderful years where you have the gift of greater maturity before you have lost any significant physical power. But if you feel that you have failed to fulfil an important part of your potential, these years can be very difficult indeed: you are faced with the fact that it may be too late to start again, that you have used up too many of life's opportunities; you may have feelings of regret about the past and see decline before you – that is depressing. Regret is a very difficult feeling to allow yourself to have, partly because there's absolutely nothing you can do about the past except change your attitude to it – but trying to evade the feeling incurs the cost of depression of spirit.

**PHYSICAL CHANGES**
**Age 40 to 60**

There comes the inevitable time when your body does not work quite as well as it used to. Perhaps it starts when you find you require reading glasses or, if you play sports, when you find yourself slower and more tired. Your body is more likely to ache and your joints tend to be less supple. None of these changes is particularly debilitating, but together they form a discomforting sign that you really are getting older.

**The menopause**

For a woman there is the much more dramatic change of the gradual or sudden loss of periods. The menopause usually occurs between the ages of 40 and 60 and the average age is around 50. The loss of periods may sometimes be accompanied by hot flushes, night sweating, and vaginal dryness as well as a number of non-specific symptoms, such as dizziness, headaches, insomnia, digestive troubles, and breathlessness which may be related more to the stress of emotional change than to the hormonal changes of the menopause. Some women find themselves very moody, irritable and depressed, which may well be related to the diminishing levels of the hormones oestrogen and progesterone (see *Hormones*, page 171). At the same time, the fact of the menopause itself may engender many feelings. You have to accept that your fertility and menstruation, and with that a particular part of femaleness, have gone forever, which is not easy to do immediately. Vaginal dryness (which is easy to change) and feelings about changed femininity may adversely affect your sex life (though for others sex life improves when the worry about conceiving another child has gone). Thirdly, the menopause tells you in no uncertain way that you are entering the last phases of your lifetime. And in addition to all this, a fifty-year-old woman may be facing the time in her life when the children have grown up and left, and when she has to reassess her marriage and her career.

**Changing looks**

At this time of life, looks begin to change at an accelerating rate. As the skin loses elasticity, wrinkles become more obvious, hair starts to grey or disappear, and for some this is very difficult to accept; but if you resist life's implacable process, you live a fight against yourself without sparkle. For those who accept the ageing process, there is the chance to begin a new part of life, which may include enjoyment of success in career, the pleasure of seeing your grandchildren grow up, and the development of personal wisdom.

**GETTING OLD**
**Age 60+**

The realization that your life is moving to its close may be very hard to accept. Most of your life is over and in the remaining years you face the possibility of illness and dependency, and the certainty of death.

**Diminishing strength**

Your body is probably slower, less flexible and less resilient. Particular disabilities, such as arthritis, may serve as constant reminders that the days of fine health are over. As your physical strength, and sometimes your memory, diminish, you are very aware of the frailty and mortality of your body – you are forced to be more and more careful and selective about what you can and cannot do.

**Increasing dependency**

The thought of the possibility of increasing dependency may be almost unbearable. And for some, the thought of death is filled with fear: fear of the final illness; fear of the shame of loss of capacity before death (for example, incontinence or paralysis); fear of pain; fear of losing friends and family; fear of being a burden; and fear of the unknown after death. It is not surprising that many people will try to repress such difficult feelings.

For these reasons and many others (see *Retirement*, page 81 and *Old age*, page 86), depression is more common at this time of life than any other. However, there are many things that you can do to change the quality of your last years. Many people feel happier and more vital after 40 than ever before and many older people continue to be creative and fully alive until the day they die (see *Positive ageing*, page 133).

# Life non-events

Lack of stimulation in life, with day following day in endless repetition, eventually leads towards apathy, a feeling of pointlessness and, ultimately, a desire to give up. A boring job or a boring home environment often lead to a feeling of hopelessness. On top of this, loneliness may create despair. Although it can be tempting to stick to the security of a well-known path, endlessly retreading that path creates a rut; the rut can sometimes become so deep you can no longer see over the edges or believe you can get out of it.

## LONELINESS

We are primarily social beings and our pleasures in life are nearly always connected with other people. What use is all the money and success in the world if, when you sit down to an exquisitely cooked meal, you have no-one to share it with? Loneliness is a large problem in our society: many people live completely alone and come home to an empty room or an empty house, while others live amongst people, but have so little genuine contact that they too are lonely and isolated.

**Living alone**  For most people, living alone is almost impossible to sustain without some degree of depression. An empty room seems to have an infinite capacity to soak up whatever you give out till you feel depleted. People, on the other hand, if they are not energy-suckers, reflect back thoughts, feelings and human energy so that the energy stays alive, bouncing from person to person, feeding all who are there who want to partake. In this way we are all dependent on people. When you are alone, almost everything that you do takes on less and less meaning: the meal that you used to cook for yourself seems a waste of effort, keeping your home clean seems to lose its point, and before you know it you are just sitting there doing nothing, feeling low and wondering what the point of life can be: without friends there seems to be little purpose. If you go out to work, the situation may be bearable, but if you do not and you are alone most of the time, life may become intolerable and you may even wish to end it: suicide is most common amongst unemployed older men living alone.

**Lack of contact**   For those who live with others but with little real contact, life can also become very meaningless. You may not be aware of being lonely and yet somehow you do not feel emotionally fed by those around you, so that you feel a sense of dissatisfaction and emptiness which may be with you most of the time. Others seem distant, or else they do not seem to really understand, or perhaps you feel they do not like you. The causes of this problem can lie either with you or with them. You may be a person who has difficulty making warm human contact, in which case you feel somewhat alone in any situation (for help with this see *Psychotherapy*, page 145). Perhaps the person or people you live with are different from you and, through no fault of their own, relate to you on a level that simply does not satisfy you. For suggestions on how to combat loneliness see *Changing the life non-event*, page 125, particularly the section on *Giving up loneliness*, page 130.

# BOREDOM AT HOME

For husband and wife, or any other long-term living relationships of people, it is only too easy for life to settle into a depressing routine of predictable action and response. If you always know exactly how your partner is going to respond, he or she will be boring to you. While weekly routines can be useful to get chores done, as soon as they become absolutely fixed, they can act as a trap which imprisons spontaneity and good feeling. When the patterns of life are rigid and you know exactly what is going to happen, the future ceases to be interesting.

In the situation of a man who works outside the home married to a woman who does not, the man is often less interested to challenge the home routines because he already has a change of atmosphere to escape to. For the woman at home most of the time, life can indeed become very dull. Housework is not very stimulating when done most of the day, every day, and the lack of stimulus at home may be compounded by a lack of variety of atmosphere if you do not get out. If you have young children, you are that much more restricted, and the work and the conversation can be mind-numbingly repetitive. Many women find that being with children all day and responding to their level of conversation really does affect their mental capacity. You find your intellect levelled to the lowest common denominator – the children's – and although this effect is not permanent, it sometimes feels as though you've lost your senses; you wonder if you would ever be capable again of going out and earning a living, and that thought may affect your confidence and make you feel more dependent. This may be another route towards depression, besides the suppression of any anger against the trap of motherhood. Confinement to the home is also one of the results of unemployment and, sometimes, retirement. If you have always had a place of work to go to, and you lose your job or retire, the restrictions of home life may well be a source of frustration and, ultimately, boredom. (See also *Unemployment*, below, *Retirement*, opposite, and *Changing the situation at home*, page 126.)

## BOREDOM AT WORK

If you are capable of doing much more than your job entails, you are likely to get frustrated and bored. A person I know was frustrated about his position but told himself: "Well, I'll wait another year and see if they offer me something else . . . I don't want to rock the boat . . . and if I left now I'm not sure if they would give me a good reference." But while rationalization for safety was going on on the surface, underneath he was feeling something like: "I'm not going to take orders from that cretin again . . . I can't stand this place . . . I can do better than this." So long as these feelings of frustration remained available to him, there was hope. But when he gave up and no longer felt his frustration, he declined into a kind of limp boredom that was very difficult to change. He had, through the expediency of safety, lost the incentive to change his lot and was in a permanent state of severe loss of sparkle.

Some people who work in large organizations are faced with the fact that they are required to be good and conscientious, but that initiative and creativity are poorly rewarded. If you have a lot of initiative and creativity, you may pay a price for the safety and perks that the big organization offers: that price is the curtailment of your talents and the repression of your self-expression (see *Underachievement*, page 82).

## UNEMPLOYMENT

As higher social beings, we need to feel useful to society. I don't mean in any grand way necessarily, but we want to feel that what we do has a use at least to somebody, we want to feel needed. When you are unemployed it is difficult to avoid a feeling of uselessness that may creep over you as the weeks and months drag on. To live for a long time without a feeling of a function in life eats at the soul and can create bitterness, hopelessness and depression. This may then create a vicious circle, for when you are depressed you do not have much energy for looking for work. Even if you do, your depressed energy is going to fail you should you get an interview, since the one thing that almost any employer wants is enthusiasm. I have seen people who have been unemployed for a long time and who have become hopeless and depressed, but who, after dealing with their low energy, have gone out and got work. One unemployed man I knew got creatively angry with his situation – that is, not only did his anger get him out of his depression, but he was also able to use his anger creatively in his energetic determination and persistence to find work. Within one week he was working 16 hours a day, employed in three different jobs. One of the jobs was gardening – he had gone round from house to house asking those with large gardens if they required help. He had no experience of gardening and no particular penchant for it, but he found a way of putting his best energy into it and even enjoying part of it, before he could find another job that suited him better.

In these days of very high unemployment, when whole areas are full of unemployed families suffering the same frustration, the situation is compounded. Many people are faced with the reality that finding satisfying work may involve leaving family, friends, an area, or perhaps even a country that they know and love.

When you are unemployed, you may find your energy sapped by boredom. You may feel angry, you may feel a sense of hopelessness and belittling uselessness, or you may feel very little because your responses have become depressed. These aspects of unemployment can be changed (see *Changing the life non-event*, especially *Feeling useful*, page 131).

## RETIREMENT

The boredom and feeling of less use that occur in unemployment can also be features of retirement, but the flavour is different. For a start, you know that retirement is usually permanent rather than temporary. Secondly, retirement is the ending of a substantial part of your life – perhaps 45 years of involved work life – and you may well experience a feeling of loss. For some, retirement is the time when you finally admit to yourself that you are indeed getting older and entering the last part of your life's journey – with all the feelings that involves (see *Life changes*, page 74 and *Old age*, page 86). Experiences of retirement may be very different in different people. It may be an enjoyable time in which you change from higher-pressure work activity to more relaxed activity of your own choosing – people who tend to enjoy retirement are those who are more accepting of their own ageing process and those who keep active after retirement. Nevertheless, even with a relatively easy transition, it is quite natural to have some feelings of loss about your position and your style of life.

For some, retirement can be insufferable. If you cannot bear getting old and your work has been your life, suddenly at the stroke of 60 or 65 it seems that your life is as good as over. It may seem that there is nothing left for you but gradual deterioration. This hopeless thought process may cause grey or black depression as well as greater susceptibility to physical illness.

You may manage to stay working and some people will work till they die. But if you cannot or do not, it is sometimes very difficult to tolerate a feeling of ineffectiveness. You may even have looked forward to having more time to tend the roses and the vegetable garden, only to find yourself, after a few months, bored. At the same time, if you are married and your spouse is at home, you suddenly find that you are with each other nearly all the time, which may be difficult to sustain with good feeling (see *Changing the life non-event*, page 125). One of the most effective ways of avoiding depression and enjoying your retirement is to stay useful, whether in the home or outside it (see *Feeling useful*, page 131, and *Positive ageing*, page 133).

# UNDERACHIEVEMENT

The balance of achieving your potential is delicately perched between the depression of feeling unfulfilled and the stress and anxiety of trying to do too much. The problem is that there are no rules to tell you just what your potential is. It is easy to assume that your potential is similar to your mother's if you are a woman, or your father's if you are a man. You may assume that your potential is similar to that of your peers, or you may believe what your teachers at school told you.

**Cultural expectations**  Barry Sheene, world champion motor-cyclist, was told at school that he would never get anywhere so long as he wasted his time fiddling with motor cycles, and Winston Churchill failed most of his exams. Sometimes very intelligent children cannot tolerate the tedium of rote-learning. Others have an intelligence that is not suited to the style of learning of most schools, but may be highly successful, if they can ever get over feeling inadequate because the school learning-system did not suit them. Many are pushed by a cultural expectation to do well in a certain manner, to learn by rote, pass exams and think with a particular kind of restricted logic.

It is not that these activities do not have value, but I think it is unfair and inaccurate to use them as a measure of "intelligence". By this standard many highly creative and original people would be (and indeed have been) dubbed "stupid". Many with an intelligence for relationships of form, who might make excellent designers or mechanics, would see themselves as inferior, while many with an intelligence closely connected to their feelings, a combination which can confer great energy and creativity, may sometimes feel stupid. Many with natural wisdom may be called irrational, ignorant and unintelligent.

**Personal potential**

I believe that every person has certain talents which, if life is to be as exciting as it can be, are required to be deployed. If you underachieve relative to your potential, even though you may initially have little idea of what your potential is, you may be left with an inner feeling of dissatisfaction. Such a feeling will probably hit you much harder over the age of 40. To find and use your talents effectively, an open and exploring attitude is necessary, followed by the courage and willingness to follow through where your talent (rather than your idea of yourself) leads. For this the support of your non-judgemental friends may be very helpful.

**Limited relationships**

For many, achievement in personal relationships will be more important or as important as achievement in a career. As father, mother, lover or friend, what you can achieve with another person is almost infinitely variable. But if you are somebody with a larger capacity for contact than you realize (and this includes a lot of people), then you may miss something by limiting your relationships within restricted bounds. Some parents deeply regret the limitations that they imposed on their relationships with their children. Perhaps their role as teacher of correct behaviour took too much precedent over warmth and friendship, and they realize too late that they have been left with an unbridgeable distance between themselves and their children. Lovers and friends sometimes miss the honesty that is available in friendship, by not allowing the expression of feelings that are judged as negative, weak or inappropriate. The man does not allow himself to admit that he is scared or that he does not know; the woman does not allow herself to be aggressive: both sexes restrict themselves and the contact that they can have together. When such restrictions go on for years, the lack of fulfilment may create an inner feeling of dissatisfaction and a loss of sparkle. For suggestions on how to change this situation, see *Dealing with the life event*, page 121, *Short-term explorative psychotherapy*, page 158, and *Creative expression*, page 207.

The whole subject of underachievement is a difficult one because it can so easily be interpreted as yet another pressure to achieve in a prescribed way. I will end by emphasizing that no two people are the same, that each person is presented with a different array of talents and opportunities (some more hidden than others), and that there are probably several positive series of choices that any one person can make in living a fulfilling life.

# OBEYING AUTHORITY

Those more influenced by external authority have a greater tendency to be depressed. Obedience to something outside yourself and lack of freedom of action involve repressing your own vitality and your own inner authority. The outside authority may be a forceful parent or spouse, or the inflexible regime of the institution you may live in or work for.

The most extreme example is being literally imprisoned. Your anger at your loss of freedom is likely to be repressed after a while; you are likely to be bored; you may well lose hope; in addition, you will lose the freedom and sometimes the capacity for self-regulation. Regulating yourself, making your own decisions, assessing your own risks and choosing your own paths are essential aspects of living life to the full. On the other hand, being in prison is very safe: it provides free housing and free food, and does not involve a great deal of personal responsibility. Most people in fact choose at least some form of relative imprisonment in order to feel safe and secure. The American psychiatrist Abraham Maslow, reckoned that only five per cent of people were truly autonomous, the other 95 per cent following without challenge the rules of life that had been dictated to them.

In a frightening study by Stanley Milgram at Yale University in 1963, subjects were asked to administer increasingly severe electric shocks to a human being who was being experimented upon. The victim was actually an actor and the shock generator was simulated, but the effect was very realistic, as evidenced by the extreme levels of emotional tension created in the subjects. The instrument was clearly marked with gradations from 15 to 450 volts. From 375 volts to 420 volts was marked "Danger: Severe Shock". The voltages 435 and 450 were ominously marked "XXX". Subjects were told that they were taking part in a learning experiment to study the effects of punishment on memory – of 40 subjects, all 40 administered a shock of 300 volts at which point the victim pounded against the wall and could no longer answer any more questions. 26 out of the 40 obeyed the orders of the experimenter to keep increasing the voltage, despite no further sounds or answers from the victim, to the very end, that is, two steps beyond the designation "Danger: Severe Shock". Observers looked through one-way mirrors and one related:

"I observed a mature and initially poised businessman enter the laboratory smiling and confident. Within 20 minutes he was reduced to a twitching, stuttering wreck, who was rapidly approaching a point of nervous collapse. He constantly pulled on his earlobe, and twisted his hands. At one point he pushed his fist on to his forehead and muttered: 'Oh God, let's stop it'. And yet he continued to respond to every word of the experimenter, and obeyed to the end."

**Freedom and security** Obedience is a very strong human trait. So long as you are obedient, you suffer less responsibility and can feel some measure of security because you are following a respected

## THE BALANCE BETWEEN FREEDOM AND SECURITY

The balance that people choose between their own "inner authority" and the outer authorities around them depends very much on their past histories, the cultures they were brought up in, their own personalities, and, perhaps most of all, their own inner strengths. The more self-regulating you are, the less likely you are to become depressed.

| | Level of freedom or security | Level of risk and responsibility | Likely level of liveliness |
|---|---|---|---|
| **FREEDOM** ↑ | You are autonomous and self-regulating. | You risk many disagreeing with you and perhaps rejecting you. | You may live in "gold". |
| | You are self-regulating in some areas but tend to hold, perhaps without realizing it, to the codes of thought or modes of expression that you have been taught. | You lessen the risk of making a fool of yourself. | You probably have some degree of "loss of sparkle". |
| | You are over-worried about what other people think of you, afraid to make mistakes and you seek the approval of those senior to you (see *"Good behaviour" personality*, page 99). | You lessen the risk of being seen to be wrong. | You are more likely to be prone to the blues or periods of grey depression. |
| **SECURITY** ↓ | You search for someone to take care of you and look after your emotional needs (see *"Dependent personality"*, page 98). | You feel little personal responsibility. | You are more likely to be prone to periods of grey or black depression. |

or powerful person or organization. If you are more self-regulating, you take more risk, for you are aware that you are responsible for the results of your own decisions, positive or negative. Freedom and security are opposites: the balance that people choose varies from physical and mental imprisonment to inner self-reliance.

# LOSING YOUR SENSE OF PURPOSE

Many people lose their sense of purpose when they are angry or disappointed with something or somebody. For others the repetition of non-events deadens meaning. At such times it becomes hard to believe that there ever could be any point to life and you lose hope of finding any meaning. As your hope recedes, even the things that used to be important to you seem pointless. Often you cannot know the purpose of your life in the present. The meaning cannot be known in advance, but comes later from "doing it" – from living life fully. The problem sometimes comes when you have completed a stage in life that is important to you and you cannot yet know what the next stage is to be. You may have just completed your life's work, retired, or your children may have just left home; suddenly you are in limbo, a transition period when you do not know what is coming next or even if there will be something coming next. During both world wars the suicide rate fell in Britain: people were kept busy and given a purpose. As soon as the wars stopped, the suicide rate rose again.

Although it is true that you often cannot know the full meaning of what you are doing till later, it is also true that it is very important to feel useful in some way. The unemployed, retired and lonely may suffer more from a feeling of uselessness than anything else. Nevertheless, it is possible to develop, initially by the use of your will, a greater sense of purpose (see *Reasons for living*, page 132).

# OLD AGE

The incidence of depression (grey or more severe) in old age is about four times that of the general population. Old people have a suicide rate in the order of 15 times greater than that of the general population. The reasons are many.

**Feeling lonely**     Many old people live alone and, because of their independence, do not feel that they should impose themselves on other people. Some try to impose themselves and are rejected, and some are taken care of, but with an underlying hostility and resentment. It is extremely difficult not to be depressed if you are old and alone, and important to find some situations where you see other people (see *Giving up loneliness*, page 130).

**Loss**   As you grow old, several or all of the following may affect you: loss of spouse, loss of friends, loss of family, loss of youth, loss of strength, loss of health, loss of mental powers, loss of work, loss of opportunities, loss of status, loss of money. All of these may be hard to bear and sometimes it is necessary to grieve for what you have lost (see *Death*, page 63). Such grief can be a positive short-term process which takes you through a disengagement from the past so that you are ready for the new possibilities in the very last phase of your life. Unfortunately, it is all too easy to hang on to the sense of loss for the rest of your life, which results in a depression of your spirit and hope. An alternative is to cultivate looking forward to the different activities that will replace the activities you disengage from (see *Positive ageing*, page 133).

**Boredom in old age**   You may be bored because you are retired and have too little to do that interests you, and you may be bored from lack of company. You may be bored because you are physically or mentally incapable of continuing with your previous interests. If your main interest was playing sport, you may have nothing to replace it when you begin to lose your physical strength, fitness and agility. If you love music, it is a terrible blow to lose your hearing, and you may have no other immediate interest to occupy and entertain yourself (see *Changing the life non-event*, page 125). Boredom and lack of activity tend to be depressing, and when you are depressed, you tend to lose interest and hope in looking for, let alone finding, activities of pleasure.

**Feeling useless**   No longer seeing yourself as an active, participating and contributing member of society can be a severe blow to your self-esteem (see *Positive ageing*, page 133). At the same time, the prospect of possible illness or of some degree of dependency on others, may be difficult for some to accept without bitterness.

**FEAR OF DEATH**   Different people have very different fears about death and dying, and there are some who are not particularly afraid of it. Most people are more afraid of dying than of death itself – perhaps you worry about how death is going to come: what illness? how much pain? will it happen when I'm asleep? Perhaps you hope that when it does come it will come fast and not leave you with a gradual deterioration of function (for instance, loss of speech or paralysis). The worst thing is that you do not know what to expect. Many people believe in a final death agony – there is no evidence for this and in fact only about one in 20 people is conscious just before death. Some greatly fear losing their dignity and being humiliated by loss of control – for instance, vomiting, incontinence, screaming. Many fear being abandoned while they are dying – and it is indeed good to have company, a hand holding yours, a friend who is with you through the uncertainty and the unknown of your dying.

For some, death itself is more feared – as you die, you give over control completely to a force you probably know very little of and a force which takes you, you know not where. Some believe that death will be the final ending and others that their spirit will in some way live on. However certain you may feel, very few people, if any, know exactly where they are going to or how it will feel to go there, even if they are not going anywhere.

**Repressing your fears**

All these fears may be repressed: "I don't want to think about that" . . . "Please, let's change the subject" . . . "This is very morbid", and many people feel very uncomfortable talking about such issues. Other feelings about death may also be repressed: you may feel bereaved at the prospect of losing your loved family and friends, and if death is imminent, you have finally to give up any future worldly ambitions. Some people get very angry before they die or will alternate between irritability and depression – they may be very angry with the doctor who cannot save them, they may be angry because they cannot tolerate being dependent, and they may be angry if those around them insist on pretending that they are not really dying.

**PHYSICAL FACTORS IN OLD AGE**

The reduction of certain chemicals (biogenic amines) in the brain is thought to be related to depressive mood (see *Chemical theories on depression*, page 104). There is some evidence that the level of biogenic amines falls in the ageing brain, which could increase susceptibility to depression.

As the brain gets older, more and more brain cells die. At the same time the arteries may get narrower, so that the blood and oxygen supply to the brain is limited. The brain becomes more vulnerable when the oxygen supply is reduced because of a respiratory condition, or when diet is inadequate. These and other factors *may* be related to longer reaction times, more inflexibility, increasing caution and decreasing ability to adjust to new situations, all of which are commoner as you get older. But it is important not to assume that these effects are physically caused, as depression causes the same effects and *is* changeable. The loss of the capacity to adjust to new situations may make any changes, such as moving house, much harder than before the advent of old age.

When old people get severely depressed, it may not be obvious. Sometimes the most dramatic symptoms are agitation, hypochondriasis (the belief that you have a physical ailment when you haven't), and paranoia (the belief that others are against you): these surface symptoms may mask an underlying depression. When depressive symptoms are more obviously there, it may be very hard to tell whether the old person is demented or depressed. Dementia, or senile dementia, is a physical deterioration in the brain, which causes deterioration in memory and mental function (this is sometimes so bad that the person has no idea what day it is, or even what year, or where he is) and eventually a change in personality (particularly the loss of social inhibitions, the person becomimg inappropriately emotional and self-centred).

In severe depression in younger adults, mental function may be slowed down and concentration poor, but basic memory and intellectual functions remain intact. In severe depression in the elderly, memory and intellectual functions are often severely affected, so that the picture looks like dementia. More confusion is created by the fact that depression in the elderly may cause such loss of appetite that starvation provokes a dementia. On the other hand, dementia may cause depression because of the difficulty in accepting the fact that mental function is going, and because the physical changes involved may affect personality. If you or a relative are depressed, and especially, if also confused, consult your doctor.

**Illness in old age**   When you are over 70, you are likely to become ill at least at some stage of your old age, and you may get depressed as a result of not being able to handle or express your feelings about your condition. Some illnesses cause depression physically (see *Specific illnesses*, page 109), and many drugs may precipitate depression physically (see *Drugs*, page 114). Finally, poor diet, combined with diminished absorption in the intestine, may lead to vitamin deficiencies; vitamin B deficiencies may cause fatigue, apathy and depression. The drug and dietary factors can very easily be changed.

**Being positive**   All in all, old age produces a lot of potential difficulties, but many of these can be changed, and even when they can't, a negative attitude to them can (see *Changing the life non-event*, page 125 and *Positive ageing*, page 133).

# Past history and personality

If you have a history of depression in your family, statistically the chances are higher that you may be prone to periods of depression. How much of this correlation is hereditary and how much environmental cannot be answered quantitatively. Although there has been some dogmatic insistence on hereditary factors by geneticists, and on environmental factors by psychotherapists, most will at least agree that susceptibility to depression is affected by both heredity and by early environment, whatever the proportions. These influences weave a complicated and inextricable pattern: a depressed parent may pass on hereditary qualities of susceptibility to the children, but the children will also learn by copying the behaviour of their parent. Depression occurs much more frequently in certain types of personality, and personality is affected by hereditary factors, by copying parents and by reactions to the family environment. The family environment is affected by the general culture, which may be more or less depressive. All these influences work together, and yet sometimes, a child of a severely depressive parent, born in depressive and hopeless circumstances and raised in a depressive culture, will grow into an adult full of hope and inspiration, who never experiences a single bout of significant depression.

## HEREDITY

This subject is included here, rather than under "Physical factors", because family influences, whether hereditary or environmental, are usually inseparable in practice.

Many studies have pointed to genetic influence in depression. These studies have mostly been done on severe depression. If any of your parents, siblings or children have had black or white depression, the chances of your having it at some time in your life are in the order of 10-15 per cent. This compares with a risk in the general population of about 0.5-0.8 per cent.

Most research shows that the hereditary influence in manic depression is stronger than that in repeated black or white depression, and this fact has led to the suggestion that manic depression and repeated severe depression may be different entities. Manic depressives tend to have a more extroverted and cyclothymic personality (see page 29) and an earlier onset of the first episode of depression or mania. Manic depression is equally common in men and women, whereas depression is commoner in women. If one of your parents or siblings has had manic depression, you are much more likely to get manic depression than just depression (within your 10-15 per cent chance of being affected at all). In other words, manic depression and periodic depression each tend to breed true, though there is some overlap.

All these comments and figures refer to severe depression. It is probable that hereditary influence is relatively more important with black or white depression. At any rate, it is almost impossible to measure hereditary influence with milder depressions since they are so much harder to define and quantify. How you interpret the figures is open to question. Using the figures given above, you could say that having a severely depressive parent gives you only a 10 per cent chance of being similarly affected – or you could say that having a severely depressive parent increases your chances of being severely depressed by thirtyfold.

# LEARNING BY COPYING

Children learn by copying what they see. Thus they learn to talk in the same manner as one or other of their parents without ever consciously trying to copy. Such unconcious mimicry, which can be funny, delightful and quite surprising, also has a problematic side: children copy the worst aspects of their parents as much as they do the best. Since parents are naturally looked up to as models of perfection, it is not possible for a young child to be discriminating or selective. Thus aspects of life which are repressed by the parents become repressed by the children.

If there is no expression of fun at home, the children learn to be serious and sombre, lacking in fun and perhaps disapproving of others' jollity. If there is no expression of sensuality at home, the children learn to repress their natural tendencies to touch and enjoy physical sensation. If sexuality is never mentioned or talked about only with embarrassment or disapproval, the children learn to repress their sexuality and may lose their capacity for sexual intimacy.

If there is never any overt aggression at home, the children learn to repress aggressive impulses. When they are adults and a situation arises that would normally create an angry response, the level of repression is required to be increased, to make sure that the angry feeling is held in. So it is that something that would make most people feel angry makes a depressive depressed.

The more reactions that were repressed in the home of your parents, the less interaction there was between you and your parents and the less available "feeling energy". Children are extremely sensitive to the amount of energy allowed in a household and unconsciously adapt themselves to fit in.

**Life patterns**

Copying is especially strong from boy to man and from girl to woman. A little boy looks up to his father as *the* model of masculinity and a little girl looks up to her mother as everything a woman should be. Although both boy and girl may later rebel against some of the overt attitudes of their parents, they will not usually rebel against the attitudes they do not know about. So it is that a woman, for example, may find herself saying "I'll never do what my mother did" and yet, without realizing it, she will say those words with the same tone of voice, the same expression and the same gestures as her mother. And sometimes she will find that her life begins to go the same way as her mother's, despite conscious efforts to make it different. For example, a girl sees her mother giving up an enjoyable life and progressively losing her spirits after the age of 30, as she becomes increasingly tied down to family life. When the girl becomes an adult, she thinks: "Whatever I do I won't let that happen to me". At the age of 30 she is married with two children but keeps an outside job. Quite inexplicably, it seems, she finds herself feeling down – somehow she is plagued by an irrational and unconscious thought: it is not possible for a married woman over 30 to feel good. If this thought becomes conscious, that is a help, because it can then be dealt with. On the surface it seems to be a silly thought, because of course not all women are like her mother and there is no necessary reason why *she* should be. But this thought was formed when she was a child when, to her, her mother represented all women.

**Emotional attitudes**

More often still, children follow the basic emotional attitudes and ways of expression of their parents. A father may not need to say to a boy "It's babyish to cry" – the boy picks up his attitude and copies, just as his own son will copy him. Thus the patterns of what is allowable and what is repressed are passed on from generation to generation.

# AVOIDING ANGER

For a child, a parent is an all-powerful figure. The baby is completely dependent on this huge person for physical care (food, cleaning and physical warmth) and emotional care (stimulation, sensitivity and emotional warmth). As a baby it is often very frustrating to be in such a dependent position, especially when you cannot make yourself understood. The problem comes when you express frustration, anger or hostility and your parent cannot handle it. A parent that can handle it reacts with warmth, even if it is a warm anger followed some time later by more gentle warmth. But if a parent has difficulty with the baby's aggression, the baby knows it. Although babies cannot understand cognitively, like some animals they are incredibly sensitive to mood and atmosphere. If the mother is frightened by her baby's anger, the baby learns to fear his own aggression. If the mother reacts with coldness and withdrawal, the baby learns that his aggression can destroy all that is valuable in the world – the warmth of his mother. Thus the baby learns to avoid (by repression) his own aggressive impulses which become turned in against himself with a logic that goes something like this: "If she reacts like that and she is the all-powerful and all-wise, I must be a bad person."

It may take some people months or years of psychotherapy to realize they are not actually "a bad person" but that their parents' opinion or reaction to them came only as a result of their parents' own limitations.

**Holding in aggression**  The mechanism of natural aggression leading to rejection, leading to the necessity of holding in aggression and a feeling of "badness" may be relevant to many people (see *"Good behaviour" personality*, page 99). Some researchers have tried to relate the holding-in of aggression to statistics on depression. For instance, the Hutterites, a German religious sect who formed self-sufficient and separate communities in the United States, place a heavy stress on duty, and allow little aggression; they have a far higher incidence of depression than the surrounding community. Depression is twice as common in women, who tend to express aggression less. In Britain there is a higher incidence of depression in the so-called "upper classes", who have been taught to curb their emotions, to keep a "stiff upper lip". Comparisons of many countries have shown an inverse relationship of homicide and suicide: the more (aggressive) killings, the fewer (depressive) suicides. But such general statistics hide an almost infinite number of human variables.

# LEARNING PASSIVITY

When pain is unavoidable, animals, children and adults learn to switch off. If a child is constantly hit, intimidated or punished with coldness, he makes the inner decision to repress the feeling of hurt. This decision is eminently sensible at the time because the child has no means of changing his environment. The problem is that the decision tends to become more or less permanent so that the adult too represses feelings of hurt, sometimes so successfully that he does not realize the need to change the hurtful environment. Instead, as a result of the repression of feelings, he tolerates a relatively depressed life, more depressed at times of greater threat or more hurt. The case history, below, illustrates the potentially damaging effect of learning to vanquish feeling.

**Negative and positive aggression**

An old Victorian saying is: "Children should be seen, not heard." Silence and repression are sometimes rewarded by approval, while the showing of feeling is sometimes punished by disapproval, or withdrawal of affection. Different styles of passivity are taught in different cultures (see *Culture and religion*, page 102). In most cultures women are generally taught to be more passive than men. Whereas men are often taught to repress fear and crying (and admitting to problems like depression), women are usually taught to repress aggression. The teaching is so strong that many believe that women are naturally less aggressive than men. There is no evidence for this, though of course it is difficult to prove either way. When I said this in a recent meeting, several women were offended because their understanding of the word "aggression" was that it was necessarily hurtful and negative. I

## CASE HISTORY

A successful English businessman of 50 told me that at the age of four he was sent to a home for children run by a "cold grey-haired woman who served tasteless mince. I remember the willow-patterned plates. I will always hate willow-pattern". He remembered his mother leaving in a red car and then not seeing her for months. She did not say goodbye as "that would only have encouraged emotion". Naturally, he was hurt, for he was losing the person most dear to him for a time that, for a little boy, felt like forever. But it was not until 46 years later that he was finally able to cry as he told the story. At the time he had to train himself not to cry and not to feel. At school in the Far East at the age of six he finally managed to prove himself capable of resisting pain. The other boys would make arrows out of thorns fixed to palm spikes with beeswax. He would stand there in his short trousers and allow them to fire the arrows into his legs. He would not run away, not make a sound, but would look down at the arrows sticking in his legs and know that he had successfully vanquished feeling. He had made himself impenetrable and the other boys admired him for it. His impenetrability, his distance from his own feelings and his loss of sparkle, had lasted 44 years.

realized that "aggression" is of course usually used in this way, especially in cultures where aggression is more repressed. What I mean by aggression here is a force of moving outwards strongly, which may be used negatively (for example, to hurt others) or positively (to protect yourself, fight for a job, protect your children or realize your ambitions). The opposite of aggression is passivity.

Whereas men tend to attribute failure to lack of effort and connect success with ability, women tend to attribute failure to lack of ability and connect success with chance. Men or women who see themselves as victims of life's circumstances are far more likely to get depressed when things go wrong. Unfortunately, once the pattern of seeing yourself as a victim or loser is set, it is very tempting to keep the label and do nothing to change your opinion of yourself. Playing out the role of the victim is fostered because being a loser has certain advantages (see below).

---

### THE ADVANTAGES OF SEEING YOURSELF AS A LOSER

- You don't have to take any action since you are going to lose anyway.
- Other people or the State will take care of you, to a greater or lesser extent.
- No-one will try to pull you down or hate you because you are successful.
- You can take the easier road of cynicism and think yourself justified in doing so.
- You can avoid the weight of responsibility.
- You don't need to think or get up in the morning. You don't need to fight for anything. In fact, you don't need to do anything at all.

Life is certainly easier as a loser. The disadvantage of being a loser is that you never really feel good about yourself and live in a more or less perpetually diminished state.

---

# INSECURITY AND LOSS

One of the most important things to a child is parental warmth and continuity. In his studies on children Bowlby, a British child psychiatrist, showed how a stable relationship with the parents created a feeling of security and a stable base from which to explore. A threat of loss of this security caused anger or fear, while actual loss of a parent or main care-giver caused a loss of interest if the child did not believe that the parent was coming back. Studies on institutions where children are kept with inadequate and inconsistent care show a distinct change in the behaviour of children in the second six months of their lives. Continual crying becomes replaced by an eventual indifference to adults, and a baby would "lie or sit with wide open, expressionless eyes, frozen, immobile face and a far away expression as if in a daze". Such babies did not babble or coo and felt stiff and wooden when picked up.

## CASE HISTORY

A 40-year-old man was talking to his therapist about his own lack of self-respect – allied to a loss of sparkle. He knew he missed self-respect and at the same time he did not really know what it meant. He spoke of how he always tried to do the right thing according to the opinions of others. After he had gone on about this for some time, the therapist said with exasperation: "I don't care what you *should* do – I just want you to be happy!"

Tears filled the man's eyes and he found the word "hospital" going through his mind. Between the ages of four and six he was in hospital with polio and for much of that time he was not allowed to move. As he allowed himself to experience his feelings about that period for the first time for 35 years, he found himself terrified and shouted "Hold me, hold me!" The therapist held him for a long time as he cried and screamed. He left the session shaken yet exhilarated by the release of feeling.

At his next session he started with his usual calm intellectual appraisal of matters. In a very matter-of-fact tone, he told the therapist how proud he had been to be the first boy in his area to get polio. The therapist asked him how he would feel if his own son had had polio when he was four (his son was eight). As he realized how he would feel as a parent, he became angry and then furious with his own parents: "You should have stayed with me . . . you should have got me out!" (They could in fact have brought him home earlier than they did.) Later he felt ashamed that he had never fought, or even been angry, but had been an understanding model boy patient. The therapist said "But you were only four" . . . and "I think I would have done the same" . . . and "Anyway, you would have calmed down in the end."

The words "calmed down" put him in a rage. For over a year he had not been able to move his body, a four-year-old boy unable to move a limb. After a while he said that he was still not satisfied that he had not fought; he knew it wouldn't have helped, but he thought he would have felt better about himself. "Is that related to self-respect?" the therapist asked. The man laughed heartily. From that moment he had greater self-respect and more sparkle. The rage about not being able to move, the terror of being alone and the anger about being left had been repressed for 35 years.

**Hospitalization in childhood**

Children who are sent to hospital may suffer greatly. Apart from the fear of the illness, which may be seen by the child as a punishment for being bad, the hospital may be an institution with little warmth and inconsistent emotional care.

The case history (above) was unusual in that it is rare for a single incident to be so crucial, and even in this case there were many other factors involved, but it illustrates the devastating effect on a child of loss, especially of parental security.

**The effects of stress in childhood**

Temporary loss of parents, childhood bereavement and parental separation may be related to depression in adulthood or may be associated with the development of psychopathy (ruthless power-seeking) or other conditions, such as a susceptibility to anxiety. The condition caused is generally not specific to the kind of insult.

When you were a child, if your parents threatened not to love you, threatened to leave you, threatened to commit suicide or threatened that your behaviour would cause them illness or death, you would naturally be left feeling insecure. Being a child you would assume that your parent was right and that you were a bad person to be capable of causing such awful things.

If your parents were over-anxious about your welfare, and therefore stopped you taking risks, that too would cause insecurity, partly because a child unconsciously picks up the insecurity in the parent, and partly because the child is not given the chance to test out life, make his or her own mistakes and build his own confidence.

**Early responsibility**

Some parents are themselves so dependent or insecure that they try to get their children to look after them and so take on responsibility much too early. Sometimes the mother will demand that the child should love her, or will tell her child "You are the only thing that is important to me." Such a statement conveys to the child the idea that the mother depends on the child for her sense of meaning in life, and that may put an enormous pressure on the child. Though they may be outwardly competent, children brought up in this way may have "grown up too fast" and lack a sense of inner security (see *"Dependent" personality*, page 98).

If, as a child, you were told repeatedly that you were unlovable or incompetent, you may have begun to believe these labels and to conform to them. When parents are unresponsive children try to alter their behaviour, to be good, in order to get the warmth they crave. They may never give up trying to be good because of course they assume that the lack of warmth is their fault due to their own inability to be good. But their attempts are in vain because warmth cannot depend on behaviour but on the capacity of the parent to love (see *"Good behaviour" personality*, page 99).

**Positive factors**

Although insecurities and losses in childhood may lead to depression, they may not. They may lead to nothing in particular: sometimes the positive factors are overlooked. A woman I know, J, who *did* have a tendency to depression, had a cold tyrannical mother who hanged herself. Her childhood was not a happy one, with her mother using the worst possible threats and demands to control her behaviour. If she cried with genuine pain she was told with a raised hand "I'll give you something to cry about." Any initiative was stamped on. She did indeed grow up with a feeling of terrible inadequacy, blaming herself rather than her mother. However, next door lived a chubby, cheerful woman who realized that J's mother could not take good care of her. As much as she was able to, she invited J into her house where she could jump on the old cushions and make lots of noise in an atmosphere of warmth and kindness. She may have saved J's life.

These observations about parents may make you wonder about what you, as a parent, can do to your child. Although you are in a position of great power and influence and it *is* important to be warm, it is sometimes reassuring to know that all parents make mistakes, that children can be pretty resilient, and that there may be many other positive influences outside the home.

# PERSONALITY

There are three main personality types that have a greater tendency towards depression: the "dependent" personality, the "good behaviour" personality and the "controlled" personality. It is important to emphasize that there is no such thing as a pure type. The three personalities described are caricatures, designed to stimulate thought about your own or others' tendencies. Many will find that they have some aspects of all three.

**"DEPENDENT" PERSONALITY**

The "dependent" type (sometimes called "oral" in psycho-analytical literature) looks to others to provide a sense of worth, emotional care, physical care and even a reason for living. His underlying attitude is that others should go out of their way to provide for him and in fact that they *owe* him care. His catch phrase is "I can't", which translated means: "You must do it for me". He believes he should not have to work, especially physically, and that one way or another the world is responsible for taking care of him.

If your attitudes were as obvious as these, you might find it hard to live with yourself without changing. Such attitudes are usually disguised – you do not think "Ah! this woman gives me a sense of worth and makes me want to live," but you fall madly in love, believing that she is everything. Initially, she may be flattered by your adoration, but she soon finds it dull never to be challenged, and begins to feel you are like a weight hanging from her. All the basic decisions are her's in the end, and she begins to feel she is looking after a child. Because of this she then tries to create more distance and breathing space. Your reaction, as a dependent type, is to say to yourself: "I'm being rejected again – that proves I'm no good", and then to cling harder. She reacts by feeling angry, though perhaps she finds it hard to be angry with such a clinging creature. At the same time you feel angry, and bitter too, because you hate the thing you are dependent on. Often the relationship ends in bitterness, and your belief that you are weak and incapable seems vindicated.

You do not consciously think, "You must do it for me". Instead you say to yourself and others with lamenting pathos: "I can't". If they do not respond by helping you, you feel slighted. You do not consciously say to yourself: "I should not have to work – the world owes me a living", but you turn up late for your job, fall ill often, do the minimum, or make little effort to find work if you are unemployed.

On the positive side, "dependent" personalities tend to be highly sensitive, and this quality remains after changing the dependent attitude.

| | |
|---|---|
| **Childhood background** | The childhood history of a "dependent" person often tells of poor care. So it is that the underlying attitude of the adult is: "Well, I didn't get it when I was young, so you owe it to me now!" The poor care is often of a particular type, the child being required to grow up and take responsibility too fast. Often there is a history of the child having to take care of his parents or brothers and sisters. The parents may have been over-anxious, and, though they may have been generous materially, may have provided little inner confidence, especially in the first year of the child's life. However, histories are not absolutely specific to character types: you are born with a tendency to develop into one type or another, which is then accentuated or actualized by the environment. |
| **Physical appearance** | Physically, a highly "dependent" type actually looks somewhat collapsed. If you try standing with your jaw retracted backwards, your shoulders drooped forwards, your chest caved in and all your muscles limp, you will find that you will indeed feel weak. There tends to be very little energy in the muscles, which is different from the "good behaviour" and "controlled" types. It is as if the energetic supply to the body has been cut off somewhere in the brain giving the dependent person a very real and actual feeling of being weak and incapable. |

The "dependent" personality is the most likely to become depressed. First of all, the lack of bodily energy tends to make you feel low at any time that you are not being fed with someone else's energy. At times of rejection, your inner confidence may collapse and you may tumble down into severe depression, in which case you really *have* to be taken care of.

| | |
|---|---|
| **"GOOD BEHAVIOUR" PERSONALITY** | The "good behaviour" type has put a tremendous amount of energy into conforming. He relies on others' opinions and likes to obey the rules. He looks down on those who do not follow the rules or do not act in the proper fashion. He is obedient and authority bound – he is always worried about |

whether the authority will approve of his actions, and he will try very hard to please. On the positive side, he may be an extremely conscientious worker.

**Childhood background**

The childhood history is often one of an over-emphasis on the control of behaviour. Being a good boy or a good girl is more important to the parents than natural expressions of spontaneity. Thus, eating up all your food, or going to the lavatory once a day, or being nice, or not being aggressive, become major issues in which the parents eventually win a battle for control. The child thinks that if he conforms, then at last he will receive the warmth and security he wants, but however hard he tries, he can never be good enough because he will never really be loved for who he is.

**Physical appearance**

A "good behaviour" type will sometimes have the appearance of somebody who has been beaten down. He will look up with doleful eyes that seem to say: "Don't hurt me, I'll be good". Sometimes the buttocks will be squeezed and held in like a dog with its tail beneath its legs. Often there is a great deal of muscular tension.

Added to the effects of constant muscular tension (see opposite), is a rather hopeless feeling, the result of always being in opposition to yourself and hardly ever having the freedom to act spontaneously. Jung described what I call the "good behaviour" type as having an over-developed persona – a mask of conformity thinly covering an inner feeling of inferiority and self-reproach. When the mask of good behaviour breaks, it can precipitate a crisis in self-esteem, for you are then forced into a position where you have to admit how little you genuinely respect and believe in yourself.

**"CONTROLLED" PERSONALITY**

The "controlled" person has his own opinions, and can stand up for himself with strength and determination. However, he tends to be inflexible and unemotional. If he has an opinion, *that* is his opinion and he will put down or avoid any evidence to the contrary. Feelings are avoided or else expressed in a very limited and controlled way. Anger will be translated to "irritation" and sensuality to "interest". The avoidance of showing feeling is seen as a sign of strength and demonstrative people are judged as weak. Confronted with too much feeling or too much physical contact, a controlled person will do almost anything to control a situation that makes him uncomfortable: he may make a sarcastic comment, change the subject, walk out of the room, get angry (or show any particular feeling that he is more comfortable with), remain aloof, stiffen and heighten his body, or openly disapprove.

## THE EFFECTS OF CONSTANT MUSCULAR TENSION

The "good behaviour" personality may suffer from the first symptoms of depression partly as a result of constantly tense muscles. A "good behaviour" type unconsciously tenses the muscles to stop them acting: the impulse to do, which on a basic animal level involves moving the body, is counteracted by the order to stop and obey. Take, for example, a kick, the most aggressive action of the leg. This involves the tensing of the hamstring muscles as the leg is drawn back, and then the releasing of the hamstrings and tensing of the quadriceps as the leg is brought forward and straightens. Kicking and stopping the kick at the same time (see the illustration, below) involves the simultaneous contraction of hamstring and quadriceps opposing each other. After years of successive repressions of aggressive impulses, little aggression is felt anymore, only tiredness and loss of zest as a result of the muscles being held in a constant state of opposition. (See also *Disagreement at work*, page 72.)

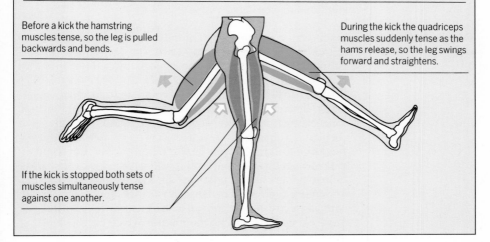

Before a kick the hamstring muscles tense, so the leg is pulled backwards and bends.

During the kick the quadriceps muscles suddenly tense as the hams release, so the leg swings forward and straightens.

If the kick is stopped both sets of muscles simultaneously tense against one another.

**Childhood background**  As a child he may have received care and love but followed the controlled example of his father and mother, the models of perfection he would have naturally looked up to. This unconscious tendency to mimic aspects of parents behaviour has its advantages and disadvantages (see *Learning by copying*, page 91, and *Unconscious allegiances*, page 190).

**Physical appearance**  Physically, the control is sometimes visible in the stiff way he holds his body. His movements may be rather rigid, with limited grace. The expression on his face may be stern.

There is no particular relationship of this type of personality with clinical (grey/black/white) depression. However, to the extent that you control your feelings, you control your own capacity for happiness and miss out on lustre and sparkle. For suggestions on trying to change this controlled tendency, see *Express the feeling*, page 122 and *Creative expression*, page 207.

# CULTURE AND RELIGION

Just as every home has different sets of patterns of what should be expressed and what repressed, so cultures and sub-cultures vary in the unwritten rules of what is, and what is not, permitted. It would be interesting to compare statistics of the incidence of depression in more or less repressed cultures. But this is not possible, firstly because definitions of depression are so variable, and secondly because the more repressive political regimes will not allow the publication of any statistic which might put the management in bad light. Thirdly, repression is qualitative as well as quantitative – what is repressed in one country may be freely expressed in another and vice versa.

**Freedom of thought and body movement**

Since comparison of cultures tends to be invidious in the stark black and white of print, I will restrict myself to the culture I was raised in, and leave you to think about your own culture. Some of what I shall say, I realized only when I worked in a different culture and country. In England, generally, there is a great deal of freedom of thought. At the same time feelings and bodily movement are usually strongly curbed. If you were deaf, you would know when an Italian was talking and even what he was talking about, but if you looked at an Englishman, you would have to look very carefully to be sure he was talking at all. The famous British stiff upper lip is a physical fact that can be measured electronically with an electro-myograph (an instrument which measures muscle tone by recording the amount of electrical activity over the muscle). The stiff upper lip is also a symbol of a certain style of resilience, which relies on control of feeling and control of movement. The lips can be used to stop facial expression, and expression of words and feelings, just as the thigh can be used to stop a kick (see *"Good behaviour" personality*, page 99). I have witnessed a psychotherapist gently press on the upper lip of an Englishman who was holding back his tears – as he allowed his lip to loosen, he began to cry. Other cultures may be freer in emotional expression or in action, but more restricted in freedom of thought. Whatever the limitation, it is very difficult to see it clearly when you are in the midst of it, since nearly everyone else has the same limitation. (If they don't, they may seem odd and may be rejected for their differences.)

A woman of 60 talked about her grandmother who had created a cold and hard atmosphere within which nobody dared to speak out of turn or behave incorrectly. Cleanliness and frugality were essential. She remembered that only a certain specific number of towels would be dealt out each week, no matter what the need. But when she thought of her own daughter, she realized with regret that she had had the same attitude – "doing it properly" had been paramount. She described with sadness how she had avoided hugging her daughter because of thoughts about her daughter's hair being unwashed. She saw how her mother had been much the same and how unfortunately, when she looked at the whole pattern, generations had all been affected. Her life was being affected even now by things her grandmother had learned over a 100 years before, and her grandmother was similarly affected by things learned by her ancestors. It is not easy to break the negative parts of the ancestral chain.

**Religion and repression**

Dogmatic religion has a sad history of repression of thought, feeling and action. There are endless examples from all religions which insist their way is THE way. I mention the influence of the Christian religion here because I have encountered this in my professional experience. People brought up in a strong Protestant tradition tend to find enjoyment very difficult to bear and even if your parents are atheist, aspects of a Protestant ethic may still have come down to you. People brought up as Catholics tend to mistrust their own thoughts, which according to the Church may be sinful enough to warrant eternal hell without even being acted upon. Since no human being can totally avoid "sinful" thoughts, such a system can create a barrier of repression, with self-righteousness outside the barrier, and self-doubt (often not consciously realized) and guilt within. This fosters a reliance on being sanctioned by the "outer authority" (which may be the Church or may have been transferred to any other institution of power).

This leads on to the interesting question of whether belief in God relates to susceptibility to depression. Logically, it would make sense that those who believe in a more authoritarian and punishing God, and who therefore act more like children towards a father, would generally be more prone to depression than those who do not believe in God or those who believe that they are part of God and therefore responsible for their own higher morality and the choices and directions of their lives (see *Obeying authority*, page 84, and *"Dependent" personality*, page 98). However, this is not my experience. The variable that cannot be measured is depth of belief. It is quite possible for someone to believe, intellectually, in total personal responsibility and yet to act very dependently, and it is possible for someone to believe in God as a punishing old man, and yet to act out of inner self-reliance.

# Physical factors

There is no doubt that severe depression is accompanied by physical changes in the body. Sometimes treatable physical diseases, hormonal imbalances or medication cause or mimic depression. It is important to rule out any treatable physical cause before anything else. Even though it is comparatively rare for depression to be so caused, it would only take one case of a brain tumour being treated with psychoanalysis to make the point.

## CHEMICAL THEORIES ON DEPRESSION

The brain consists of about ten thousand million neurones, or nerve cells, each cell having the capacity to conduct a tiny electric charge to others, via seven or eight thousand inter-connections. The tail of each cell spreads into thousands of fibres, each ending with a swelling called a terminal button. The electric charge passes from the head of the cell to the tail, and ends in the thousands of terminal buttons. Between the terminal buttons of one cell and the head of the next cell are microscopic gaps called synapses. The electric current cannot jump the synapse, but instead causes a change in the chemicals within the synapse, this change then causing a current to start in the head of the next cell. These chemicals are called neurotransmitters because they effectively transmit electrical charge from one neurone to the next. A few neuro-transmitters have been isolated. They are divided into two groups, called the monoamines and the catecholamines.

The main chemical theory of depression is that a depletion of brain monoamine transmitters reduces the amount of "excitement" in the brain. The first evidence of a possible link between such chemical changes and depression came from observation of the effects of certain drugs, including some drugs which used to be used for high blood pressure, which sometimes caused depression and which reduce monoamine levels. Many researchers tried to correlate depression with actual levels of brain amines (or at least their breakdown products) but the results were variable and inconclusive. On the evidence, there can be no simple chemical cause which explains depression. If it were only a matter of monoamine depletion, it would be hard to explain why the drugs that deplete monoamines (and they do this in a gross way compared to the body's own subtle changes) do not always cause depression: in fact, they do so fairly rarely. It is also difficult to explain why some other drugs which deplete monoamines are not known to be associated with depression. Perhaps the presumed chemical changes often follow, rather than initiate, depression.

There is no doubt that someone in dark grey or black depression undergoes physical changes way beyond a mere change of mood (see *The case of Mr. X*, page 15), and such changes could well involve a change in brain amines. But since gross drug-induced amine depletion does not usually cause depression, there must be many other factors involved.

# PRE-MENSTRUAL TENSION

The pre-menstrual syndrome is a group of symptoms which occur regularly before menstruation and during early menstruation. After menstruation you are, by strict definition, entirely free from symptoms.

The symptoms are variable, ranging from migraine, backache, joint pains, asthma, tension, irritability, pimples and blotchy skin to swollen breasts, swollen ankles, bloatedness and tiredness. If the symptoms include the triad of tiredness, depression and irritability, this is called pre-menstrual tension. To find out whether you are susceptible to pre-menstrual depression or tension, it is useful to record accurately the timing of symptoms in relation to the menstrual cycle. This means using a diary or a chart every day for several months, and recording the presence or absence of symptoms and the presence or absence of menstruation. Only if there is a regular correlation and if the symptom disappears after menstruation, can you be sure of the diagnosis.

Whether physical and mental changes are monitored or not, many women are very well aware that their mood is different pre-menstrually. A study in Los Angeles showed that half the suicide attempts by women occurred in the four days immediately before, and during the beginning of, menstruation. The majority of violent crimes committed by women are carried out during the pre-menstrual week. On a more everyday level, most women feel different during this time. A 34-year-old woman said:

"I feel fat, worthless, everything's twice as much effort. I lose my sense of humour. I want to cry but I can't. I get spots, I get really puffy, my eyes get baggy and I feel ugly. My fingers get puffy. I get cranky with the kids and I have to stop myself from being hard on them. I forget it has anything to do with my period and wonder 'what's the point of living?' Then my period starts and I think 'oh, that's what it was', and I suddenly feel OK.''

**Hormonal changes during the menstrual cycle**

The pre-menstrual syndrome occurs when there is normally a rise in the hormone progesterone in the menstrual cycle (compare the diagram of pre-menstrual depression, below, with the diagram of progesterone levels, page 60). Women with pre-menstrual syndrome tend to have a lower than usual level of progesterone in the second half of the menstrual cycle.

Hormonal changes are responsible for the retention of water in the body pre-menstrually, which may lead to a feeling of being bloated as well as aches and pains, including headaches. Pre-menstrual loss of potassium may make you feel weak and lethargic, while changes in blood sugar may make you feel hungry, faint and irritable. If things at home or at work have not been going well, the symptoms feel worse and the mood change may be greater (see graph, below). (For treatment, see *Hormones*, page 171. See also *Childbirth*, page 58, and *Physical changes*, age 40 to 60, page 76.)

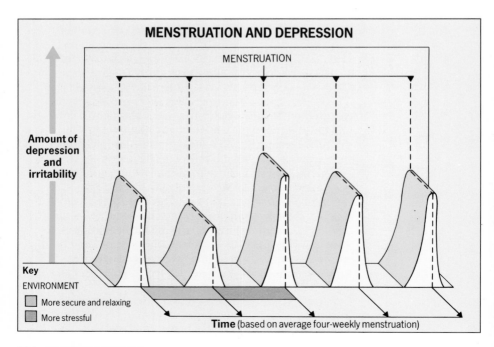

# INFECTION

Any infection that is serious enough to tax your body and deplete your energy will make you feel physically depressed, quite apart from any reaction you may have to being temporarily incapacitated.

However, some viral infections seem to have a very definite depressant effect, which often lasts longer than the physical symptoms. This is more commonly true of influenza, glandular fever and viral hepatitis (infection of the liver). It is quite common to feel low for several days after a bout of "flu". After glandular fever or viral hepatitis it is possible, though not usual, to feel depressed for months.

Sometimes depression or emotional stress is a causative factor in becoming infected. For instance, a study on streptococcal throat infection in families, measured by culturing the bacteria and estimating levels of antibodies, showed that the onset of illness was related to incidents of family stress, such as children's examinations. Heart attacks are more common in the six months after being bereaved of a spouse. Emotional stress and depression may create susceptibility to any infection (see, for instance, *The case of Mr. X*, page 15).

# SEVERE ILLNESS

Any severe illness and some medical measures, such as operations, radiotherapy and the use of some drugs, may deplete energy and therefore mimic depression. At the same time the prospect of long-term illness or of facing life with debility creates all kinds of feelings which may be repressed.

**LOSS AS A RESULT OF ILLNESS**  Losing the function of part of your body, being permanently debilitated, losing part of your body through amputation, or knowing you are going to die naturally cause grief (see page 63). An initial numbness or disbelief about your condition may sometimes amount to a complete denial of the facts. Sometimes people who are told they have cancer manage to block the fact so effectively that they have no memory of knowing or of ever being told. More often the fact is known but there is remarkably little worry, or an unrealistic optimism. Some degree of denial may continue for a long time.

When reality is faced, there may be many different feelings. There may be fear of pain, fear of death (see page 87) or fear of a changed life. The feelings of loss are hard for someone else to imagine – losing your own life, losing your family and friends, losing your own capacities and abilities.

**Loss of image**  If you lose a visible part of your body, you have to face the fact that your old body contour was not an inviolate boundary. It is quite natural to grieve over your loss of image: you feel not a whole person, blemished, odd, and you miss the part that has gone, which was a part of you. Women who have had mastectomies (removal of the breast) or hysterectomies (removal of the womb) often take time to adjust to a new body image – the result, sometimes, of feeling depleted or less of a woman. Depression tends to be more common both before and after hysterectomies: *before* because hysterectomies are usually carried out as a result of menstrual difficulties, which are sometimes secondary to emotional difficulties; *after* because any pre-existing emotional problems may not have changed and because it may be difficult to adjust to a body image without a womb. One of the hardest changes to tolerate is a colostomy, where your intestine ends in a hole in your abdomen to which is attached a plastic bag. Often people try valiantly to put a brave face on things while underneath they feel ashamed, depleted and isolated. If such feelings exist, it can be helpful to talk about them.

**Anger**  It is also natural to feel some anger about your condition. Sometimes the anger gets repressed, whilst sometimes it is directed at hospital staff, and sometimes it emerges through being irritable and difficult. If you are faced with a terminal illness, you will be angry that you are losing your life. You may be angry that you are going to have to depend on other people, that you cannot work any more or that you have to change to less "difficult" work. You may be angry with life or with God.

Acceptance of your new condition may involve coping with relearning how to use your changed body, accepting a new role in life and accepting a changed relationship with others. For help with coming to terms with your new condition, see *Dealing with the life event*, particularly *Talking to somebody*, page 124.

**STIGMA**  It is often difficult to tolerate being different. If you are obviously different, for example, paralysed, people tend to look at you with a mixture of sympathy and avoidance, which makes you feel somewhat apart from the human species. Because people tend to be awkward with their own feelings about what they see, they don't say "My God, what happened to you?" but ignore what they see, and you become isolated by politeness. Some handicapped people respond by living a life of depressed solitude. It is also difficult to live with a condition for which people do not make allowances because they cannot see what is wrong with you. People with respiratory failure, for instance, get little sympathy, but their life of hardly being able to move without gasping for air may be intolerable. Again, talking about your feelings may be helpful (see *Talking to somebody*, page 124, and *Short-term explorative psychotherapy*, page 158).

**ILLNESS IN OTHERS**
It can be very difficult to tolerate illness in your family or close friends, or to watch your parents die. It is inevitably *sad* to see what is happening. What may be *depressing* is to block your feelings. You may feel sad about their condition or that they are going to die. People tend not to share these feelings with the person who is ill, which is a pity. Although it may be initially awkward, it can be a relief to talk about the sadness and the possibility of death. Such conversation can create moments of great intimacy and friendship. On the other hand, you may also feel angry with them for being ill. This may sound unfair, but if you are inconvenienced by their illness (for instance, having to look after them), it is natural to have feelings of resentment. You can express these feelings outside the situation (see *Creative expression*, page 207) or with humour to the ill person – both solutions being preferable to becoming cold or bitter with them. You also may need to get some more help with looking after them. You may feel angry with them for using their illness to manipulate you or get their own way. This is common with people who are chronically ill. If you are on the other end of such manipulation, it is up to you to tell the person to stop it. You have to be insistent and avoid falling for the guilt. If their manipulation consistently fails to be successful, they will stop. The ill person may also remind you, uncomfortably, of your own fears about illness and mortality. It may help to talk about your fears with others (see *Talking to somebody*, page 124).

# SPECIFIC ILLNESSES

Although physical diseases can cause or mimic depression, they are a comparatively rare cause. Most of the specific illnesses mentioned here are uncommon and, with the possible exception of hypothyroidism, they start with depression in only a relatively small number of cases.

Several hormones have an effect on mood. As well as the female sexual hormones (see *Childbirth*, page 58, and *Premenstrual tension*, page 105), hormones from the pituitary gland, adrenal glands, thyroid glands, parathyroid glands and pancreas may all affect energy and mood. However, such effects occur only when there is a significant disease in the relevant gland, which is fairly rare, and in which case there are usually also physical symptoms.

**Hypopituitarism**

The pituitary gland fails to produce six hormones which normally stimulate other hormone-producing glands. The symptoms include a combination of Addison's disease (see below), hypothyroidism (see below), loss of menstruation and infertility. Both Addison's disease and hypothyroidism can cause symptoms of depression.

**Addison's disease**

The adrenal glands fail to produce enough steroid hormones, leading to loss of appetite, loss of weight and increasing tiredness and weakness, which may mimic depression. You may also have diarrhoea, constipation, nausea or vomiting. Your skin becomes strikingly darker.

**Cushing's syndrome**

This is caused by the presence of excessive steroid hormones, usually the result of taking steroid drugs, but occasionally due to an overproduction of steroids by the adrenal glands. Your face and body become fatter while your limbs get thinner. Your skin may bruise easily and stretch marks may appear. You may develop diabetes (see opposite) and high blood pressure. You may feel weak, tired and depressed.

**Hypothyroidism**

This is underactivity of the thyroid gland, resulting in the production of less thyroxine (thyroid hormone), which causes the basic rate of chemical processes in the body to slow down. The symptoms may develop gradually over months or even years. Your whole body slows down and you feel tired and lethargic. You tend to get constipated and gain weight. You may feel very depressed. Of all the glandular disturbances, this is the one that is most easy to miss, for initially it may be very similar to a severe depression. However, there are characteristic symptoms which differentiate hypothyroidism: you tend to feel the cold more, your hair tends to become sparse and dry, your skin becomes dry and thickened and your voice may become rather hoarse and deeper. A single blood test makes the diagnosis clear.

**Hyperpara-thyroidism**

Increased activity of the parathyroid glands causes excess parathyroid hormones, which leads to higher levels of calcium in the blood, partly by removing calcium from the bones. The first symptoms may be indigestion and depression. Later, minor injuries may cause bone fractures and the excessive calcium in the blood may be deposited in the kidneys, causing kidney stones.

**Diabetes mellitus** Insulin is necessary in the transference of blood sugar from the blood to the cells of the body. When the pancreas fails to produce enough insulin, there is too much sugar in the blood, which causes excessive urination and thirst, and too little in the cells of the body, which causes tiredness, weakness, apathy and loss of weight.

**Cancer of the intestine and pancreas** Very occasionally, cancers in these areas are preceded by depression, sometimes over a year before there is any medically detectable sign of cancer. There is no obvious medical explanation of this phenomenon.

**Organic brain disease** Sometimes a physical disease in the brain, like a brain tumour, becomes manifest through a change of mood, such as depression. This is very rare.

**Anaemia** Loss of red blood cells means the blood can carry less oxygen, which makes you tired, lethargic and perhaps depressed. More severe anaemia causes shortness of breath.

---

### IMPORTANT

I want to emphasize that these causes of depression are very rare. If you do have any of these conditions you should see your doctor. If there are no other reasons for being depressed, the depressive symptoms will disappear as the disease is treated.

---

# WEIGHT CHANGES

This is a complicated subject because mild depression can make you fat, severe depression can make you thin, while being thin or fat can make you depressed.

**Gaining weight** Occasionally, weight gain can be due to a particular medical problem (see, for example, *Hypothyroidism*, opposite), which also causes a depression (see the *Physical factors chart*, page 49). Much more often weight gain results from relative overeating (some people can eat vastly more than others without putting on weight), or lack of care about the body. Eating is very comforting and an easy way to provide yourself with at least some stimulation. If life is dull, or you are mildly depressed, a vicious circle ensues – you feel low and bored, so you eat. As you get fatter you feel worse about yourself and eat more. As you feel worse about yourself, you care less about how your body looks and feels, so you don't stop yourself from eating even more. As you get still larger you dislike how you look, but since in your depressed state you dislike yourself anyway, eating more makes complete sense. Then, as your excessive weight causes tiredness and inertia, that adds to your depressed state . . . and so on.

**Losing weight**    More severe depression tends to cause a loss of appetite and weight. You simply do not feel like eating or if you do, you cannot be bothered to do anything about it. It is not unusual for someone in dark-grey or black depression to lose 6 kg (14 lb) fairly rapidly.

Weight loss may also be caused by a number of illnesses (see the *Physical factors chart*, page 49). You should always see your doctor if you have lost weight without explanation. (See also *Diet and depression*, below).

# DIET AND DEPRESSION

We are built of what we eat and the balance of our diet can affect both our physical and mental well-being. Many dietary imbalances may cause some depression of mood.

**BLOOD SUGAR**    If you take in too few calories, as you may during a fast or a period of dieting, you may feel tired, lethargic and low. This is because your level of blood sugar has decreased – energy, well-being and clear thinking require an adequate level of sugar in the blood so that the brain, muscles and other organs can help themselves to as much immediate energy as they require from moment to moment. The brain and nerves are completely dependent on blood sugar since they cannot get energy from other foods in the blood, such as protein.

The effects of low blood sugar levels do not only occur during periods of not eating. The level of your blood sugar depends on the kinds of foods you eat. Carbohydrates, particularly sugar, tend to produce a rapid rise in blood sugar, which does not last long and which may be followed by a period of fatigue, lowered efficiency and lowered mood. Protein, however, especially when combined with some carbohydrate and fat, causes a more gradual rise in blood sugar, which is often sustained for six hours or more and which may be associated with efficiency and a feeling of well-being. It seems paradoxical that carbohydrate, which is a source of quick energy, can actually cause fatigue and depression. The mechanism is probably as follows: a sudden surge of carbohydrate overstimulates the pancreas, which then produces too much insulin; the insulin, in turn, causes the liver and muscles to withdraw too much sugar from the blood resulting in weakness, irritability and low mood.

**BODY SALTS**  Imbalance in body salts – lowered potassium, lowered sodium or raised calcium – may also cause depression, but these balances are closely determined by hormonal balance. Imbalance nearly always indicates hormonal disease rather than faulty diet. The one exception is that raised levels of calcium can be caused by taking too much vitamin D in tablets or cod liver oil.

Calcium levels decrease in women during the menopause and pre-menstrually (at the times when oestrogen levels are lower). It is possible that lowered calcium may be a factor in creating depressed mood, but the evidence is conflicting.

**VITAMINS**  Vitamins are essential substances that need to be eaten because the body is not capable of manufacturing them. A deficiency of thiamin (B1), niacin, pyridoxine (B6), B12, folic acid and ascorbic acid (C) may cause depression.

The chart (below) outlines foods rich in these vitamins, those people most at risk of deficiency, and the possible reasons for depression as a result of deficiency.

**Vitamin deficiencies**  Gross deficiencies in the vitamins mentioned here most commonly occur in those who are severely ill, in alcoholics and in the elderly. It may be that small deficiencies affect mood and it is possible that many other substances and different

## VITAMINS AND DEPRESSION

| Vitamin | Good sources | People at most risk of deficiency | Possible mechanism relating to depression |
|---------|--------------|-----------------------------------|-------------------------------------------|
| B1 | Cereals, nuts, peas, pork. | Old people. | Essential in enabling the brain cells to take in energy from sugar. |
| Niacin | Meat, fish, wholemeal cereals. | Alcoholics, vagrants. | Essential in breaking down food to provide energy. |
| B6 | In most foods. | Women on the contraceptive pill. | As in Niacin (above). |
| B12 | Only in animal products, particularly liver, kidney and sardines. | Strict vegetarians. People with "pernicious anaemia" cannot absorb B12. | Deficiency directly affects nerve cells. Also causes anaemia, which mimics depression. |
| Folic acid | Liver, fresh vegetables, yeast. | Pregnant women. Women on the contraceptive pill have a higher requirement. | Causes anaemia, which mimics depression. |
| C | Fresh vegetables and fruit, especially citrus fruit. | Those with a poor diet, lacking in vegetables and fruits. Alcoholics. | Important in response to stress. |

balances affect how we feel. Eating more monoamines, in cheese or chocolate, for example, might affect your mood (see *Chemical theories on depression*, page 104). Various specific allergies may also affect mood. It is difficult to be sure as there is much conflicting evidence and many conflicting views and fashions on diet. Too much diet consciousness may be depressing in itself.

# DRUGS

Many drugs have a depressant effect on the mind and body. Others have a stimulant effect, lack of which makes you feel depressed when you stop taking the drug.

**Alcohol**    Although alcohol relaxes the muscles, reduces anxiety and often removes social inhibitions, it can be a stimulant or a depressant – it tends to accentuate an existing mood. Sad people often become morose, especially when drinking alone. Whatever your mood at the time of drinking, afterwards, during the hangover, you may have a headache, feel lethargic and in low spirits.

Both alcoholism and depression are often mechanisms for avoiding feelings. Some genetic studies suggest that depression and alcoholism tend to go together in families, but that more men become alcoholic while more women become depressed. Depressives and alcoholics are the most likely to attempt or commit suicide. People who can cope while drinking regularly may get depressed when they stop drinking.

Drinking may cover up depression or bring it about. However much an alcoholic denies the drink problem, somewhere underneath there are feelings of inadequacy and a loss of self-respect. Usually they are obliterated by the next drink, but sometimes they emerge as self-blame, disgust and depression. Conversely, depressed people sometimes drink more, hoping for some relief. If you have a mild depression, caused in part by too much control of feeling, letting go with the help of a little alcohol can be a very good idea. But if alcohol becomes an addiction and therefore an instrument of damaged respect, it only adds to the depression.

**Tobacco**    Giving up cigarettes causes depression, irritability, anxiety and loss of concentration. Since 50 per cent of smokers try to give up and only 15 per cent succeed, stopping smoking is a common phenomenon, sometimes carried out by one person several times a day. The effects are not primarily psychological but are related to the level of nicotine and can be allayed by injections of nicotine or eating nicotine chewing gum. However, there is also pleasure in the rituals of smoking which may be missed. Some people eat more after stopping smoking and then feel bad about their weight gain. Others blame themselves unnecessarily for not being able to stop.

**Anti-anxiety drugs**
Anti-anxiety drugs, otherwise known as anxiolytics, sedatives or minor tranquillizers, are very similar in effect to alcohol. They reduce muscle tension, repress anxiety and acute feeling, but at the same time, repress normal social inhibitions so that the feeling may be more flamboyantly expressed. Unfortunately, these drugs are highly addictive. There are many people who are spared anxiety through their use, but only at the expense of losing sensitivity to the finer feelings in life.

**Sleeping tablets**
The majority of sleeping tablets now prescribed are benzodiazepines (for example, nitrazepam or Mogadon), which contain the same group of chemicals as the anti-anxiety drugs, only with different advertising and packaging. Most sleeping tablets have an effect that lasts through the next day, making you less anxious, less responsive, and a little less alive. These drugs are addictive and when they are stopped create a rebound effect – it is even harder to sleep than it was in pre-tablet times. This effect lasts several days.

**Stronger tranquillizers**
These drugs are prescribed mostly for psychotic conditions, including the manic phase of manic depression. Although they may be highly successful in stopping and preventing psychosis, they may occasionally result in some depression of reaction and mood.

**The contraceptive pill**
The incidence of depression in those on "the pill" is not statistically higher than average, but it seems that in a few women there is an individual response of depression which is probably drug-related. One possible explanation is that the

---

## STRONGLY ADDICTIVE DRUGS

Coming off drugs that made you high can make you feel low for some time. If, for example, you have regularly been taking amphetamines (speed), you have to face mundane slow reality when you stop taking them. Apart from getting over the physical problems of addiction, you have to confront an immediate history of self-destruction and the knowledge that responsibility has been avoided. You have to cope with a whole host of problems that you once ignored. A fractured image of yourself stares at you uncomfortably, almost inviting you to go down a hole of self-castigating depression or back up on to a cloud of drugged oblivion. This applies to any addiction, from heroin to alcohol.

synthetic progesterone-like substance (progestogen) used in the pill actually causes depletion of the body's own natural progesterone, and the lower level of natural progesterone may be related to mood change (see *Childbirth*, page 58, and *Pre-menstrual tension*, page 105). Another possible cause of depression is a deficiency of vitamin B6, which is fairly common in women on the pill (see the vitamin chart in *Diet and depression*, page 112).

**Anti-hypertensives** These drugs are used to lower blood pressure. Occasionally they lead to depression, possibly by the mechanism of depleting brain monoamines (see *Chemical theories on depression*, page 104). This effect is increasingly uncommon, however, as modern anti-hypertensives have more selective effects.

**Steroids** These drugs can occasionally cause severe depression when taken internally in relatively high doses over a long period (see *Cushing's syndrome*, page 110). Local steroid applications to the skin or the nose do not enter the blood stream in sufficient quantities to be able to cause depression.

**FIND OUT WHAT YOU ARE TAKING** Nearly all conventional drugs are also poisons. In many conditions, the benefits of the drug are well worth the side-effects, but this is your choice. Many people allow themselves to be prescribed drugs without knowing what the drugs really do and what their side-effects are. Thus side-effects, such as depression of energy and mood, may be unwittingly produced and unnecessarily endured.

# THE WEATHER AND THE STARS

Mood is affected by many kinds of outer influence. Most people are affected by the weather, by dampness dampening the spirit, by dreary grey days which correspond with dreary grey moods, and by sunshine which nurtures good feeling.

**NEGATIVE IONS** Just before a thunderstorm, the weather is usually sultry and heavy, which makes you feel heavy and look forward to the thunder breaking. After the storm, the air feels fresh and you feel better. Putting aside the symbolic imagery, some of the effect on mood may be due to the balance of negatively and positively charged particles in the atmosphere. Basically, negative ions make you feel positive and positive ions make you feel negative. An electrical storm produces a lot of negative ions as does the breaking of the water on the sea shore. An electronic ionizer creates a similar effect.

**THE SEASONS AND THE HEAVENS**

We are affected by all kinds of rhythms, from outside us and from within. The tilt of the earth relative to the sun creates the rhythm of the seasons, which has an obvious effect on how we feel. Depression severe enough to warrant admission to hospital, and suicide, are both more common in the spring and autumn. Autumn depression, apart from the obvious connection with dying and cold, may be related, in part, to day length. Some autumn depressions have been treated successfully by supplying extra doses of bright light, effectively increasing the length of the day.

**The moon**

The rhythm of the moon may have a strong effect on mood. Some women find that their periods correspond exactly with the changing moon. The moon is thus affecting the timing of all kinds of hormonal change, which are often related to changes in mood. The old term "lunacy" was based on the belief that madness and the lunar cycle were connected, lunatics being active at the time of the full moon. This has been repeatedly confirmed statistically – at full moon there are more admissions to psychiatric hospitals.

**Night and day**

The rhythm of night and day seems to have a powerful effect on complex timing mechanisms relating to mood. There are a number of cases of manic depression in which the cycle is a regular 48 hours, changing every 24 hours from mania to depression or from depression to mania. One such person was given an artificial 22 hour day by changing the timing of light and dark. The cycle changed to a regular 44 hours, changing direction every 22.

**The planets**

If we can be affected so much by the relative positions of earth, sun and moon, it would not be surprising if something as subtle and delicate as mood could be affected by the more distant influences, the position of the earth relative to planets and stars. Such influences may relate to "biorhythms" – rhythms of physical functioning, of intellectual functioning and of sensitivity which may affect us. The evidence for the exact periodicity of these cycles is conflicting. If you get to know your own personal rhythms well, you may be able to predict the best times for making decisions and to time your activities more effectively. Some people keep accurate charts of their own physical, intellectual and emotional rhythms. Whether or not you get to know your own rhythms, it is anyway reassuring to know of the existence of often unseen external influences, to know that it is sometimes natural to feel a little low for no very obvious reason, and that the mood will change in time, just as the sun will surely reappear.

# Part 3

# LIFTING DEPRESSION - THE MANY WAYS UP

# Introduction

There are hundreds of different therapies for depression, and what you decide is right for you depends as much on who you are and your own preferences as it does on how bad your depression is or what caused it. Just as there are many causes (see *The complexity of cause*, page 35), there are also many types of treatment which are not necessarily contradictory. One sort of cause does not mean that a certain treatment is necessarily required. For instance, a depression may have been precipitated by a marital separation, but if it is severe enough to cause strong physical symptoms, initially it may be best treated physically.

## CHOOSING AN APPROPRIATE THERAPY

On looking through the possible causes charts (see pages 38 to 55), you may have picked out some causes that perhaps seem relevant to you and some that really strike a chord. Perhaps you find that your early family situation provided you with very little emotional support and a poor opinion of yourself – it is possible to explore these avenues with in-depth psychotherapy (see page 145), which may be useful: but you may, on the other hand, decide that this is not right for you and that you would prefer to focus more on changing your lifestyle and environment. A purist may say, "But then you are not really getting down to the nitty-gritty, the real cause". This does not necessarily matter for two reasons: first of all, this "real" cause may be one of many, and it may not be the most important one. Secondly, it is sometimes possible to change your feelings about yourself without analyzing them, as long as you have the strength and determination to make your present environment and experiences of life different and positive.

Reading through the sections in this part of the book may give you an idea of the kind of treatment you might prefer. You may also need to discuss it with somebody, in which case talk to your general practitioner (see *How to approach your GP*, page 170), or else consult one of the agencies listed in *Useful addresses* on page 218. In general, there are four factors which affect your choice of treatment: depth of depression, cause of depression, personal investment, and personal preference.

## Depth of depression

There usually comes a point in deepening depression when words become less effective than physical treatments. As a general guideline, loss of sparkle, blue and grey depression can often be treated through self-help (see page 121) or psychotherapy (see page 145), while black and white depression generally tend to respond more effectively to physical treatments (see page 169).

## GUIDE TO CAUSE AND TREATMENT

While there is obviously considerable overlap, in general the four sections on causes relate to the following ways out:

| Cause | Main action |
|-------|-------------|
| Life events | Self-help or psychotherapy |
| Life non-events | Self-help or psychotherapy |
| Past history and personality | Psychotherapy: see a psychotherapist (either through your doctor or through one of the organizations listed on page 218) |
| Physical factors | Physical treatments: see a doctor or psychiatrist |

**Cause of depression**  Cause and treatment may not be obviously related. For instance, a life event may precipitate a depression too severe for psychotherapy to be helpful. Although the above guide is generally true, it is worth noting that there may be several causative influences, and that depth of depression, personal investment and personal preference are also important.

**Personal investment**  It makes sense to try self-help before seeking professional help, both in terms of the investment in time and money and in terms of the dividend of more self-reliance. If you need or want professional help, psychotherapy and physical treatments involve very different kinds of investment.

In terms of personal effort, time and money, psychotherapy is usually more expensive than physical treatment. Financially, this is because physical methods are more likely to be paid for either by the State or by insurance companies. There is only a limited amount of psychotherapy available through the State. Although short-term psychotherapy may sometimes take less time than a long series of physical treatments, in general it takes more time than physical treatment. In addition, psychotherapy, when it is effective, always requires personal effort, a willingness to explore pain as well as pleasure, and an openness to changing a view on life.

The other side of the equation is that your greater personal investment may pay longer-term dividends. If you can learn to handle your depression without drugs, you are more likely to be able to deal with a recurrence, if it arises, yourself.

**Personal preference**  To an extent, it is important to find a form of therapy that feels suitable for you. Most people will want to try some forms of self-help. Those with a more mechanical and materialistic view of life are more likely to prefer physical treatments, while those who like to find inner meaning and motive are more likely to prefer psychotherapy.

# Self-help

The problem with depression is that you seldom feel like helping yourself at all. The section on self-help is therefore purposefully directive. There are two main ways you can help yourself. Either you can deal with the cause of your depression by dealing with the life event or changing the life non-event, or you can deal with the symptoms. The best option is to do both. In the following sections, there are some suggestions that may strike a chord and others that will put you off. Although you are more likely to take up your preferred activities with more enthusiasm, you need to balance this against the need to try something different in order to challenge some of the views and rigid patterns which may have contributed to your depression.

If you are deeply depressed, you may find it very hard to find the motivation to even look for, let alone try to deal with, a cause of your depression. If this is so, you may need to work on changing the symptoms first, either by helping yourself (see *Changing the symptoms*, page 136) or by getting professional help (see *Psychotherapy*, page 145, and *Physical treatments*, page 169). As soon as there is an uplift in your mood and motivation you can then return to looking at the cause.

## DEALING WITH THE LIFE EVENT

If there was a significant life event, or even one that seemed insignificant, that occurred before, at or around the same time as the beginning of your depression, it may be helpful to look at the following questions and suggestions.

● *How do you really feel about it?* After diagnosing the life event as a possible cause of your depression, go back to the event and ask yourself how you really feel about it. If the answer is "depressed", do not accept that, but find the feeling before the depression – even if that feeling was only transient. If you can't find the feeling after reading what you have read in this book so far, make a guess as to what the feeling could be.

Then ask yourself what it is that does not allow you to feel that kind of feeling. For instance, as a mother, you may have felt moments of anger with the children which you quickly shut off and tried to ignore. You may find that you have a belief, even though you may never have thought about it in these terms, that a "good mother" should always think well of her children and should always feel love and gratitude. Or perhaps you find a general injunction that anger is wrong.

● *Whose opinion is it, anyway?* Next, ask yourself where that attitude comes from – perhaps your parents or your friends. It is important to know who it comes from, because as soon as you know, you realize you are not dealing with a universal law, but with someone else's opinion. Now challenge this other person's opinion. Consider the opposite or alternative possibilities. Perhaps a "good mother" is primarily warm (as opposed to "correct" in feeling) and warmth means giving out what you feel inside, anger included. Perhaps warmth means being more human than perfect. Perhaps women have the right to get angry. Perhaps men have the right to cry and to share disappointment and failure. So far you have been dealing with the internal judgements that stop expression of feeling. For some, it is unnecessary to do this. For others, freer expression is not possible without clearing up some of the inner doubts first.

**EXPRESS THE FEELING** When you have dealt with some of the doubts that stopped your feeling, you may find that you can allow the feeling to "live" within you without repression. Often, however, it is helpful to find a way of expressing the feeling. You do not necessarily need to know what the feeling is in advance. If you are mindful of the possibility of the feeling arising and free to let it arise if it will, you will find that some of the following activities can create an opening for the rediscovery of the feeling you stopped. If you don't feel anything, don't worry, the exercise itself is helpful. Try one of the following sugges-tions, depending on the nature of the feeling.

**1** Difficulty in expressing anger:

● Take part in an aggressive sport like squash or football.

● Hit a punch-ball, imagining each blow is directed at the person or the situation (if that is easier) that makes you angry. Use all your force and with each blow, grunt. After some practice, try hitting and grunting with your mouth wide open and then increase the volume of sound till you are yelling at the top of your voice. All this can be done equally well hitting a cushion, a pillow or a bed. As you get more into it, try putting words to each blow, for example, "I'm sick of dirty nappies!" or "I'll smash your face in!".

● If it is difficult to find enough privacy to shout at home, try shouting while alone in a car. Or else shout in the woods, hit the ground or punch the air.

● Do a physical job such as cleaning, digging or chopping wood, putting all your energy and anger into the activity.

**2** If you have withheld tears or have difficulty in crying, and after challenging the idea that people like you should not cry, find your own way of relaxing. For instance, take a hot bath or get someone to massage you (see page 197). You may be relaxed after aerobics or other exercises or sports. Then in a more relaxed state try any of the following:

● Listen to music that moves you and allow yourself to get lost in the music or the words.

● Touch yourself very gently, with love and tenderness, around your eyes and mouth. Tell yourself it is alright to cry. If you do not cry, it does not matter, you have still given yourself some care.

● Be held by someone who loves you. If you are a man and would not think of crying in front of somebody else, don't forget to challenge that idea too. It can be a wonderful relief to cry with somebody. If you cannot, do not worry – being held and touched can give you a lot.

**3** If you have withheld sexual feeling or have difficulty with sensuality or sex:

● Try touching each other sensually with absolutely no pressure to have sex, just purely for the experience of feeling the touch. If you have too little sexual feeling to feel like initiating sex, you can wilfully organize sensual activity. You could, for instance, spend half an hour being together naked. Decide which one of you wishes to be touched first. The toucher then explores the body of the touched, while the touched says exactly what he or she likes. There is no pressure on the touched to respond in any way and therefore, since he or she is not under any pressure to perform, it is easier to allow the experience of pleasure. However, when you are depressed don't expect to feel as much as you normally do.

● Buy some new clothes or wear an outrageous outfit. Changing how you look outside can affect how you feel inside and it is also a small act of hope.

● Go out dancing late into the night. You will be giving yourself four anti-depressants simultaneously: encouraging sensual contact; hearing music that moves you; moving your body; and disrupting your sleep patterns.

**4** If you have unfinished business with another person, that is, there were things you did not say that you wish you had:

● Take the plunge and talk to that person. It may be a little embarrassing to reopen a subject, but giving up a little pride is a small cost to pay for lifting your depression. If the person has gone to Australia, ring Australia. If you are scared, be scared, but don't let that stop you.

● In a couples problem, try changing the old pattern. If you never fight, perhaps you need to. Perhaps you need to say as directly and honestly as you can some of the things you have never said, not with the intention of hurting, but with the intention of remaking contact.

● If you fight all the time or too much, ask yourself if you are fighting about the right subject – you may be fighting about the washing up when the real problem is lack of sex. Ask yourself if the fight is not an avoidance of other feelings. Perhaps you are uncomfortable with softer feelings.

● See if you can get beyond blame. If you blame the person, he or she becomes defensive and contact becomes impossible. If you blame yourself, it may help you to realize that self-pity and self-castigation are selfish – your own energy is directed at yourself and there is no contact with another.

● Talk to the person in your imagination if you cannot talk to them directly. Imagine the person you have feelings about standing in front of you. It may help to close your eyes. Imagine how he or she looks in detail. Now say, perhaps out loud, everything you want to say to that person as honestly, feelingly and as directly as you can.

● With someone who has died, do not be afraid of the pain of telling them how much you miss them, how much you would like them to be able to see what you are doing with your life, or how much you love them. However unfair it may seem, don't stop yourself from being angry if you need to. Their death may not have been a malicious act, directed personally against you, but their leaving hurt you and you may feel angry with them about it.

● Talk to life or God. Speak your grievances out aloud. Again, don't be afraid to be as angry as you want. Life and God can take anything you throw at them – and they will not punish you.

**TALKING TO SOMEBODY**

Talking to a third party – a friend, a relative, a priest – can provide both a relief of tension and a new perspective; speaking your thoughts often clarifies them. It can be a relief to share your problem with another person who is warm and understanding. Even if he or she doesn't understand, perhaps the dialogue makes you angry enough to break a few depressive cobwebs, or a completely erroneous suggestion may set you thinking on a different course. The very act of talking about troubles sometimes provides an answer as well as a relief of tension. In other words, the more important aspect of talking to somebody is what you give out and not what you get back. You are breaking through the depressive shut-down of communication.

Holding on to fears and feelings is both a cause and a result of depression. When you are depressed, you are going to feel like resisting any desire to initiate conversation. Make yourself. For instance, muster your will, arrange the meeting and tell the person that you have some important personal things that you would like to discuss. That way you are committed, and it is harder to pull out at the last minute. Most times when people do broach hitherto forbidden subjects, they are thankful for it and feel not only relieved but also closer to both the other person and themselves. Here are a few examples:

● Mothers with young children often think that other mothers cope more easily, and that their feelings of resentment about their loss of freedom are not natural. What a relief to be able to talk freely about the frustrations as well as the pleasures, and to let go of the pretences of motherhood bliss.

● Going through any of the life changes (see page 74) can be very hard. What a difference it makes to allow yourself to talk about your regrets of not having achieved your dreams, or your fears of getting older. So often you find that an open listener has similar concerns, or different concerns – either way his or her humanity helps you feel less alone.

● Going to hospital may be a time of great fear. Being incapacitated (for instance, paralysed) can make you feel isolated and different. Sharing your feelings can remind you that you are still one of the family of Man.

● When you, or a friend, are dying, pretending to each other that it is not happening creates distance. Talking about it and sharing the fear and sorrow can transform those last weeks or months, leaving a memory of intimacy and friendship.

You may be wary of talking to somebody because you don't want to burden them or because, in your depressed state, you cannot imagine that anybody could be interested in you. But if you share some of your feelings, you are *giving* to somebody else and providing someone with the pleasure (or challenge) of helping. Sharing joy increases it. Sharing pain lessens it.

# CHANGING THE LIFE NON-EVENT

When you are depressed you get into such a state that you don't believe you *can* change what is around you. In a depressed state you feel like a victim of circumstances and it seems quite unimaginable that life could be better in any way.

So, in general, this section applies more to lighter states of depression – before the barrier of hope and especially before the barrier of will (see *Different levels of liveliness*, page 16). After these barriers it is much harder to find the energy to change outer circumstances, but not impossible. Again, you may need to deal with the symptoms first (see *Changing the symptoms*, page 136). Or you may take a jump and, against all the dead weight of hopelessness, use your intelligent thought to make a decision that, objectively, could alter your depressive situation to the good.

## CHANGING THE SITUATION AT HOME

It is easy to become accustomed to a certain way of living, so much so that sometimes you forget that you actually do have the freedom to change it. You don't have to eat three meals a day, watch television in the evenings or stay all day at home with the children. You don't have to live with your mother-in-law, your parents or even your spouse. It is your life and you have the freedom to choose how you want to live. This may seem obvious, but it is sometimes difficult to act on your freedom because:

● You are too depressed to act. Sometimes it is a good idea to wait for the slightest upswing in your mood and then act, make yourself act.

● You are too depressed to know what the best action is. You probably need to talk to somebody (see page 124).

● You judge your considered action as unfair on another. This may well be a false argument, which you are using to stop yourself from acting. It is far more unfair on both yourself and the other when you live in an atmosphere of repressed resentment.

● You are out of touch with any feeling that would give you some impetus. It is useful to find a way of reaching emotional or body feeling (see *Psychotherapy*, page 145, *Sports*, page 194 and *Creative expression*, page 207).

● You are under the thumb of another – spouse, parent or anybody else (see the case history below) – and do not dare to challenge the rules. Consider what you have got to lose if you do challenge the person or their rules.

### CASE HISTORY

A footballer related the following story to a psychotherapy group. His mother had been trying to get him to look after her for many years. Her flat had recently been burned down in a fire that she had started in her kitchen. He felt compelled to take her into his house indefinitely and felt depressed as a result. He felt she was a burden, and he stood slumped as if he were carrying a huge weight on his shoulders. Rationally, he thought that the situation ought to make him angry, but he judged any anger as unfair to his mother, and he was too depressed to feel anything much at all.

It was only when he could imagine the aggression he felt when fighting for the ball on the football field (aggression that he did not judge as bad) that he knew and felt his anger. At that moment his stance changed, he stood erect, smiled and decided there and then to find another place for his mother to live until her flat was rebuilt. Within a week his mother had left, with no bad feeling.

**Time away from home**

There may often be situations at home that make you irritated and deplete your energy. If you are a mother or father stuck at home with young children, there are little things you can do to help. You can find a way of expressing your frustration creatively (see *Creative expression*, page 207) and you can talk to somebody (see page 124). Remember that most other parents of young children have all the same problems as you. You can make sure that you give yourself time away from the home – perhaps you could find another mother who could look after your children, and vice versa, so you can take an afternoon off a week and later a day off. There may be a good crèche your young child can go to while you keep your body and mind in trim (see pages 194 to 205). If you find it difficult to leave your children with someone they don't know very well, make sure you get some time off by leaving them with your partner. You do not need to be housebound. Some mothers do not get out for fear of hurting their children and feeling "bad mothers" but:

● There is no evidence of any damage to children if the person looking after them can cope and is not emotionally cold.

● When you have had a break, you can give much more to your child with heart rather than duty. Quality of time is more important to both you and your child than quantity.

When you do get off, do something completely different and exciting and don't let anyone talk about children.

**CHANGING THE SITUATION AT WORK**

If you are bored or unhappy at work, or the pressure feels too great, consider changing jobs. You do not have to do the job that you are doing. You can speak to your boss or supervisor about changing departments at the place where you work, or you can leave altogether. This may be difficult when you are depressed, and there may be considerable pressure on you to maintain a steady income. However, even if you decide not to change jobs, the knowledge that you can will take some of the pressure off. The thought that this is your lot, that your fate is to work like this till retirement, is a thought of your own making. If you don't want to change jobs, consider:

● **Dealing with authority** There is a story of a man who suffered from epilepsy who felt bad about his pay but was too afraid to approach his boss. Very rarely, after an epileptic fit, a person goes into "automatic" behaviour in which he seems to function normally but is quite unconscious. This is what happened to this man, and during his period of automatic behaviour, he asked his boss for a rise, and got it.

At work there are two levels of authority: there is your position relative to someone above you, which you have to respect if you are to keep your job. On the other hand, there is an emotional level, which may lead you to act in an inferior fashion towards someone to whom you hand over more power than is necessary (see *"Dependent" personality*, page 98, and *"Good behaviour" personality*, page 99). If you feel intimidated by your boss or someone above you, take the plunge and say what you need to say in a manner that is not designed to threaten their position.

● **Dealing with unfinished business** with colleagues and peers (see *Express the feeling* page 122).

● **Making your work environment look as good as possible** You could, at least, bring something with you – a plant or an ornament that means something to you, for example. Make yourself feel at home. Give yourself some pleasure at work.

● **Changing the routine** If work is boring, consider ways of changing the routine. If the main routine is fixed by the nature of the work, consider any way you can make the work more interesting. Listen to music, chat to your workmates, make plans about what you can spend your hard-earned money on.

● **Changing your attitude to work** Consider how important the job is in the perspective of your whole life. This may reduce the feeling of pressure.

● **Allow yourself to dream about the work you would most like to do** It may seem impossible to achieve initially, but consider whether there may be some small, real step that you can take towards that dream.

● **Taking a rest or holiday** Sometimes a period away from the pressure or the routine is all you need to feel better. However, if you are so depressed that you have lost much of your initiative, you may find work is the one place where you can stay productive because there is constant outside pressure to keep you going. If depression gets so bad that, even with outside pressure, you become less and less productive and therefore feel worse and worse about yourself, despite trying self-help or help from others, then it is best to take a long time off from work, until you are better. Provide your employers with a doctor's certificate and, initially, consider giving yourself at least a month off so that you are not bent by the pressure of return, and have a clear break which can be extended if necessary.

● **Taking a job lower down on the scale of social ranking or financial reward** If your work is generally too pressured and you find yourself getting depressed at times of mounting pressure, consider doing a job that gives you more pleasure. It may, initially, be difficult to move down without a feeling of failure but in the long run you may find the pleasure far more important than the position and the money.

**CHANGING THE PHYSICAL ENVIRONMENT**

A psychotherapist who had been depressed many years before told me that after weeks of lying in bed feeling hopeless, the first change came when he got up, changed his sheets, cleaned his room and opened the windows in order to let the air and sun in.

Whether or not the state of your room, your home or your work-place was significant in depressing you, changing your environment can be very helpful because:

● The act of cleaning outside makes you feel cleaner inside.

● The activity gets your body and mind moving.

● You can give yourself small tasks which are accomplishable. Completing a task, however small, provides a glimmer of better feeling about yourself.

● You end up with a brighter environment to be in, which reminds you of the positive step you have made, and feeds you with a good feeling every day.

Even if you do not usually do these things, consider some of these as possibilities: cleaning your house; dusting and shining indoor plants; cleaning and re-arranging cupboards and drawers; doing any gardening job you enjoy; cleaning your car; re-arranging the furniture in a room; decorating a room. It is important not to take on a job that is too big. One completed task gives a little hope.

**CHANGING BORING HABITS**

Habits can provide comfort, security for children, an efficient way of coping with things that are repeatedly necessary, and/or a dulling restriction of spontaneity. If you are stuck in a routine and feel mildly depressed (down to light grey), you can improve things. Here are some possibilities:

● **Food** Spice it up, experiment, change your diet, change the times you eat, go out for a meal.

● **Drink** If you do not drink much alcohol, have a few drinks. Go out for an evening with friends and drink a bit too much. If you drink a lot regularly, try cutting down or stopping, or changing the timing.

● **Sleep** Many people, especially when depressed, get obsessed with how much sleep they should have. There is no general rule about how much sleep is necessary. Lack of sleep is *not* harmful and your body will always take as much as it needs in the end. What *is* harmful is worrying about how much sleep you need. If you don't sleep well, try going to bed later but still get up at the same time in the morning. Sleep deprivation has been used successfully as a treatment for depression: this involves being kept awake for 36 hours, perhaps once or twice a week. You can try doing this yourself by, for example, going out dancing all night or reading an exciting book that is hard to put down.

● **Sex** If you are not too depressed to feel any sensual feeling, try varying the routines you may have slipped into. If you feel able to do so, vary positions, change who usually initiates sexual contact, talk about sex, try touching in different ways.

● **Routines** Alter your schedules and routines. If the morning paper depresses you or has no effect on you, do not read it for a few days, or stop reading it altogether. Change the time of the dog's walk. Go out to a film instead of watching television. Do the opposite of what you usually do – just as an experiment for a while. Try giving people different answers from your usual ones. See what happens. You may find that a great deal of what you do is habit and open to intelligent challenge.

**GIVING UP LONELINESS**

Loneliness is probably the biggest single cause of depression. It is usually possible to prevent it.

If you live alone and are lonely, you may be too depressed even to consider living with somebody else. Perhaps it is helpful to remember that there are many other lonely people in the world, longing for company. Maybe there is someone you know who might be interested in sharing with you, even if, in your depressed state, you cannot imagine that anybody could be. To ask requires the risk of rejection. If there is nobody you know, you can advertise. There are many people who have changed their lives by contacting a dating agency or by simply advertising to share a flat or a house. Everyday contact with another human being is nearly always worth any loss of pride it might cause you to ask or advertise, and is also worth some loss of privacy. How much privacy you lose is to some extent up to you – you might, for instance, prefer not to share a living room or prefer to live in adjacent flats.

**Living alone**

If you prefer to live alone, make sure there are times when you have contact with others. Join clubs and, if you can, get involved in activities. If you join an organization with an undercurrent in your manner of "talk to me, I'm lonely", people will probably try to avoid you. A better bet is to make yourself useful and active and allow the contact to come naturally through the activity.

**Living with other people**

If you live with others and are still lonely, you need to find out whether the problem is with you, with them or with something between you. You could try opening the subject up by saying, for instance: "I don't know what it is, but I feel a bit distant from you". If that's too serious, perhaps you could say, with a little humour, "Have I done something wrong?" Quite often, distance is created by an unspoken judgement or feeling. Talking such things out is often enough to recreate a feeling of contact (see *Creative expression*, page 207). It may simply be that you are with the wrong people. A 30-year-old woman who lived with other 30-year-olds always "felt out of it" until she moved in with much younger friends – she had "missed" her teenage period and still somehow felt a teenager, though she did not realize this until it was suggested to her. You may find that your depth of contact with others is at the wrong level for you – you may want more or less, or a different type, and need to seek people who want the same kind or level of contact.

**Distance from other people**

If you have a recurrent problem of being distant from other people, there may well be something in you that seeks and maintains the distance, even without your being aware of it. Such an inner attitude can be changed with psychotherapy and a great deal of motivation. If you are too depressed to do something about your loneliness, please take the step of seeking professional advice. Either see your doctor, or contact one of the organizations listed on page 218.

**FEELING USEFUL**

The most debilitating effect of unemployment and retirement can be the feeling of uselessness. Such a feeling may prevent you getting another job and render you of less use than you need to be. If you feel like this, consider the following:
● Do something useful. It does not matter how small it is. Choose a small, though useful task, such as putting the children to bed, cleaning something or repairing something in the house or garden. Any completed task will give you a better feeling about yourself (see *Reasons for living*, overleaf).
● If you are unemployed, remember that an attitude of despondency will stop you getting another job. If you feel despondent when you go to a job interview, act. Muster all the enthusiasm you can, practise it on friends and act eager and interested at the interview. It quite often happens that the initial pretence breaks through a barrier to your genuine enthusiasm. Do as much research as possible on the job you are applying for and gather every bit of available information on potential jobs. Consider doing jobs that you would not normally consider, just to get yourself started and to regain some self-respect.

You may need to give up the idea that there is someone who ought to supply you with a job, and consider creating work for yourself, filling a need in your area that no employer ever thought of. When you are depressed it is difficult to find the creativity, initiative, and self-belief to start on such a project, but perhaps you can consider it as a possibility for when you begin to feel more confident. Find out about courses which may help you start your own business. Talk about such ideas with friends: this keeps your own interest moving, and can give you valuable feedback and support.

Meanwhile, keep yourself moving by taking regular exercise (see *Keeping your body in trim*, page 194), and by doing other useful tasks around your home (see *Changing the physical environment*, page 129). Consider doing voluntary work and involving yourself in the community.

● If you are retired, see the section on positive ageing (see opposite). You may want to look for part-time or full-time work, but consider first whether this is something that will give you pleasure or whether it is something you are driven to out of a fear of ageing. If your job gave you a major reason for living, you need to find other tasks. If you have recently retired and are married, you and your spouse may, initially, find it hard to get used to spending so much time with each

---

## REASONS FOR LIVING

If you wonder about the point of continuing your existence at all, consider:

■ The possibility that if you are alive, your mission on earth (whether you know it or not) is not yet completed.

■ That any mistakes you have made are not mistakes – they are part of your life education.

■ Giving something. Giving is one of the greatest anti-depressants there is – it makes you feel good. Consider doing something for somebody else, for instance, helping a friend or writing letters for people in hospital who can't write, or joining a voluntary help project. Consider getting a cat or a dog that you have to care for – any mess or disorder in your house may well be worth the feeling you get through giving. Consider teaching what you know. If giving is the last thing you feel in the mood for, remember you are doing it for your own spirit.

■ Achieving more of your potential. Think of some of the aspects of yourself that you have not developed fully. If you have been very outwardly orientated, you could consider exploring more within; for instance, with some form of meditation. If you have been more inwardly orientated, you might want to develop your intellectual interests or your physical skills. You may be surprised that your capacities are far greater than you think. (See *Underachievement*, page 82.)

■ Doing a project you have always wanted to do. Perhaps you would like to study a language, travel, or design a garden. Do it. One man I know loved walking – after he retired he organized walking trips for older men which he enjoyed and which gave him a small income.

Living your own particular dream gives your life meaning. If your dream is bigger than your income or beyond your situation, it is often possible to take a step towards your dream or to realize your dream in a different form. Many people do not let themselves dream of what they really want because they discount their dream even before it has had time to reach consciousness. It is important to let yourself dream first, and then tailor your dream to reality later. If you start with what is realistic, you cannot dream creatively and your life is then in danger of staying the same for ever or of being greatly limited. Most changes we make originate from a dream of a different possibility.

■ Take on a challenge. If you do a task that taxes you, you do not have time to think of why you live. Meanwhile, the full engagement of your own energy *is* a reason for living.

■ Friends and family. Remember how much friends or family, and the pleasures of personal contact, are central to feeling good and alive. When you are feeling good, you do not worry about the meaning of life or reasons for living.

other. Both of you may need to keep yourselves a little busy, unavailable and out of each other's way – go out with somebody else; keep some of your own separate friends if you have them or develop your own friendships separately from your spouse – perhaps through activities such as cards, music, bowls or golf. Then when you do see each other, it can be a lot more exciting.

**POSITIVE AGEING** A study of behaviour in ageing by the American psychologist, Suzanne Reichard, revealed five basic types of attitude:

● **Constructiveness** An intelligent acceptance of old age, with few regrets and an optimistic approach to the future.

● **Dependency** A passive, "rocking chair" uninvolvement, with expectations that others will provide material and emotional support.

● **Defensiveness** A rigid, self-controlled, compulsive attitude means that old age may have been well prepared for materially, but that emotionally it is simply not acceptable. The result is a pretence at not ageing, upheld by working as hard and as long as possible.

● **Hostility** Unacceptance and anger with the ageing process spills over into a generally aggressive attitude, especially towards the young, who are envied. The aggression and competition may hide fears of dependency and death.

● **Self-hating** Criticism of past achievements, disappointment with life, and an attitude of self-disgust lead to a desire for death to come soon.

These attitudes are worth looking at, because if one or more is wholly or partially your own, recognizing what may be a negative attitude is a first step towards changing it. The second step, even if it is only a small one to start with, is actively to do something different. Some negative attitudes to ageing could be challenged in the following ways:

○ *Dependency* Make yourself get up and do something for yourself. When you are with others, surprise yourself and them by offering to do something for them – it will benefit you much more than anything they could give or do for you.

○ *Defensiveness* Although it is quite uncharacteristic for you to speak to others about your concerns, try telling somebody about how ageing really makes you feel deep down.

○ *Hostility* As you feel the anger rising, take a deep breath, close your eyes, take another deep breath and ask yourself "What am I frightened of?"

○ *Self-hating* Write down a list of everything positive you have done in your life. Every day do at least one more thing which you consider positive. At the end of the day write it down. Then start each day by reading the list.

**Disengagements**    A positive attitude to ageing involves accepting a lot of good-byes. Some of the losses listed in the section on old age (see page 86) can be seen as disengagements. In the final stage of life you disengage yourself from:
- Some of your responsibilities.
- Your physical strength and stamina.
- Your working life.
- Particular kinds of opportunities (for instance, starting up a new business).
- A particular kind of status (for instance, running a committee or having status at work).
- Some friends and family who die before you.

Whether you see these things in terms of loss or disengagement depends on your attitude. Feeling the loss can be a positive short-term process of grieving, but it is a great pity to hang on to the feeling for the rest of your life. An alternative is to look forward to other activities that will replace the disengaged activities and possibilities, such as:
- Spending more time with family or friends.
- Looking after grandchildren.
- Renewing and deepening old friendships.
- Involving yourself in community activities.
- Developing hobbies or interests that you did not have time for previously.
- Giving yourself enough time to foster more *quality* in any activity you choose to do.
- Using your experience of life to entertain others with stories and anecdotes of times gone by.
- Developing your understanding of life and death so that you may be more ready to die when the time comes.
- Developing your own wisdom and depth of spirit.

**Adopting a positive outlook**    If you have a positive attitude to ageing, you are far more likely to be fulfilled and content in your later years. The following points may be helpful.
- Do not take any notice of any information you may have heard (or are just about to read) about losing brain cells as you get older. Although it is true that brain cells are gradually lost throughout your adult life, the capacity of the brain is vast. There is a well-known case of a man with hydrocephalus (water in the brain) who gained a university degree with nine-tenths of his brain volume missing. You will lose only a small percentage of your ten billion cells, and your mental abilities may be sharp until you die – it depends very much on how much you practise. Using your brain maintains your mental agility, whereas lack of practice may steadily lessen it. However, whether you practise or not, you may well find that

your short-term memory gets worse. Don't worry about this: use a note pad and always keep it in the same place.
- It is normal to require less sleep as you get older.
- Do everything you can to avoid getting lonely. You may want some time by yourself and you may not want to be a burden, but do not allow the time alone to become oppressive or depressive. Join clubs or organizations connected with an activity you enjoy – for instance, if you enjoy playing bridge, meet others through this activity. If you want to live with somebody, don't pressurize them by telling them how ill you are or by making them feel guilty. Instead, just ask them directly, and give them a genuine opportunity to say "no". If they say "no", consider asking other old people you know to share with you, either in the same house or flat, or in a group of flats that shares a caretaker. Often the greatest difficulty is that once you are alone and depressed it is hard to initiate a move. If you are lacking the energy to change your situation and you do not have friends who can help, please see a social worker for advice.
- If you do become physically more dependent on others, try to accept this with humour and grace.
- If you feel bored, *make* yourself do something – either a hobby, something in your home, or going out to see somebody or something that interests you.
- If you feel useless, do something useful. If you don't feel up to anything complicated you could help care for somebody's plant or pets, get involved in meals on wheels, or do some other small but useful job in your neighbourhood.
- Keep your body as well as your mind active. You might do some light jogging, or perhaps play an easy game of tennis or golf. You might try stretching exercises or yoga to keep yourself supple. If you can move only a little, exercise the little that you can move (see *Keeping your body in trim*, page 194).
- Try to keep your sense of humour. Organize times of recreation and fun.
- Make sure you dress and groom yourself in a way that feels good to you. Looking good, even if nobody else sees you, can make you feel good (see *Changing the symptoms*, overleaf, and *Caring about your physical appearance*, page 199).

If, nevertheless, you are depressed, consider:
1 Is your diet adequate? If not, make sure you are not anaemic (see your doctor who will give you a blood test), change your diet and discuss with your doctor the possibility of taking vitamin supplements.
2 Are you on any drugs that might have a depressant effect? You are likely to be far more sensitive to drugs as you get older. If this is a possibility, see your doctor.

**3** Talking to somebody about how you feel. It may be a relief to talk to someone (preferably someone who is not afraid of old age) about what it is really like, for you, to get older. You may find you can do this with a friend or you may find it easier with a professional whom you do not know. Your doctor may be able to refer you to somebody, or else you could ask to see a social worker. (See also *Useful addresses*, page 218.)

**4** If you are too depressed to have enough initiative to do any of the above, go to see your doctor. He may suggest you take anti-depressants or suggest you see a psychiatrist. If you see a psychiatrist, it does not mean you are going crazy or demented, but it may help you to deal with your depression or sort out some of the problems connected with getting older.

# CHANGING THE SYMPTOMS

At first sight, altering symptoms may seem a superficial and therefore less effective approach. But this is not necessarily so. Depression is a vicious circle in which hopelessness creates non-activity, which feeds hopelessness. Symptom and depressive process are inseparably intertwined, for nearly every depressive symptom makes you more inadequate at dealing with the world, and every inadequacy makes you feel more depressed. Where you break the vicious circle is not so important as breaking it.

What follows over the next five pages is a list of a series of possibilities and activities related to changing specific depressive symptoms. However, not all the suggestions will be appropriate to you even when you do have the relevant depressive symptom. Some of the suggested activities will appeal to you more than others. For instance, you may not particularly like music or dancing, or you may hate sport. Also the suggestion may not fit your level of depression. You may be too depressed to start, unless you can use your will to get over the hurdle of initiating something.

Some of the suggestions are likely to be useful no matter which depressive symptom you have. This applies particularly to exercise and physical movement. In general try to keep an open mind and be willing to experiment – you may surprise yourself and find that some suggestions and activities are helpful though you may never have previously considered trying them.

If you start an activity and then fail to carry it through, don't be hard on yourself. Choose something you can achieve and try it on the next upswing of mood. Expect setbacks and don't be too ambitious initially.

# CHALLENGING EVERY SYMPTOM

| SYMPTOM | ACTION |
|---|---|
| **Loss of feeling; lack of reaction; numbness** | ■ Get angry. See the suggestions in *Express the feeling*, page 122.<br>■ Cry. See the suggestions in *Express the feeling*, page 122.<br>■ Laugh. Consider the possibility that some of your loss of humour and inability to laugh is, like a child in a sulk, because you won't. One moment of humour can change your whole day. Even a wry smile may help.<br>■ If you have a partner, try a period of sensuality together (see *Express the feeling*, page 122) even if you have to make yourself start. |
| **Loss of sensation; everything is dulled and dimmed; the world seems grey** | Strong sensory stimulation can be a good way of jolting your senses back into action. Here are some possibilities:<br>■ Play some music very loud and feel the reverberations inside you. Move your body with the music if you have the feeling to. If not, just let the music go through you and take you over. Alternatively, play some quieter music that moves you or used to move you.<br>■ Physical pain. Heavy exercise can cause you aches or pain. The pain is at least a sensation of life and feels better than being depressed.<br>■ Go to a sauna or Turkish bath, followed by a cold plunge. Take a hot bath or cold shower. Go for a swim.<br>■ Use a perfume or after-shave that you enjoy or used to enjoy.<br>■ Change the colour or style of your clothing.<br>■ Redecorate your room or house.<br>■ Eat tasty and spicy food. Have a drink you are not used to so that it challenges your taste buds.<br>■ Have a deep tissue massage, that is, a firm, hard massage. |
| **Loss of creativity; loss of self-expression** | ■ Get a large piece of paper and some liquid water-colour paints. Put aside any training you may have had in drawing or painting and put aside any thoughts you may have about not being good at painting. The point is not to make a good picture but to give yourself the freedom to express whatever you want to. Close your eyes for a couple of minutes while you breathe quietly but deeply and let your head drop forwards with your neck relaxed. Then, when you are ready, open your eyes; dip your brush, or your fingers, into the first colour that feels right (without thinking about it). Carry on in this way, and for the first picture at least, paint very fast, without thinking. If you feel angry, splash the paint on. Feel free to express yourself in any way. When you have finished, don't waste your time with judgement – the point is the process of doing it, not the result.<br>■ Pottery. If you can, find a room or a piece of ground where you can make a mess if you want to. Get a lump of clay and hold it in your hands. Read through the section on painting (above) to free yourself of the restrictions of training and self-judgement. After relaxing and breathing, knead the clay in any way that feels right (without thinking about it). If you feel like throwing it on the floor, throw it on the floor. Feel free to make a mess. After getting the feel of the clay in your hands, make a couple of objects (which do not need to be representational) according to your feeling, in the space of a few minutes. Then, if you want to, go on to spending more time making an object, keeping in mind that the only thing that matters is your process of expression, not the result. If you like the piece you've made, keep it – it may remind you that you have both feeling and creativity.<br>■ Dance. (See also *Express the feeling*, page 122). |
| **Distance from other people** | ■ Say what you think and feel (see *Express the feeling*, page 122).<br>■ Put judgement and blame of others aside. Put judgement of yourself aside and say what you need to say (see *Creative expression*, page 207). |

## Challenging every symptom (continued)

| SYMPTOM | ACTION |
|---|---|
| **Difficulty in sleeping** | ■ Change your sleeping habits (see *Changing boring habits*, page 129).<br>■ Get so tired physically from doing physical work or heavy exercise that you need more sleep. For example, a day of digging in the garden, a day's walking, a long run, or an "outward bound" course will make you tired, as well as more relaxed and even satisfied. |
| **Difficulty in getting up in the morning** | ■ Set an alarm. If that's not enough, put the alarm on a plate on the other side of the room, or buy an alarm that does not stop ringing until you turn it off.<br>■ Give yourself an incentive to get up. For instance, make sure that any food or drink is in another room so that you have to get up for it.<br>■ Set up something that you are responsible for, such as taking the children to school or the dog for a walk. |
| **Feeling worse in the morning** | ■ Get your body moving. Do some stretching exercises and then some more vigorous exercise (see *Keeping your body in trim*, page 194).<br>■ Postpone any activity that involves concentration and initiative till the morning period is over. |
| **Difficulty in getting moving; tiredness; feeling there is little energy in your body** | ■ Do some cleaning (see *Changing the physical environment*, page 129).<br>■ Take some form of exercise. Consider swimming, jogging, aerobics, dancing. All these forms of exercise mobilize energy in your body. Often a period of temporary exhaustion after the exercise will be followed by a feeling of more liveliness. Gradually, you may regain a feeling of pleasure in movement.<br>■ Play an aggressive sport, such as squash, boxing, karate, judo, football or hockey. The combination of the exercise and the aggression can have an incredibly strong anti-depressant effect. Don't expect to play as well as when you are not depressed.<br>■ As long as you are not suicidal, do a challenge sport which puts your life at risk. Sports like rock climbing, horse riding, sailing, parachuting, hang gliding, deep-sea diving and car racing may give you a sensation of being in danger or near death which often helps to appreciate living. This is combined with concentrated use of mind, body and feeling (anxiety) which can break the reverberating depressive circuits. Join a local club through which you can receive qualified tuition in the sport of your choice. |
| **Slumped body; bent back** | ■ Stand up straight.<br>■ Do a few stretch exercises (see *Keeping your body in trim*, page 194).<br>■ Get an orthopaedic mattress or, cheaper, put some boards or a plank of thick chip-board under your mattress, so that you sleep on a flat surface.<br>■ See an osteopath. Your doctor should be able to recommend one. If not, consult the list of organizations at the back of this book. |
| **Slowness of movement** | ■ Run – make yourself. Many people with depression keep themselves going by running every day. Running can make your body feel alive and change the whole feeling of the day. |
| **Miserable expression** | ■ Smile. This is not as absurd as it may sound. Every morning look in a mirror and force yourself to smile at yourself. You will, grudgingly, smile back. It might sometimes amuse you, but that is not so important. The point is that the act of changing a bodily gesture or expression can have, after a while, a feed-back effect on the feeling. |
| **Constipation** | ■ Make sure your diet includes plenty of fresh fruit, vegetables and fibre. Try not to worry about being constipated. See your doctor if the constipation causes pain and you do not get better. |

## Challenging every symptom (continued)

| SYMPTOM | ACTION |
| --- | --- |
| **Indecisiveness** | ■ Consider the fact that it is indecisiveness rather than the direction of your decision that is more likely to create failure. Therefore decide, one way or another, and take that course of action without further thought. If you really can't decide, use a coin or a dice and obey the result. This advice does not apply to major life decisions when you are depressed, and should never be used if you are suicidal. If you are wondering whether to kill yourself, don't. Hang on. |
| **Loss of initiative and difficulty in getting started at anything** | ■ If your job does not involve too much initiative, keep working (but see *Changing the situation at work*, page 127). <br> ■ Get someone else to give you orders and to organize you. <br> ■ Make a list of everything you need to do. From that list take out two things, one that you will hate doing and one that you will like doing. Both must be things that you know you can do and that can be done in a short time – a few hours at the most. Your goal must be small, realistic and achievable. <br>   Start with the thing you hate such as writing a certain letter or completing a tax return. You may have been putting it off for a long time. Doing it may be tedious but can relieve you from a large amount of wasted energy worrying about, or avoiding worrying about what you haven't done. Set yourself a deadline and start straight away. If you miss the deadline, rather than berating yourself, set another that is more realistic and start again. Completing the job provides satisfaction and hope. Then do the job that you enjoy doing. <br> ■ Do things with other people. Make an appointment with somebody else so that there is a little pressure to be somewhere by a certain time. Do the shopping with a friend. Arrange to go to a friend's house and have him or her come to yours on alternate occasions so that you can work together. |
| **Loss of concentration and short-term memory** | ■ Write things down. If you find yourself continuously forgetting things, keep a pen and note pad close at hand to remind you and help you concentrate. |
| **Loss of care about your appearance** | ■ Suspend any judgement you may have on the superficiality of appearance and try some of the following as an experiment. How you look can not only be an expression of yourself or of what you hope for, but can also have a strong effect on how you feel. <br> ■ Buy some new clothes. Try some different colours and different styles. You may look good in many things besides the ones you are used to. <br> ■ Work on your body. If you are fat and do not want to be, diet but without harshness or self-recrimination – in other words don't focus on what you don't like, but focus on how you would like to be and slowly work towards it. Perhaps go to a daily exercise class (wear some exciting clothes to exercise in) and work especially on the parts of your body you want to firm up or develop. <br> ■ Try out some new looks with make-up or try a facial. <br> ■ Get your hair done: try a different style, have it dyed an exciting colour or have it permed. <br> ■ Have a manicure and pedicure. |
| **Loss of care about your environment** | ■ Clean and decorate (see *Changing the physical environment*, page 129). |
| **Sulking; self-pity** | Consider these points: <br> ■ If life were easy, how could you ever achieve anything? <br> ■ Any expectation that life should not give you pain or problems will cause you pain and problems. |

# Challenging every symptom (continued)

| SYMPTOM | ACTION |
|---|---|
| **Sulking; self-pity** (continued) | ■ Pitying yourself for your fallibility is not productive. Perhaps the worst mistake you can make is to spend your life trying not to make mistakes. The willingness to make a mistake provides the freedom to respond more openly – there is no longer the need to repress your responses for fear of error. The making of a mistake is often the richest source of learning: when this is so, even though you may not see it for years, can you still call this teacher a "mistake"?<br>■ To sulk when things do not go your way is, first of all, a punishment of life or of those who make things go wrong, yourself included. Remedial action is more profitable than punishment.<br>■ Criticism is only someone else's opinion of you; you have the right to disagree with that opinion. |
| **Giving up responsibility of action; blaming yourself** | ■ Consider the possibility that blame of self or others is virtually the opposite of responsibility. If you say "I am to blame", the emphasis is on I. In self-berating and self-recrimination, the emphasis is on self. In an extreme form, self-blame is an obsession with yourself. While it may masquerade as concern, your only real concern is for your own ego, and the only thing you can give to another person is discomfort and a disguised demand to be soothed. Responsibility, on the other hand, involves an ability to respond, the willingness to take action and the generosity to give some kind of reaction or to take care of your own or another's needs. If you believe in free will, you must be ultimately responsible for your recovery, and the more responsibility you feel, the more you can help yourself. The humility to accept your own free will is the opposite of the arrogance of self-blame.<br>■ Ask yourself if your depression gives you a way out of responsibility and therefore if there is not a genuine temptation to stay depressed. Don't be afraid to admit this if it is true. Accepting it is the first step towards changing it.<br>■ Make yourself responsible for something or somebody. Look after somebody else's plants, or, better, an animal. Get a dog and take care of it. Concern yourself with somebody else's needs.<br>■ You can be helped by others, but there is no doubt that you have the final say. The powers of self-healing are already within you. |
| **Hating yourself; losing self-respect; hating the world; believing the world is bad; believing you are bad** | Consider these points:<br>■ Forgiving yourself and forgiving others are both healing processes. The more you can forgive yourself, the more you can forgive others, and vice versa, for the two are intimately connected.<br>■ If you have had an unhappy past, you can change your history. If you were not loved as a child, you can find a way to love the child within you. One possibility is to make a list of things you enjoy, or used to enjoy doing, for instance, making a model, baking a cake, planting seeds. Then, treating yourself as you would have liked to be treated as a child, choose an activity on your list and do it just for fun with no concern about results.<br>■ If you find yourself using the newspapers to support your view of how bad things are in the world, don't read them for a while, or better, write to your paper with a positive opinion. Even if they don't print it, you may feel better for the activity of writing and getting your own thoughts in motion.<br>■ Note that there are miserable people living in affluence and good fortune and happy people living in great hardship. It is your attitude, not the circumstances, that is ultimately important in your own happiness.<br>■ Put love into the things you do. Whether you are preparing a meal, tuning a machine, or looking after somebody, do it out of love rather than duty. The love you put out with trust and no expectation will come back to you somehow. |

## Challenging every symptom (continued)

| SYMPTOM | ACTION |
|---|---|
| | ■ If the world is in trouble, you can at least change the little bit of the world that is yourself; as the old Chinese proverb says "Better to light a candle than curse the darkness".<br>■ You may have made mistakes. Right now, you may be miserable and boring, but you are probably not a bad person. |
| **Believing there's nothing inside you** | ■ Give. If necessary make yourself give something. There is no greater proof that there is something inside you. |
| **Negative thinking; loss of faith** | ■ Don't forget that positive thought is just as powerful as negative thought. When you consider the vicious circle of negative thinking (depressive thoughts reducing your effectiveness, which verifies your depressive thoughts), consider too that positive thinking has a similar circle which feeds itself. If you can stay positive in your thoughts for long enough (a few seconds is all that's required) to initiate a positive activity, the result will then support your hope and positive thinking. Positive thinking cannot exist in a vacuum; it requires an activity to affirm it. Be patient with the activity and don't expect miracles.<br>■ Don't tell yourself you have no faith. You have faith that you will take another breath and that after you sleep you will wake up. You therefore know that there are powers which are beyond your control. If they are beyond your control, who are you to say that such powers cannot heal you.<br>■ Write down a list of your assets (this can include your personal assets of character, your material assets, and assets of friendship and family) and then another list of your liabilities. After you have looked at them, considered them and perhaps added more items, throw the list of liabilities away. Keep the list of assets and read it every day. |
| **Negative coloration of the past; on looking back everything seems awful** | ■ Make a list of all the positive things you have done in your life and of all the people you have helped, even in the smallest way. If you are too depressed to do this on your own, get someone who knows you to help you remember. Read the list every day.<br>■ Make another list of moments of pleasure you have had. If you can, get someone who loves you to help. Read the list every day. There may be thoughts like "Yes, but this will never happen again". Put them aside for a moment and read your list. |
| **The future seems blank and everything is getting worse; negative coloration of the future; loss of purpose; loss of hope** | ■ Consider the possibility that your loss of hope is a statement of pride. There is an element of bragging about the statement "My situation is hopeless", and since you cannot be in control of all the elements within and around you that affect your recovery, you cannot *know* there is no hope for you.<br>■ Sometimes you need to accept that there is nothing you can do for the moment. Accepting your own limitations or powerlessness can be a relief.<br>■ It may not be your privilege, yet, to know what your purpose is.<br>■ After your worst part of the day (perhaps the morning), and after taking some exercise or completing an activity successfully, do the questionnaire in Part I (see page 12) and write down the score. In the same manner, repeat the questionnaire, answering as honestly as you can, once a week, and put the results on a graph. If the graph goes down, knowing you are getting worse is better than fearing it. If, as is more likely, it goes up, you have documented proof that your thinking is coloured.<br>■ When you have a slight upswing in mood, *and* after vigorous exercise, write down some goals that are realistic and achievable in the future.<br>■ If you cannot feel hope, remember there is always hope of hope.<br>■ Know that depression, even when untreated, gets better. |

**DEPRESSION CAN BE A POSITIVE EXPERIENCE**

This seemingly contradictory statement is perhaps the most important in this book. Depression *can* be a positive experience. When you are depressed, nothing could seem further from the truth. But to the extent that you can temporarily lose some of the most valuable aspects of your life, to the same extent you can gain, because:

● You can learn what is valuable to you. Being depressed may seem like a hard way to learn, but it is difficult to appreciate something you have never lost.

● You may learn that your own life force is more valuable than anything else.

● You may completely reassess your life priorities. Self-esteem and self-respect may take on a value beyond material security. Acting from the heart may transcend dutiful obedience. Money, possessions and position may be seen in a more balanced perspective.

● You may learn that it is acceptable to need other people.

● If you are searching for more understanding of life or for more depth of feeling it is sometimes necessary to know periods of emptiness, hopelessness and despair. Avoiding these chasms can keep you merely surviving on the surface. Sometimes, it is only by allowing a descent to despair that, on the other side of the depressive chasm, life can attain fullness and you can acquire greater depth of feeling.

● You may feel stronger because you have gone down that far and have been able to come back. When you have come back you may have more faith and hope than you ever had before. In the midst of hopelessness you have reascended. This suggests that there are powers beyond your control, and hope beyond your feeling of hopelessness.

# LIVING WITH A DEPRESSIVE

Living with someone who is depressed can be an exasperating and difficult experience. If you are honest and tell the depressed person how exasperating he is, he agrees with you, feels confirmed in his negative view of himself and gets even more depressed, which makes you even more exasperated. It seems there is nothing you can do to help and that everything you do is wrong. What to do depends, to some extent, on the level of depression.

**Disguised depression**

Sometimes depression is completely denied. The first sign of disguised depression may be resigning from a job for no very good reason, drinking more alcohol, or feeling physical pain – perhaps an old injury or ache getting worse (see *Warning signs*, page 189). If you suspect something is wrong with your partner or friend, try to get him to talk. In his desire not to drag you down or not to admit to himself how bad he feels, he may try to talk on the bright side. It may be helpful to ask, "But in your darkest moments what are your worst fears or your worst thoughts?" This way you may learn the reality of the situation.

**Mild depression**  At this level (loss of sparkle to light grey), it is usually possible to make contact. Here are some possible suggestions:
● Encourage him to talk about what is really bothering him. Be sympathetic to him and his expression of his problem, and try to understand his perspective.
● React to perpetual sulking and self-pity as you will. If it makes you angry, be angry. If he reacts by withdrawing more, demand a reaction. If you succeed, you will feel better, and he will feel better from having reacted, even out of provocation. He may not like your angry attitude, but if you are acting out of care the final result is often positive. If he is too depressed to respond, don't worry; it may be a relief for you to express yourself and for him to hear the truth (which he knows anyway). However, don't get repeatedly angry if there is no response. You also need to express your own feelings outside the situation (see *Express the feeling*, page 122, and *Creative expression*, page 207).
● Ask yourself, without any self-blame, if there is anything you have done or are doing which encourages the depression. In a struggle for power, the loser may become depressed. If one partner in a relationship is subordinate, he or she may well become depressed (see *Marriage and families*, page 66). If your partner is depressed you may derive a feeling of strength from looking after your dependent. In any situation such as this, your honest awareness can be the first step towards changing your position.
● Beware of the enormous power of the depressed person. It is easy to get manipulated by somebody else's weakness and to start doing things for them which encourages their dependence and passivity. It may be very difficult to differentiate this from genuine need and it may be helpful to talk to somebody else to clarify when to take over and when to insist that the "victim" takes action (see *Talking to somebody*, page 124).
● Do everything you can to keep him active. For instance, insist he goes out or takes exercise (see *Keeping your body in trim*, page 194). Be firm but caring.
● If he has depressive thoughts such as "I have never enjoyed life", feed back the truth unremittingly. Remind him of a time when he did enjoy something, even if it was only for a

moment. As soon as he has admitted it, say with relish: "Therefore you do have the capacity to experience enjoyment and pleasure."

● Use the tiniest upswing in mood not only as a herald of hope but as a time for him to be most active so that the hope can produce a result. The smallest result (an extra length swum in the swimming pool or a letter written, perhaps) can be built on.

● Spend time away from the depressive situation, so that you can rejuvenate yourself. Talk to your friends. Express your frustrations. Talk to a social worker or a counsellor about the best ways to handle the situation. Give yourself regular times off so you can go out and have a good time.

● Whatever happens, keep your sense of humour.

**More severe depression (darker grey, black, white)** Whereas mild depression is often helped by more human contact, severe depression is usually aggravated by intimacy. It may be important to try to make contact because you may succeed, and if you don't, you at least know that you have done as much as you can on that level. Make sure the depressed person sees someone soon. If he is reluctant to see his doctor, tell him you are going to take him. He will probably be relieved, but if he refuses (which is very unlikely in his passive state) and you are worried about him, you can always get his doctor to visit. Don't forget that sooner or later he will get better.

**Threatened suicide** If suicide is being threatened in order to manipulate you into taking some kind of action, or to punish you for an action already taken:

● Make sure the threatener understands that it is his responsibility as to what he does with his life.

● Make sure that he also understands that you don't want him to do it (but you will not sell your soul to stop him).

● Ask him what is really wrong, or tell him if you know. If he is willing to admit that he wants to hurt you, he almost certainly will not need to act it out.

● Get him to see a doctor, counsellor or psychotherapist.

**Suicidal intent** When a depressed person is suicidal, even with no threat, the result is unpredictable. Get him to talk about it, which will diffuse some of the tension and give you more warning if thoughts turn into intent. When there is suicidal intent:

● Get him to hold on. At least there is hope of hope.

● Hide all dangerous drugs.

● Get him to see his doctor straight away. (See also *Suicide and attempted suicide*, page 30).

# Psychotherapy

Talking to someone, counselling, removing a single symptom by expression and understanding, changing an attitude by deeper exploration, or delving into the creative resources of the spirit – all these activities are often included in this very large term, "psychotherapy". This chapter discusses different therapeutic approaches and gives advice about choosing a psychotherapist. If you are unsure about the differences between the therapists mentioned, refer to the definitions on page 166.

**Reasons for psychotherapy**

There are three main reasons for having psychotherapy:
1 When you have a problem, you may want to talk to somebody, without analysis or exploration. This is "supportive psychotherapy" (see overleaf).
2 You have a symptom or a group of symptoms which you want to get rid of by exploring their psychological origins. Only those aspects that are directly related to the symptoms are looked at – you do not want to explore the rest of your life. This I have referred to as "short-term explorative psychotherapy" (see page 158).
3 You are not so concerned about particular symptoms, but because of a general loss of sparkle you want your life to be better, and hope that by exploring at depth many of your attitudes and preconceptions, you may be able to lead a life of more spontaneity and freedom. This I have referred to as "long-term explorative psychotherapy" (see page 163).
Of course there is overlap between these three types of psychotherapy. If you want to get rid of a symptom by exploration (2), you are likely to touch some other aspects of your life (3), as well as receive non-analytical support (1).

**Admitting your need**

Whatever form of psychotherapy you choose, sometimes the hardest part is simply admitting that you need help. If the problem is medical or treatable with a drug, it is often easier to accept your need. If it is a human problem it is all too easy, especially when you are depressed, to consider your need as even more evidence of your failure. But the opposite is true. It takes courage and strength to allow yourself to be vulnerable before another person, and sharing a problem will often make you feel better.

# SUPPORTIVE PSYCHOTHERAPY

A supportive psychotherapist offers a listening ear to subjects and problems that you might not want to discuss with those you are closely involved with. You may be helped simply by hearing yourself speak and by organizing your thoughts and you may be relieved by sharing your problem with another person. You may receive some simple advice, and objective feedback may make you reconsider some of your opinions about yourself.

Ideally, all doctors who see patients would be capable of supportive psychotherapy. But sometimes this is not the case and often a doctor will just not have the time. If this is so, ask your doctor to refer you to a counsellor (see *How to approach your GP*, page 170), or you can find a counsellor yourself through one of the organizations listed on page 218.

Supportive psychotherapy can be useful for anyone with a problem and it has no contra-indications. You may need to have only one supportive psychotherapeutic session to realise that it is permissible and a relief to share a feeling that has been repressed.

Supportive psychotherapists do not necessarily require formal training, since their effectiveness depends very much on their human qualities of warmth, care, understanding and integrity – as well as on providing the chance for you to speak your mind. You may sometimes prefer to see a counsellor rather than a friend because: you may find it easier to be open with somebody outside your circle of family or friends; a counsellor who has never seen you before may be more objective – though not necessarily so, and a counsellor may have, though not necessarily, more experience with handling problems and with helping people to see what their problems may be.

The difficulty with seeing someone you do not know is that you may not know in advance the quality of the counsellor, or how well you will get on. If after a few meetings, you feel your counsellor is not the right person for you, don't be afraid to say so. Discussing it may clear the air or dissolve an impediment to progress. If discussing it does not help, find somebody else. If your therapist tells you you are being defensive, that is, you are leaving in order to avoid hearing what he or she has to say, this may be the case, but perhaps you will find someone who is more able to cope with your defences.

You may find a supportive psychotherapist or counsellor who is one of the following: a social worker; a priest; a doctor; a nurse; a marriage guidance counsellor; a Samaritan; a psychologist; a psychiatrist, or a psychotherapist.

# EXPLORATIVE PSYCHOTHERAPY

The exploration of thoughts, feelings, tension patterns and inner attitudes, with a caring and skilful therapist can, potentially, provide any of the following:

● A channel through which you can express your thoughts and feelings in a safe and controlled setting, in which there is no criticism or negative judgement of you.

● Feed-back from a third party who has some objectivity and life experience.

● A relationship of trust with another person and the development of a greater capacity for intimacy.

● Advice.

● A short-term treatment for specific conditions such as psychosomatic symptoms and grey depression.

● An understanding of present, past and future possibilities.

● The discovery of aspects of yourself and talents which were previously hidden or only partially realized.

● A release from rigid patterns of behaviour.

● An acceptance of the world as it is, or of your own self, limitations included, so you learn to like yourself.

**WHEN TO CHOOSE EXPLORATIVE PSYCHOTHERAPY**

Most people who start a course of explorative psychotherapy want to discover more about themselves. Some are sent to psychotherapy because someone else thinks it will be good for them – such people often drop out and gain little because they simply do not want to explore in that way.

The major indication for psychotherapy is motivation. Wanting to explore your past, your feelings or your inner self is a very subjective matter, which depends on a personal desire for a particular kind of self-knowledge. If the basic motivation to explore is there, you may have a number of different reasons which spark off your interest, for instance:

● You may have periods of blue or grey depression, or other particular symptoms, which you believe you may be able to change through exploring your own attitudes.

● You may not feel too bad but want your life to be more fulfilling or exciting. You realize that these feelings depend more on your attitude to life than on life's circumstances.

● You may have a feeling that there is something missing in your life and you want to find out what it is.

● You may feel that somehow you are trapped in the past or by restricting fixed attitudes, and you want to break free.

● You may want to develop a greater capacity to be intimate and to love.

● You may want to learn to handle life's changes (see *Life changes*, page 74) more adroitly.

The last five reasons all imply some loss of sparkle; all six incorporate the desire to change yourself, which is an essential ingredient for success. You may not know in advance that you want to change, but it soon becomes apparent as you are faced with the possibility of change and the chance to sacrifice comfortable, known ways of being. Naturally some people explore and change themselves through their own life experiences, or through many other ways besides psychotherapy.

**WHEN NOT TO CHOOSE EXPLORATIVE PSYCHOTHERAPY**

The most obvious reason is if you do not want to explore thoughts and feelings. Sometimes, for purely personal reasons, people do not want to explore or choose to change, and sometimes people respond to the pressure of the norm of their culture. In England it is not quite culturally acceptable to see a psychiatrist or psychotherapist or to explore feelings; this stigma often inhibits people who are, underneath, very willing to do so. In America it is perfectly acceptable to see a psychotherapist, and someone might see one who, underneath, had no interest in change at all.

In general, you should have serious doubts about psychotherapy in the following circumstances:

● If you are psychotic (out of touch with reality), or prone to psychosis; exploration and higher levels of emotional contact can spark off another episode.

● In manic depression; psychotherapy is not only useless during attacks, but is often of little avail between attacks. This is not always true, but usually someone prone to manic depression is simply not interested in psychological exploration. Maybe this is because manic depression often has a more hereditary/biochemical basis (see *Heredity*, page 90). Sometimes exploration sparks off a manic attack, which seems to protect the person from feeling pain or discomfort. There are definitely exceptions, and it is sometimes possible to combine psychotherapy with lithium prophylaxis (see the drug *Lithium*, page 181).

● In white depression, as you are psychotic and unreachable by means of reason.

● In black depression you are very often unreachable because circles of negative thinking form an almost impenetrable barrier to other people. Sometimes, intensive psychotherapy combined with a heavy programme of exercise can help. Occasionally, long-term explorative psychotherapy has been used for those with recurrent black depression.

● In grey depression you may be too passive to explore. (For this reason, exercises before your session or intensive exercises at the beginning of the session may be helpful and prepare you to work hard both mentally and emotionally.)

● If you do not want pain, psychotherapy is possible as a means of confiding in someone and feeling some support, but not as a means of exploration. Exploration may involve feeling pain from the past, pain from letting go held back feelings, pain from what you are missing (which brought you to psychotherapy) and the pain of losing some familiar and comfortable, but counterproductive, ways of being.
● If you do not want to risk altering your view on life, explorative psychotherapy is a waste of time.

# PSYCHOTHERAPEUTIC APPROACHES

Particular people have stamped their own particular style on psychotherapy and some have deliberately tried to create an organized system. Although many psychotherapists can use several approaches and will adapt their learning to form a style that suits their talent and personality, some adhere more rigidly to a single approach. In this section there is a selection of ideas and approaches that have been used and that may have influenced your present or prospective psychotherapist.

**ANALYTICAL APPROACHES**
Originated by Sigmund Freud, the analytical approaches to psychotherapy were the basis from which psychoanalysis developed. The aim was to uncover hidden wishes and motives by an intellectual analysis of unconscious material. Such material was made manifest by the interpretation of dreams, and by inviting the patient to speak freely, without censorship, about whatever thoughts might arise.

**Freudian ideas**
Freud (1856-1939) believed that nervous problems, including depression, often resulted from repression of unconscious impulses. Patients were often "resistant" to exploring such unconscious material, but when they did so with feeling, there could be a relief from neurotic symptoms. Freud considered that many people never grow out of early phases of development – thus the "dependent" personality (see page 98) would be seen as someone whose energy ("libido") was stuck in the oral phase – that is the phase of early babyhood when the baby is wholly dependent and sucks. His method of exploration through free association – allowing the patient to talk completely ad lib about anything that came into his head – provided the clues of unconscious significance that might relate to a phase of development or repressed material.
Freud's ideas and his courage to go against orthodox belief created the beginning of a whole new era in therapy, though his own system had several drawbacks:

● Freud was a rigid man who tried to fit everything into his system, and many of his disciples do the same. The danger of this is that psychotherapy can then become more of an indoctrination than an exploration.

● His use of complicated jargon created an intellectual system that can disassociate people from their feelings.

● Freud believed that the unconscious was infantile, animal and objectionable, and that it needed to be repressed. This judgemental attitude comes through in some of his disciples.

● Dependency of the patient was effectively encouraged (see *Psychoanalysis*, page 163).

**Jungian ideas**

The Swiss psychiatrist, Carl Jung (1875-1961), believed that the unconscious was positive, the source of consciousness and of the creative spirit. Whereas Freud was more interested in dealing with neurosis (a more medical standpoint), Jung was interested in personal growth (a more educational standpoint – educational in its original sense of "leading forth"). Jung believed that, by exploring within, you can find different aspects of yourself, new creativity and a greater understanding of the universe and your own inner self. This dichotomy between cure and growth has existed ever since (and long before), those clients with a more medical orientation looking for what is wrong with them and searching for a therapist who will tell them what is wrong, and those clients with a more educational approach looking for a therapist who will stimulate them to search for their own way of self-improvement.

The Jungian approach suits those who want to explore extensively inwards. Jungian therapy usually involves long-term psychoanalysis (see page 163).

**Existentialist ideas**

The Danish philosopher, Sören Kierkegaard (1813-1855), first wrote of existentialism. He stressed the essential freedom of existence and vehemently opposed the view of the German philosopher, Hegel (1770-1831), who believed that freedom meant handing over responsibility to the state.

Existential therapists have stressed the ultimate responsibility of each person for his own life. While it is true that you have been influenced by your culture, by your genetic make-up, by your family and by your experience, in the end you always have a choice of which way to go. Most people avoid this choice and like to pretend they are trapped by circumstances so that they don't have to feel anxiety. Those who recognize that they are fully responsible for their own life choices can be free, but must feel anxiety. Unfortunately, some of the stricter existentialists get bogged down in one or both of the following:

● Complicated intellectualizing. If you read "Being and Nothingness" by the French existentialist Jean-Paul Sartre, you may discover more about nothingness than about being.
● Pessimism. An enormous tragedy is sometimes made out of the fact that those who allow themselves choice must suffer anxiety. An optimist would call it excitement.

**ALTERNATIVE APPROACHES**

Many different therapists challenged what they believed to be the over-intellectual approach of analysis and encouraged more exploration and expression of feelings, including bodily expression. The orientation of therapy moved from an understanding of problems with the mind to an attempt to help a person feel more alive and whole by developing feelings, body, spirit and mind in proportion. This approach is sometimes called "Humanistic Psychology".

**Psychodrama**

This technique was developed by Jacob Moreno (1892-1974), a Viennese contemporary of Freud, who noticed that a particular actress became "nicer" in her private life when she played "nastier" roles in the theatre. People often found it easier to be honest while acting out a role. In psychodrama, former situations, or situations that are feared, can be acted out in a group setting. The acting out of the situation makes it more real and emotive than a verbal description.

For instance, a man, John, with cold angry eyes and a jutting jaw, has suppressed resentment against his father. The therapist might ask John to act out a scene with another man in the group, Frank, acting as his father. John would have licence to say anything he wanted. He might for instance start by standing at a distance from his "father" and by being cold and cutting. The way he stood in relation to his "father", and his tone of voice, would convey a very real impression of how he sees himself in relation to his actual father. In the group Frank would be encouraged to respond either in the manner of John's father, or in his own manner, formed from how he sees a father (which would relate to his own past and might help him learn more about his own attitudes).

Perhaps Frank says, accusingly and critically, "You're distant and cold!"

The edge of criticism sparks off an emotive memory in John, whose father *was* very critical, and suddenly he expresses some of the anger he has held back for so long: "You were the one that was cold, you bastard!" ... and later, "I never want to be close to you again!" As the therapist recognizes that such anger covers pain and hurt, he might, after some time, direct the drama in a different direction. He could make an interpretation, saying something like "That coldness must have hurt you a lot." Or he could suggest words that John could say, which he knows are just beneath the surface, for instance: "Dad, why didn't you hold me?" If the therapist is wrong, the client will say so, or else will repeat the words with no feeling. If the therapist is right, the words will be spoken with feeling and lead to further memories.

John says: "Dad, why didn't you hold me?" . . . "I wanted you to hold me" . . . "I missed you, Dad" and begins to cry. Frank holds him, and, moved by his own memories, cries too. As Frank holds him, John cries much more freely. As the crying stops naturally, they hug each other again, stand back, look at each other, smile and perhaps thank each other. John feels as if he's glowing inside. From this experience, John may gain the following:

● He learns to feel the difference between his cold state (which is without sparkle) and a state of warmth (anger, tears and then pleasure).

● He learns that anger does not need to be destructive but can lead on to greater contact.

● He learns that it can be acceptable to have close contact, even close physical contact, with another man.

● He learns that it is not only acceptable for a man to cry, it is a tremendous relief.

● By feeling the pain of what he missed with his father, he could be on the road to changing his coldness, for his coldness was in part designed to protect himself from his pain.

● He might change his actual relationship with his father, or he might change his relationship with men in general, since the child in us assumes that all men are like our father.

**Precautions** All contra-indications to explorative psychotherapy (see page 148) apply even more, since this is a powerful and therefore potentially threatening technique. Because of the power of the technique, it is even more important for the therapist to have integrity and creative skill.

**Gestalt** Fritz Perls (1893-1970) was originally a psychoanalyst in Berlin who later moved to America and challenged many psychoanalytic ideas.

As a reaction to the excesses of psychoanalysis, which examined the patient's past, "making him deader and deader", Perls stressed what has now become a catch phrase, the "here and now", and the following ideas:

● It is only immediate experience that makes you feel fully alive, and the past is therefore useful only if it helps to free you in the present.

● To *feel* fully alive you need to be feeling, and hence too much thinking is counter-productive.

## THE PROBLEM WITH TECHNIQUES

The ideas described in the section on Gestalt are not peculiar to it and are found in many of the more modern therapies. Although founded on an attempt to find more vitality, they can be misused, because as soon as any technique becomes inflexible it creates an act rather than a vital expression. Because the techniques are exciting, some people also use them to get a temporary "high" on human experience, rather than to learn to be more themselves. The important point is that any technique is only a tool of the trade, a "gimmick" to get through to the more alive part of a person. Tools can be used in many ways, and some tools work better in some people, and in some eras, than others. What is most important to you as a client is the skill with which the tool is handled and the integrity of the handler.

● The "what" and the "how" of a situation can bring more immediacy of experience than the "why".

● Saying what you really mean in the most direct fashion is encouraged, even if this may be temporarily hurtful, since ultimately genuine contact is valued more than a phoney image of yourself.

● Personal responsibility is emphasized.

● Body language and tone of voice often convey more direct information than words.

Perls was interested in how the parts of a person (which on their own might be difficult to make sense of) could make a whole shape (Gestalt) which had a meaningful form.

A Gestalt therapist might, for instance, use a technique based on this idea with John. Noticing that John is cold and aloof, he comments on this and later, asks John how he feels about his own coldness. John says that he is not sure, but he thinks that somewhere it makes him angry. The therapist then invites John to stage a dialogue between these two aspects of himself. The demarcation between the two aspects can be emphasized by using two chairs facing each other. John is in one chair when he is speaking from the 'cold', and in the opposite chair when he is speaking from the 'angry'.

Perhaps the dialogue goes something like this:

*Cold part:* "You should always keep your distance. Emotions are unnecessary. They cause pain. Emotions hurt people."

*Angry part:* "I want to get out of this! I want to express myself. I have a right to express myself and I have a right to be angry. So go away!"

*Cold part:* "Now calm down. You are getting over-excited. You were rude to me and you will regret that."

*Angry part:* (now really angry) "Shut up! Just shut up! Just go away. I don't need you. All that cold control. Cold control! I've had enough! You won't stop me! . . . ."

The therapist might allow the dialogue to reach its conclusion. Perhaps with John, the anger would win and in winning, find that it did not have to be quite so angry when the control was no longer there. In other words he was only angry because he was controlled – the anger in his eyes and his cold control both made sense as reactions to each other. Another possibility would be for the therapist to ask John who the control side reminded him of. "My father", he would say and realize that he was carrying around his father within him (see *Learning by copying*, page 91). The dialogue could then be continued between the "father" within him and the "boy" within him (see *Transactional analysis*, below).

**Transactional analysis**

Transactional analysis, developed by the American psychiatrist Eric Berne (1910-1970) in the 1950s, is a far more approachable way of understanding some of the best of Freud, and applying it to relationships. The theory is that every person has within him three basic states of being, a Parent, an Adult and a Child. When you are in your Parent state, you are acting as your parent would act and perhaps responding with similar gestures, use of words and so forth (see *Learning by copying*, page 91). When you are in your Adult state, you are capable of objective and autonomous judgement and action. When you are in your Child state, you act as you would have when a child.

All three states exist together in each person and all are necessary, in proportion. The Child creates charm, creativity, intuition, spontaneity and fun, though it can also create

---

## CONFUSED TRANSACTIONS

Modes of communication are often illustrated in Transactional analysis, as in the following example of an entangled exchange between husband and wife.

**Wife:** *(hoping to control the activity of her husband)* "What time will you be back?"

**Husband:** *(pretending not to notice the design of the question and with exaggerated coolness of tone)* "Er . . . between 2 and 2.30, probably nearer 2.30."

While pretending to ask a simple "Adult" question, she has spoken from a position of control, that is, from her "Parent" to his "Child". He pretends not to notice and on the surface replies with "Adult" to "Adult" information. However his intent, manifested by the over-exactness of his reply and his tone of voice, is to pay her back by making her angry (through ignoring the intent of her question). Such indirectness often creates confusion and lingering bad feeling.

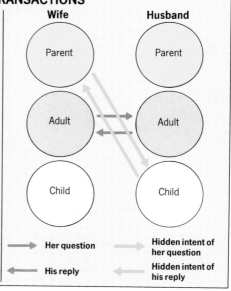

---

dependence and whining manipulation. The Adult is essential for dealing effectively with the outside world, though out of balance it creates a boring, functional existence. The Parent is necessary in order to make automatic responses which saves time in repeated situations, though out of balance creates a doctrinaire approach.

The three states connect with the three personality states (see *Personality*, page 98) which relate to depression:
• Overbearing Parent with "Good behaviour" personality
• Overbearing Adult with "Controlled" personality
• Overbearing Child with "Dependent" personality.

A healthy person can move freely between all three states. Problems between people occur when modes of communication ("translations") get muddled, as in the example on the previous page.

**Bioenergetics**    Wilhelm Reich (1897-1957), a pupil of Freud, extended analytical ideas on repression of thought and feeling to include the physical level. He showed that people literally tense against an uncomfortable or socially unacceptable thought, by tensing muscles and thereby creating an "armouring", rendering the body physically less vulnerable. When the body is harder, the person feels less vulnerable emotionally. Many people are aware of their bodies tensing in a tense situation, for instance, their necks stiffening in a moment of anxiety. Lowen and Pierrakos, both patients and pupils of Reich, took the best ideas of Reich and developed what they called "bioenergetics". In this form of psychotherapy they made use of physical movement to help release old tension patterns, which Reich had recognized to be related to old patterns of thought and feeling.

For instance, when you cry you hold your jaw back and when you are angry you hold your jaw forwards. Even if you have not noticed this as a conscious objective observation, when you see someone's jaw go forwards you will probably know, perhaps without being aware of why you know, that that person is beginning to get angry. The person who holds his jaw forwards perpetually tends to believe the world will fight him and that he must fight back or resist, whereas the person who holds his jaw backwards tends to believe the world will hurt him and that he must retreat.

In this way physical stance is related to attitudinal stance, or character. A good bioenergetic body-reader will be able to tell a fair amount about somebody's character without having seen that person before, simply by looking at his body. Sometimes this amazes people who have never before seen how much a body can reveal.

There are three main ways of working bioenergetically.

**1 To increase the ease and depth of breathing** It is ancient knowledge that breathing and feeling are closely related. An example is that moment before a car crash or a near miss, when you hold your breath, concentrate on the best avoidance and feel very little – this is sensible since feeling fully the terror of death at that moment might convert a possibility into a probability. When you are safe, you take a deep breath, sigh, and suddenly you are flooded with delayed fear which makes you feel weak. Another example is your breathing pattern while watching a thriller. In a moment of suspense, you hold your breath in order to reduce the feeling of fear, then take a deep breath when the tension is relieved. The relationship between breathing and feeling is used therapeutically to help someone connect with deeper feelings through breathing more fully. More relaxed and full breathing is related to more energy felt in the body.

**2 To relax the tension of some of the muscles which "armour" the body** "Armour", or life stance, limits your flexibility of response and therefore your creativity, spontaneity and energetic capacity. Tension can be reduced by breathing more fully, or tension can be released by initially exaggerating the degree of tension.

The therapist working with John might describe his case: "John had rather a protruberant jaw and a kind of permanent stance of silent aggression. He was the tough, taciturn type. I asked him to exaggerate the jutting of his jaw and make a sound; he was angry. A little later I pushed his jaw down and back, firmly but not hard, and asked him to breathe more deeply. After a while, tears began to well in his eyes and his jaw began to quiver, but in his inner view it was not acceptable for a man to cry (even though, intellectually, he disagreed with this idea) and so he could not let himself cry. He told me that his father never cried and was always tough and distant, "a hard man". Then he began to feel what he had missed with his father – no warm contact, no softness, no tenderness – and he began to cry."

**3 To make sure there is good contact with the ground** As taught in Eastern sports of self-defence, if you stand your ground in a stable yet flexible posture, your opponent will find it hard to knock you over. Such a stance conveys confidence and non-rigid stability, which allows you to be able to take more feeling and excitement in your body without becoming hysterical, frightened or out of contact.

Much of the emphasis in bioenergetics is on the need to increase your capacity for feeling and excitement. The body is seen as a container for feeling and has the capacity to squeeze feeling (by blocking it with tension) or to let feeling flow. Since we cannot be happy without feeling (since happiness is a feeling), the aim is to develop the capacity to loosen your body so that you can feel when you choose to.

Increasing body energy is particularly appropriate for depression, for which bioenergetic exercise can be very useful (see *Short-term explorative psychotherapy*, overleaf). One of the difficulties with bioenergetics has been its particular use of language, explaining processes in terms of "energy" blocks, and even calling itself "bioenergetics". Although this may make sense to someone experiencing this kind of therapy, it has created a credibility gap with medicine, science and those wishing for a more exact and mechanical understanding. I have therefore translated it into more mechanically understandable terms (see *Disagreement at work*, page 72, and *"Good behaviour" personality*, page 99). From these ideas and others, many forms of body-work have developed. As they can be a powerful and fast form of psychotherapy, the same precautions apply as in psychodrama (see page 151).

**Hypnotism and meditation**

Hypnotism and meditation are methods of focusing the mind so strongly on a bodily sensation, a visual object, a sound or a thought, that all other thoughts and worries temporarily "disappear". In this state, you are more freely available and sensitive to a suggestion from another, a suggestion from yourself, your inner feelings, imagination and spirit.

Such a "trance" state is associated with specific patterns of brain waves measured on an electroencephalogram, a machine which records electrical impulses from the scalp. Ten cycles per second (alpha waves) increase sensitivity without dampening reasoning power. This occurs in day-dreaming and in light hypnosis. Five cycles per second (theta waves) increase receptivity more, but block reasoning power. These waves occur in deeper hypnosis.

There are an enormous number of methods of achieving these states, which have been practised for thousands of years. In hypnosis you may be asked to concentrate your vision on an object, as the suggestion is made to you that your eyelids are getting heavier. If you choose not to fight this suggestion, you can sink into a relaxed but sensitive state. Another method is to focus on body relaxation, feeling your body getting heavier and more relaxed from your feet upwards. In light hypnosis, which is a more useful state for psychotherapy, you do not lose your reasoning power or your sense of discrimination. Exactly the same methods can be used on your own, in self-hypnosis, which is in many ways similar to meditation (see page 198).

Whatever the method of induction, the trance state can be useful for the following:

● In psychotherapy, memories may become available and conscious. You are often able to remember back long before any previous conscious memory. You may touch previously repressed inner feelings.

● It is a powerful form of relaxation.

● It can help to reconnect you to a deeper sense of your spirit or life force.

● It can release your imagination. This facet can be used as a tool to tap the body's own healing power. It is well known that trained yogis can direct parts of their body that medicine used to believe to be completely automatic. In these matters, the imagination must take ascendancy over the will. You cannot will yourself to salivate, but you can imagine your favourite food. Imagination is used in techniques of "visualization", in which you imagine your defences attacking your disease while you are in a relaxed or trance state. In a similar way, you can imagine yourself in a more positive state, and you can make the positive suggestion to yourself that tomorrow morning you will wake up feeling better.

**Precautions** Hypnosis is generally safe. However, it is not useful for deeper states of depression. It sometimes seems to encourage passivity, even in grey depression. Sometimes trance states are used to escape from worldly reality. It depends on your intention. Removal of symptoms by suggestion may be superficial, though not necessarily so.

For these reasons, trance states as used in the psychotherapy of depression can be most useful for those with loss of sparkle, who have a good sense of reality and who are searching for finer inner resources and spirit.

# SHORT-TERM EXPLORATIVE PSYCHOTHERAPY

You can try short-term explorative psychotherapy (S.T.E.P.) for any depressed state down to grey. Those in black depression could try to deal with their depression in this way but are advised to see a psychiatrist, perhaps in conjunction with their psychotherapy. Any of the techniques described in *Psychotherapeutic approaches* can be used for S.T.E.P., but in general the alternative approaches (see page 151) tend to work faster. In particular, S.T.E.P. can be useful for:

● Reactions to life events
● Breaking through grey energy
● Dealing with couples problems
● Dealing with family problems.

# REACTIONS TO LIFE EVENTS

The following case histories demonstrate how people can benefit from S.T.E.P. in relation to a life event. Those with held back grief can often be helped with S.T.E.P. Feelings about severe physical debility or about becoming chronically ill (see *Severe Illness*, page 107) can be aired in a supportive psychotherapeutic approach, or explored briefly in S.T.E.P. The same applies to the difficult feelings often encountered at life changes (see page 74), and mothers' feelings about family life and their children, as illustrated in the second case history.

## Case history: 1

Mrs. G was aged 36 and had been depressed for seven years. She was originally referred for psychotherapy because of heavy, painful periods, which her doctor thought might be related to her emotional state. Anyway, she wanted to find out, before making the final decision to have her womb removed. She was seen a total of four times between February and May 1982 and then once again two years later to see how she was getting on.

Her depression varied from loss of sparkle to grey, but she had not felt good for seven years. Seven years earlier, her younger son had been killed in a road accident. As she spoke of him dying at the age of three her body stiffened, the muscles of her face tensed up as if trying to stifle her facial expression and her voice rose in pitch and wavered. She then lightly stroked her cheek as if wiping away an imaginary tear.

The therapist encouraged her to go on. David, aged three, and his brother John, four years older, had gone together to cross a road and David was run over. She told the story matter-of-factly, with no overt emotion. The therapist intervened to say that she had not grieved over David's death. Tears welled in her eyes and with encouragement she began to cry. The therapist asked her to speak directly to her son as if he were present in the room. She began to say "Why did you go? . . . I miss you . . . I miss you so much." She wept bitterly.

Later, the therapist asked her if she had anything to say to life or to God. She demanded "Why did you take him away from me?" As there was anger in her voice she was encouraged to express this feeling fully and shouted: "Why did you take him away from me? . . . Why? . . . Why?" She was in a rage.

At her next session she said that she had spent four hours talking to her husband about David's death, a subject that had been completely avoided since it happened. They had felt the pain openly together for the first time, and that had created a feeling of togetherness more than at any other time in the last seven years. She felt more energetic, better about herself, and relieved. But though she had made remarkable use of her therapy, she still looked rather pallid and tense. The therapist considered that either there was more grief to come or that there was some other particular barrier.

In her third session, the answer became clear. She talked of her first son, John. She said that he was always difficult. He slept very little, was discontented and often cried. In every way, she explained, he was the opposite of David, who had been gentle, placid and had slept through the night. There was an element of bitterness in her tone of voice as she spoke of John. The corners of her mouth turned downwards and tensed.

The therapist suggested that she had not forgiven John for David's death. He, after all, had been the older brother leading David across the road. With no hesitation, Mrs. G said that this was true. However, because she felt so bad about feeling this way, she did not know how to go on. The therapist encouraged her once again to express herself openly, using her voice fully, and with licence to be irrational. After some time, with fists clenched tight, she shouted: "You killed him, you killed him! It was your fault . . . it was your fault! . . . I hate you . . . I'll never forgive you!" The therapist witnessed the fury, the hate, the pain and sadness, with tears in his eyes. He explained that in his opinion it was better to clear it up and try to make a different relationship with John – it was not too late. But rational explanation did not of course stop her from feeling herself as a bad

## Case history: 1 (continued)

mother. She had never admitted such feelings to herself before. It was only when the therapist related his own personal experience of negative feeling, that she began to accept herself as human and was grateful for some comfort.

Her final therapeutic session was four weeks later – by her own choice. She said that after the last session she had cried for many hours. She had gone for a long walk with her husband in the woods, told him everything and cried with him. For two days she felt weak and shaky. After two days she began to feel a surge of relief and noticed that her relationship with John was different. He appeared to act differently towards her, he was more friendly and enthusiastic, and she, for her part, had genuinely forgiven him. She talked to him about David's death, and he admitted to her that he had always felt guilty and known that she blamed him. She had had two menstrual periods since the beginning of her psychotherapy, both normal and not excessive nor painful. Her face was less tense, with more colour. She was relieved and grateful.

She was given a follow-up appointment two years later and her case was discussed with her general practitioner who knew her well. Her periods had worsened after the psychotherapy and in August 1982 she decided to have a hysterectomy. Her mental and emotional gains continued, however. She looked lively two years later and had had no further depressive episodes. Her relationship with John became better. Now they were "as close as anything".

It is unusual for explorative psychotherapy to be both so intense and so brief, but this example shows what can be possible. The success depended on a number of factors, some of which were:

■ She was well-motivated. She really wanted to change, though this was not obvious at first because of her depressed state.

■ She was a capable and receptive woman.

■ She had support from outside; her husband was sympathetic and supportive of her change.

■ She was willing to explore possibilities, even though it caused her pain and anguish.

■ She trusted and had good rapport with the therapist who was warm, caring, and good at his job.

■ The therapist encouraged vital expression rather than discussed the loss of vitality.

## Case history: 2

A woman with two young children, of six months and three years, went to see a psychotherapist because she was depressed. It was soon evident that beneath the lowered energy, she was frustrated with her children, who she felt took away her imagination, creativity and intellect. With encouragement from the therapist, she eventually got to the point where she stamped her feet on to the floor and told her children what she would like to do to them. At one point in the midst of her tirade, moved by her own painful memory of what had happened to her as a baby, she said: "The only worthwhile teaching is coldness and hate because that's training for real life." Later, she added bitterly: "At least nothing could shock me when I had to face the world!"

"That's not true," the therapist said, "you were shocked by love and tenderness."

"But I don't have any love in me," she replied, again with bitterness.

"I know you do."

"But I didn't get any love so why should they?" she asked angrily. Then her whole expression softened and she said that she did not feel ready to leave her children for any length of time yet. The therapist pointed out that she didn't want them to go through what she had gone through. This made her cry. When she went home she was able to regain her intimate feelings for her children. As is so often the case, the clear expression of the negative, spoken with the intent of healing by honesty, had cleared a path for feelings of love. However, she still needed to learn how to manage herself, how to face the frustrations that most mothers have to face, and give herself time for her creativity and her intellect, so that she could keep some of these good and intimate feelings on a day to day basis.

**BREAKING THROUGH GREY ENERGY**

When you are depressed, your thoughts are likely to be negative, circular or unproductive. Whatever anybody else says, you can always interpret it gloomily. An effective way of bypassing this kind of thinking is to work with the body (see *Bioenergetics*, page 155), to reduce muscle tension and to encourage more movement of feeling. Once the body becomes more energetic and alive, the circular thinking disappears, so long as the depression is not too deep (grey or lighter).

It is interesting that "pushed" body movement, an exercise without feeling, can lead to a reduction of muscle tension, which then allows more feeling to be experienced. If the exercise is an aggressive movement, aggressive feelings are more likely to arise. If the aggression is genuinely felt, no matter why, the aggressive movement is a potent anti-depressant in itself. Release of tension in particular muscles tensed against a particular feeling may lead to release of that feeling. A therapist requires considerable skill to know the difference between fabricated feeling (which is initially being encouraged) and genuine feeling (which can be therapeutic).

This technique does not work beyond a certain barrier that is usually somewhere between grey and black depression, but this varies in different people. If the thinking is absolutely fixed in the negative, the benefit of a good energetic body feeling will be completely lost. The mind will think something like: "Yes, I know my body feels better and I am feeling more, but it won't last long and soon I'll be back in exactly the same state – only with less hope because I achieved a bit and lost it", and this self-fulfilling prophecy is then promptly fulfilled. When your thinking is so negative, psychotherapy may not be useful, and you may need to consider medical treatment. Before that point, working with the body to release tension and feeling can be the fastest and most effective way of breaking through depressive deadness.

**THERAPY FOR COUPLES**

If you have a problem in your relationship you can see a therapist on your own or else go as a couple. On your own, you can work out your own part and responsibility in the problem between you, and sometimes that clarity is enough. You may go back to your partner and find that your changed attitudes spark off a change in him or her. If you go back with more directness, your example may encourage the same in your partner.

Sometimes couples problems become so entangled that it is helpful for partners to see a therapist together in order for the therapist to get a clearer idea of what is going on. For instance, a husband and wife both feel depressed. She sees a therapist first and complains bitterly about the restrictions of marriage. As soon as she seeks to liberate herself by going out more and expressing herself more openly she feels that her husband is stopping her and she seriously considers leaving him. The therapist sees them both. The husband has a controlled nature, and clearly too much feeling makes him anxious. But with encouragement in two joint sessions he comes out of his shell and realizes it is actually permissible to have intense arguments with his wife – in fact, she is longing for that bit of excitement. For a while they have a good time together and neither is depressed, though their freer expression brings up some other issues which may then be dealt with in further joint or individual sessions.

You may find a good couples therapist in many different forms of therapy. You can go to a marriage guidance counsellor, see your doctor who may refer you to a therapist, or choose any good psychotherapist directly (see *Choosing a psychotherapist*, page 166, and *Useful addresses*, page 218).

If you want therapy for your relationship and your partner does not wish to go to joint sessions, the best thing to do is to take sessions yourself so that your choices become clearer. If your partner refuses to believe there is a problem at all you may have to be willing to break off the relationship before the point is made clear. It is not worth living a depressed half-life for anybody, not even for someone you love.

**THERAPY FOR FAMILIES**

Similarly, for family problems, a single member of the family can go to see a psychotherapist, or the whole family might have therapy together. A family meeting tends to be more threatening because each member of the family has a certain position or status within the family which could be changed. But on the other hand, a family approach can be very rewarding, because it is easier for the therapist to see what is going wrong in the various family interactions. Sometimes the therapist only needs to help change a particular balance of power for the family to be able to live in a more positive way. As the therapist has to deal with inputs from several directions at the same time, and as family sessions tend to be emotive, the therapist needs to be experienced and to have a certain kind of non-defensive strength.

Family therapy is particularly useful when the children are in trouble, because there is nearly always a problem between the children and the parents (see *Life changes*, page 74 and *Obeying authority*, page 84), which may be relatively simple to sort out. If the children are willing to speak and if the parents are willing to give up a position of absolute authority, it can be moving and inspiring to witness lines of communication clear as old grudges are aired and love is rediscovered.

# LONG-TERM EXPLORATIVE PSYCHOTHERAPY

Changing more basic attitudes, or learning to live with pleasure with the characteristics that we have, usually takes a long time, sometimes a life time. Often those who undertake long-term explorative psychotherapy (L.T.E.P.) want to "grow" – searching to find the best of themselves and to be in "gold". But L.T.E.P. can also be used for more severe mental symptoms (for example, recurrent black depression) in an attempt to help somebody "grow-up again" with a different "parent" (the therapist). All the ideas and approaches discussed in *Psychotherapeutic approaches* (see page 149) can be used.

**PSYCHO-ANALYSIS**
This involves seeing a psychoanalyst for between three and five 50-minute sessions a week, usually for a minimum of three years. Usually you will be asked to lie down on a couch and the analyst will sit in front of you or out of sight according to his form. You will be encouraged to speak whatever comes into your mind. The analyst may remain silent or may make an interpretation, the type of interpretation depending on the system of analysis he uses.

**Advantages**
● With such a constant and long-term contact you may regress to such an extent that you are able sometimes to "go through" some of the earliest life phases again. This can be useful for intensive long-term therapy for those with severe symptoms who need to "grow-up" again.
● It is a slower and less threatening way of facing yourself, compared to some of the alternative techniques.
● If you successfully manage to get through the dependency, that experience of growing up will be valuable to you.
● You may find an analyst of personal wisdom and warmth who will transcend the technique.

**Disadvantages**
● Time and money. 3 to 5 separate sessions per week is a considerable, and often expensive, commitment.
● Over-intellectuality. The intellectuality often takes people away from their feelings so that they may *understand* what's wrong, without *feeling* any more alive or spontaneous.
● Dependency. Most psychoanalytic systems lay great stress on "transference" – the transferring of feelings from a parent, for instance, on to the therapist. Although it is undoubtedly true that people do transfer their earliest ideas of a man or a woman (see *Learning by copying*, page 91) on to a male or female therapist, and this can be a useful way of seeing their preconceptions, the use of "transference" has often turned

out to be negative and over-used. Firstly, not all the feeling between client and therapist is transference – there may be genuine human warmth and love for another person, and in fact this is one of the most important requirements for success. Secondly, the encouragement of transference can create more power for the therapist and more dependency for the client, which is not useful if you are looking for autonomy.

• Different systems of psychoanalysis tend to adhere rigidly to their own dogmas.

• The client learns from the therapist's example of lack of expression; this can be a devitalizing and depressing process.

• For those who are looking for more specific help, psychoanalysis tends to be all-embracing and not focused on a particular problem of development.

**ALTERNATIVE APPROACHES AND L.T.E.P.**

All the alternative approaches described on pages 151 to 158 can be used for long-term psychotherapy. The form the therapy takes is very variable. A fairly average example would be one session a week for three years, possibly combined with attending a group for group psychotherapy for one evening, every two weeks.

**Advantages**

A therapist who uses some of the alternative techniques may provide the following:

• A far faster process costing less time and money.

• A more effective route to self-expression.

• The possibility of exploring body, feeling and spirit as well as the intellect.

• An emphasis on being more vital rather than understanding why you are not.

**Disadvantages**

• As in psychoanalysis, therapists tend to try to make their systems of therapy all-embracing, which may not be what you want or need.

• As in psychoanalysis, some therapists get rigidly identified with a particular technique, which then becomes a dogma.

• As in psychoanalysis, there is a danger of a certain kind of unreality. In psychoanalysis it is in intellectual abstruseness, divorced from everyday life. In the alternative therapies the unreality can be in a certain kind of spurious optimism – everything is beautiful!

• As the therapy is often exciting, there is a temptation to get "high" on a few week-ends without making any long-term change in your life.

• The power of the therapy makes it more dangerous for anyone psychotic (out of touch with reality), or near-psychotic, as exploration can spark off another episode.

● The power of the therapy requires even greater integrity from the therapist.

Generally, the quality of psychotherapy depends much more on the quality of the therapist than on the choice of techniques used. But, given therapists of equal integrity, skill, warmth and so on, there is no doubt that the alternative techniques generally have more to offer.

**GROUP PSYCHOTHERAPY**

In this form of therapy, a number of people, who usually have not known each other previously, meet at regular intervals with one or two therapists to discuss and "work on" their problems. Group psychotherapy is often more productive over a longer period of time. Any of the various techniques described in *Psychotherapeutic approaches* (see page 149) can be used in a group setting. An example of a group is the psychodrama session described on page 151. Some people take individual psychotherapy sessions at the same time as joining a group – this can be complementary. Issues may arise in a group (for example, the way in which you relate to others) which might never have come up in private sessions, but which could be explored further individually.

**Advantages**

● Seeing others express themselves often makes it easier for you to be less inhibited.
● Feedback from other members of the group may be very useful in seeing yourself more clearly.
● Seeing others change over a period of time gives you hope about what is possible.
● How you relate to other people becomes visible in a group and may be useful information in your therapy. You may see and react to some members of the group as you saw and reacted to some members of your family.
● Real friendships may develop in a group. (This is often frowned on in psychoanalytic group psychotherapy where distance is the more general rule.)
● The group contains more energy of reaction: the more people there are, the more potential interactions. This can make an electric atmosphere, which cuts through unnecessary resistance.

**Disadvantages**

● Because of the last advantage, group psychotherapy can be more threatening than individual techniques. The contra-indications listed in *When not to choose explorative psychotherapy* (see page 148) apply even more strongly.
● There is a lack of privacy. Though a group can be intimate and deal with private and personal matters, there may be some subjects you would rather deal with individually.

# CHOOSING A PSYCHOTHERAPIST

Choosing a psychotherapist is not an easy task. Some of the following questions and answers may help you clarify what you are looking for, whilst the definitions in the box (see below) provide a guide to the different kinds of people who practise psychotherapy. The quality and integrity of your therapist is far more important than the technique used. Nevertheless, what you hope to gain from therapy is to some extent related to the technique and form that are most appropriate for your needs.

**Choosing a therapy**
- If you have the blues temporarily, consider supportive psychotherapy (see page 146).
- If you want to go slowly and with caution, use a more analytical approach (see page 149).
- If you want to go fast, find someone who is familiar with some of the alternative approaches (see page 151).
- If you tend to be over-analytical, consider a technique which stresses feeling and vitality (see *Bioenergetics*, page 155).
- If you are prone to depression (down to grey) and wish to learn how to mobilize your own body energy, consider body-work (see *Breaking through grey energy*, page 161).
- If you have long-term loss of sparkle or grey depression caused by an inhibited reaction to a life event, consider short-term explorative therapy (see page 158).
- If you have loss of sparkle or grey depression caused by family problems, consider individual short-term explorative psychotherapy, or else therapy for couples or for families (see pages 161 and 162).

## SOME DEFINITIONS

■ **Counsellor**
Those who consult, give advice, and do supportive psychotherapy, but who are not psychoanalysts, psychologists or psychiatrists.

■ **Psychiatrist**
Medically qualified practitioner who goes on to specialize in mental health. May or may not have training in psychotherapy.

■ **Psychologist**
In most countries has a university and post-graduate training. May specialize in different areas – testing and measurement of abilities and dysfunctions; using behavioural techniques, for example helping somebody to do the thing he is afraid of; psychotherapy.

■ **Psychoanalyst**
May have no academic training, but has undergone a personal analysis over a period of at least a few years, usually followed by a year or more's training and supervision with the same or a different psychoanalyst.

■ **Psychotherapist**
A general term for any of the above who practises psychotherapy (psychoanalysis is a form of psychotherapy) and for many other officially qualified practitioners (who may have done courses in marriage guidance, for example) and unofficially qualified practitioners (who may have unregistered experience of personal psychotherapy and/or group psychotherapy).

● If you have long-term loss of sparkle or grey depression caused by a long-term attitude, perhaps relating to childhood, or personality traits predisposing towards depression, consider long-term explorative therapy (see page 163).

These are only general considerations. What is important is what appeals to you and what you connect with, since in individual therapy you will be at least half of the psychotherapeutic interreaction. Personality and personal preference are important for both client and therapist. For instance, an approach with more drama might be more or less appealing to you than a more verbal approach. For some, a body-work technique just does not work because it is too alien, while for others such a technique is highly effective for changing from an over-analytical level to one of more spontaneity.

Some therapists have several techniques at their disposal and will have developed their own flexible style which suits their personality and talents, and which they can adapt to find the best way of getting through to the most "alive" part of you. The following questions and answers should help you decide what particular qualities you are looking for when choosing a psychotherapist.

**1** *Should my psychotherapist be medically qualified or in any other way officially registered?*
This depends very much on your problem. If you are in black or white depression, or have a history of depression of this severity or have had episodes of mania, it is better to see a psychiatrist who is experienced in these extremes and trained to be aware of the earliest signs of a deterioration. If you have grey depression and prefer physical treatment, you should see your doctor or a psychiatrist.

If you are in light grey depression and want explorative psychotherapy or if you want to improve the quality of a life without enough sparkle, then you need to look for some of the following qualities in a therapist, most of which cannot be related to any form of official qualifications.
● A zest for life. You cannot be taught to be lively by somebody who is dull.
● Creative intelligence. This quality cannot survive restriction within a dogma.
● An ability to listen without being judgemental.
● Warmth.
● A capacity to love, and yet to be objective.
● An interest in people.
● Skill and experience in human relations.
● Self-awareness. The therapist should have had his own personal exploration so that he is comfortable with his own feelings and inner processes.

- A sense of humour.
- Integrity.
- The humility to recognize the knowledge and the qualities he or she lacks. Though some therapists pretend to be a cross between a god and a brick wall, the best therapists are able to show their humanity.

**2** *Even with mild depression, would it not be safer to find these qualities in someone who is also officially registered?*

Registration will guarantee some minimum of learning. If you are one of the minority who will get seriously mentally ill, this is more likely to be recognized earlier by someone with the proper training.

If you are looking for exploration and personal growth, you have a dilemma. I have seen supremely "qualified" psychotherapists, working in the most prestigious institutions, who are almost incapable of making human contact; and I have seen psychotherapists with no formal qualifications who are no less than brilliant at making human contact with love and precision. If you want long-term explorative psychotherapy, which relies on creativity and qualities of human contact, registration gives you no guarantee. With an analytical approach, registration will offer you some guarantee of analytical knowledge but no guarantee of skill or sensitivity.

**3** *If qualifications give so little guarantee in explorative psychotherapy, what do I have to go on?*

Initially, the word of mouth of a person you trust. In the end you have to rely on your own feeling. It is a very personal matter. Only you can decide if a certain person is a good guide for you, and so the responsibility must finally be yours. If you need to, shop around till you find someone whom you feel you can trust and whom you feel may be helpful. Remember that in your first interview you are interviewing your therapist, as much as vice versa, to see if he or she has something to offer. If it seems that the therapist does and you are thinking of long-term explorative psychotherapy, you could make an agreement to try out an initial series of, say, six sessions.

**4** *Is there any scientific evidence for any of these techniques?*

No. Because of the enormous number of human variables (variability in the client, the problem, the therapist and the technique) it is quite impossible to standardize results. You cannot measure qualities of inner warmth and even final results, such as more spontaneity and sparkle, are subjective. Objective results have been possible with asthmatic patients in whom breathing capacity can be measured and standardized – psychotherapy has repeatedly been shown to be effective in increasing air flow. As for increasing feeling-flow and energy-flow, that remains a personal matter.

# Physical treatments

Whether or not physical treatment is appropriate for you depends on your personality and preference, as well as the severity of your depression, and the cause or type of your depression. In general, you are most likely to want or need physical treatment if you do not wish to have psychotherapy; if your depression is caused by a treatable physical factor, as in pre-menstrual tension; or if your depression is dark grey or worse. In the depressive continuum (see *Different levels of liveliness*, page 16) it is when more physical symptoms begin to appear that physical treatment tends to be more effective.

## PHYSICAL TREATMENTS

The following table suggests various physical treatments for different kinds of depression. This does not exclude methods from the sections on self-help and psychotherapy, which may often be appropriate and useful at the same time as the physical treatment.

| Type of depression | Possible medical treatments |
|---|---|
| Loss of sparkle | None, unless caused by physical ailment, e.g. anaemia, poor diet. (See *Treating the physical cause*, page 171.) |
| Blues (including maternity blues) | None, except as above. |
| Grey depression | Often none. In some depressions with special features – monoamine oxidase inhibitors (see page 179). |
| Black depression and white depression | Tricyclic anti-depressants (see page 175). ECT (see page 185). Hospitalization (see page 183) – nearly always necessary in white depression. |
| Depression while on the contraceptive pill | Pyridoxine (see page 171). Stopping the pill. |
| Pre-menstrual depression | Progesterone (see page 172). |
| Post-natal depression | Progesterone (see page 172). Other physical treatments if the depression is severe. |
| Menopausal depression | Often none. In rare cases, hormone replacement therapy (see page 171) may be useful; other physical treatments if the depression is severe. |

# HOW TO APPROACH YOUR GP

If you have read most of this book so far, you probably know far more about depression than most GPs. Most doctors have surprisingly little training in mental illness and handling people, though some are naturally good at it. This is partly because medical education tends to lag behind society and discovery. Though it is now well known that at least 50 per cent of people who see their family doctors do so partly or wholly for social or emotional reasons, and though medicine is gradually accepting Pasteur's belief that the host and its resistance or susceptibility is much more important than the bug, it is likely to take medicine at least 50 years to catch up. This is because:

● Medicine is basically conservative; this is sometimes useful in an institution which has such power over important decisions, often those concerning life and death.

● Medical educators were themselves educated with the old medical model of an outside agent causing disease and the patient being largely irresponsible. Also, those doctors, trained before any basic change in training, may use the teaching they learned for up to 60 years.

● It is an enormous task to change not only a doctor's but a whole institution's emphasis, that is, to switch from an overridingly technical emphasis to a mode that combines technical expertise with an approach of sensitivity, human understanding and equality between doctor and patient.

If you regard your doctor as an ordinary person with a limited education, but with some knowledge that may be useful to you, that may help you frame your questions with more authority. Make sure you know the basic function and side-effects of any prescription before you take it. Don't be afraid to ask "Why?" The professional before you is a servant in the best sense and is being paid by you either directly, or through taxes or insurance premiums. Together, you are tackling you and your problem.

Just as you have the right to choose your doctor, your doctor has the right to choose the kind of medicine he wants to practise and may or may not prefer a more technically orientated approach. You may find your doctor is naturally warm, sensitive and understanding, in which case you will find that you can talk openly about what you want and need. If he does not have time to discuss your problem at length, he may well be able to refer you to someone else. If, on the other hand, your doctor is not so interested in emotional problems, he may be able to help you with drugs or through knowing where you can get further help.

# TREATING THE PHYSICAL CAUSE

With the possible exception of pre-menstrual tension, which can sometimes be treated hormonally (see below), depression is rarely caused by a treatable physical ailment. However, when it is, it is important to know so that the cause can be treated. If, after going through the physical factors chart (see page 49), you are concerned about a possible physical condition, have a medical check-up as soon as possible, so that you can remove that doubt and get on with treating and changing your depressed state.

**DIET**
If you think your diet may be inadequate or imbalanced (see *Diet and depression*, page 112), look into it seriously and experiment with a healthier *and* more appetizing diet. Preparing your food well and concerning yourself with what goes into you is itself an exercise in caring about yourself and thus a powerful antidote to depression. However, don't be depressingly strict and over-conscientious. If you start to feel low and lethargic in the late morning, as opposed to waking up feeling bad, consider the possibility that your breakfast contains too much carbohydrate and too little protein, and if it does, try changing the balance. Increased intake of the B and C vitamins may make you feel better if you are currently deficient in them (see the chart on page 113). They have no known side-effects.

**PYRIDOXINE**
Sometimes depression while taking the contraceptive pill and pre-menstrual depression may be related to a deficiency in pyridoxine (vitamin B6). This can be both diagnosed and corrected by taking pyridoxine – if pyridoxine helps, you needed it, and if it doesn't, it's harmless.
● *Side-effects:* none.
● *Dose:* 50 mg tablets: one tablet, two or three times a day. Try them for one month to see if they are effective.

# HORMONES

Many hormones affect mood. With the exception of female hormones, hormonal treatment is indicated only when there is disease of the gland secreting the hormone. In these uncommon cases the gland may be treated, by surgery for example, or the missing hormone may be replaced – thyroxine given to a hypothyroid person removes depression. There is considerable controversy in medical circles about the use of female hormones. They have been used to prevent and treat post-natal depression (see *Childbirth*, page 58), for pre-menstrual tension (see page 105), and for menopausal depression (see page 76). The clearest useful effects have been in the prevention and treatment of pre-menstrual tension.

**PROGESTERONE IN POST-NATAL DEPRESSION**

The biological function of the hormone progesterone is to prepare the womb for a possible pregnancy. After childbirth the level of progesterone plummets down and this may be one of the hormonal factors in some cases of post-natal depression. Two out of three women who have had post-natal depression will have it again after subsequent children; for these women, prevention with progesterone therapy is a possibility. This involves organizing in advance for progesterone injections to be given daily from the onset of labour, to be replaced by progesterone suppositories eight days after birth or on returning home. Progesterone injections and suppositories have also been used in the treatment of post-natal depression though at the moment there is some debate about their effectiveness. The reason progesterone cannot be taken by mouth is that the digestive juices destroy the hormone. Synthetic progestogens (like Norethisterone used in the contraceptive pill) can be taken by mouth, but they lower the body's natural progesterone levels, which may make post-natal and pre-menstrual depression worse.

**PROGESTERONE IN PRE-MENSTRUAL TENSION**

In pre-menstrual tension in general, as well as pre-menstrual depression specifically, there may be a deficiency in natural progesterone, which can be corrected by using progesterone suppositories every month before menstruation. Before trying this, it is first of all necessary to make sure of the diagnosis (see *Pre-menstrual tension*, page 105). There are no side effects from, or contra-indications to, using natural progesterone suppositories.

## MENSTRUAL CHART

If you are prescribed progesterone to prevent and treat pre-menstrual tension, you will have to keep a record of your symptoms, perhaps on a chart like the one included here, in order to know when to start taking the progesterone, before the onset of symptoms is expected.

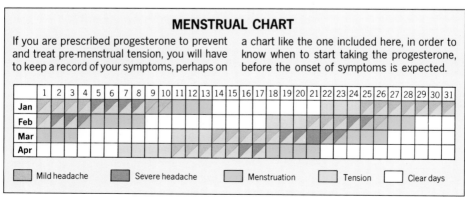

Mild headache    Severe headache    Menstruation    Tension    Clear days

**Dosage**  This varies in different women. Usually it is necessary to start the suppositories four days before the onset of symptoms is expected, which is judged from the recording of symptoms on a chart (see the sample on the previous page). Suppositories come in two doses, 200 mg and 400 mg. A total dose of between 400 and 1600 mg per day should be taken in two divided doses. Pessaries (placed in the vagina) can be used instead of suppositories, at the same dosage.

**HORMONE REPLACEMENT DURING THE MENOPAUSE**  Hormone replacement therapy (HRT) should not be used without due cause. Its role in treating depression is highly debatable. It may be that some degree of irritability and depression (similar to that found pre-menstrually) is hormonally caused, but some may also be due to your reaction to what is happening to your body (see *Life changes*, page 74), and perhaps to the upheavals of children leaving home and the prospect of a different kind of life ahead of you. Talking to somebody may be of more use to you than HRT – though one does not preclude the other.

**How it works**  As hormonal levels of progesterone and oestrogen decrease at the menopause, there seems to be a mid-level, particularly of oestrogen, that causes some menopausal symptoms. Below this level these menopausal symptoms disappear again.

It is during this mid-phase that hormone replacement can effectively remove *hormonally caused* symptoms. After this phase, therapy can be stopped and, as long as your oestrogen levels are below the sensitive mid-phase levels, your hormonally caused symptoms will not recur.

**Side-effects and risks**  Oestrogen replacement alone carries a slightly increased risk of cancer of the uterus and is not recommended. Gallstones *may* be more common in women who have HRT. There is no evidence that oestrogen used with progesterone in the second half of the menstrual cycle carries any increased risk of cancer, blood clotting or heart disease.

**Contra-indications and precautions**  Because of the association between oestrogen use (at the higher effective doses of the contraceptive pill) and blood clotting, your doctor may consider HRT more risky if you have high blood pressure, a history of thrombosis of any kind, a strong family history of heart disease, or if you smoke. It should not be used if you have fibroids, cancer of the uterus or breast, undiagnosed vaginal bleeding, or kidney or liver disease. Before you start you should have a physical examination, including a cervical smear, which should be repeated once every year.

**Dosage** Packs of measured doses of oestrogen and progestogen (a synthetic progesterone-like chemical), which mimic the natural production of hormones during the menstrual cycle, are commercially available. An example would be oestrogen from day 1 to 28 and synthetic progesterone from day 17 to 28 in a pack with each day's tablet(s) clearly marked. Alternatively, synthetic progesterone may be replaced by natural progesterone suppositories, which are more likely to have an effect on mood.

If your mood change is hormonally caused, you should notice a difference within a few days. If your mood change is secondary to hormonally caused menopausal symptoms, then hot flushes, night sweats and vaginal dryness should also change within a few days.

# ANTI-ANXIETY DRUGS

Also known as "minor tranquillizers", anti-anxiety drugs should not generally be used for depression. The exception is to provide a temporary relief from overriding anxiety accompanying depression. Unfortunately, they are enormously over-prescribed in Europe and America and often wrongly prescribed for depression. Below are examples of such drugs.

Since these drugs can cause depression and are addictive, it is best to stop taking them as soon as you can, after due consultation with your doctor. If you are anxious as well as depressed, you can always take an anti-depressant that also has a sedative action (see opposite). When coming off the drug, it is best to stop it gradually over a period of about two weeks, as there is likely to be a rebound effect. You may prefer to wait until a period of greater security in your life and you may need the support of your doctor or friends.

## ANTI-ANXIETY DRUGS

| Drug | Trade examples | Drug | Trade examples | Drug | Trade examples |
|---|---|---|---|---|---|
| alprazolam | Xanax | diazepam | Alapram Atensine Evacalm Solis Tensium Valium Valrelease | lorazepam | Almazine Altivan |
| bromazepam | Lexotan | | | medazepam | Nobrium |
| chlorazepate | Tranxene | | | meprobamate | Equanil Milonorm |
| chlordiazepoxide | Librium Limbitrol* Tropium | | | oxazepam | Serenid D |
| clobazam | Frisium | ketazolam | Anxon | prazepam | Centrax |

*chlordiazepoxide combined with anti-depressant, amitriptyline

# TRICYCLIC ANTI-DEPRESSANTS

These drugs can be useful in dark grey, black or white depression. Sixty-one out of 93 different studies have shown them to be more effective than placebo (tablets with no effective drug) in double blind trials (the patients and the doctors not knowing who was taking anti-depressants and who placebos). This is a significant finding, since placebo drugs are themselves fairly effective in reducing almost any kind of symptom. The drug is called "tricyclic" because the chemical structure contains three "circles". More recently drugs of the same group but with four "circles" have been synthesized, called "tetracyclics".

**How they work**

The theory is that the drugs increase the effective quantity of monoamine neurotransmitters, thereby counteracting the possible depletion of monoamines due to depression (see *Chemical theories on depression*, page 104). Although the effect on transmitters is fairly rapid, for some reason not well understood, it takes the drug between ten days and two weeks to have an anti-depressant effect.

**Who are they suitable for?**

They are the drugs of choice for black depression. The more physical symptoms you have (see *Different levels of liveliness*, page 16), the more likely such drugs are to be effective. As people descend into more and more severe depression, they seem to pass a barrier beyond which the appeal of reason and feeling is impotent. In the chart of the different levels of liveliness, I have called this the "barrier of hope". What the chart does not show is that the barrier can be different for different people. I have seen those with features of black depression respond to a vigorous programme of exercise combined with intensive psychotherapy, and I have seen those with very few features of black depression who seemed completely stuck until they had taken anti-depressants.

**Side-effects**

**A**
- Dry mouth *(very common)*.
- Difficulty in focusing vision *(less common)*.
- Constipation *(less common)*.
- Delayed ejaculation in men *(less common)*.
- Retention of urine – greater difficulty in urinating *(less common)*.

**B**
- Sedation – the degree of sedation depends on which anti-depressant is used. Even though the drugs are normally taken at night, drowsiness may continue in the daytime.

**C**
- Changes in blood pressure – up or down. This can lead to fainting on getting up too fast *(uncommon)*.
- Changes in the rhythm or speed of the heart *(uncommon)*.

**D**
- Confusion, delusions, hallucinations, nightmares, anxiety, uncoordination, tremors, numbness, tingling, ringing in the ears, loss of sensation, convulsions, hypomania or mania in those prone to manic depression *(rare)*.

**E**
- Nausea, vomiting, diarrhoea, inflammation of the liver, breast enlargement, production of milk from the breasts, testicular swelling, changes in levels of blood sugar, loss of hair, skin rashes, itching, swelling of the face, severe anaemia, jaundice *(extremely rare)*.

Lists of side-effects look awful. To put them in perspective, several trials have shown that placebo drugs (no active ingredients) produce all sorts of side-effects. Apart from a dry mouth, all these side-effects vary from uncommon to extremely rare. However, the spectrum of effects does indicate the profound effect that such a chemical has on the entire body system.

**Drug interactions**    Tricyclic anti-depressants potentiate the effects of the following drugs, which should therefore be taken with care:
- Alcohol
- Barbiturates
- Other anti-depressants. Tricyclics must not be used within 14 days of using a monoamine oxidase inhibitor (MAOI)
- Local anaesthetics
- Some drugs used for high blood pressure, e.g. bethanidine
- Some drugs that dilate the bronchi of the lungs
- Drugs that dilate the pupils

### WHEN TO AVOID TRICYCLIC ANTI-DEPRESSANTS

| Medical condition | Reason for avoidance |
|---|---|
| Urinary retention or enlarged prostate gland | Side effects **A** – retention of urine. |
| Pyloric stenosis (constricted exit from the stomach) | Side effects **A** – slowing of intestines. |
| Glaucoma (high pressure in the eye) | Can interfere with drainage from eye. |
| Diseases of the heart | Side effects **C** – the drug should not be used in the recovery phase after a heart attack. |
| Epilepsy | Side effects **D** – convulsions. |
| Diabetes | Side effects **E** – blood sugar changes. |
| Pregnancy, lactation, impaired liver function | Be careful of any drug during these conditions. |

● Drugs used for Parkinson's disease

● Some drugs used to control vomiting.

If you are taking any of these drugs as well as tricyclics, ask your doctor if any dose adjustments are necessary.

**Contra-indications and precautions**  Tricyclic anti-depressants should be avoided or taken with great care in the conditions listed on the previous page. Tricyclics are highly dangerous in overdose because of the effects on the heart. People with suicidal intent should be given only small quantities of a drug at a time. If someone is determined to take an overdose, he will find a way, and save up the small quantities to take as a larger quantity. The small quantities serve to remove only unplanned momentary temptation to die.

**Which to take**  With all drugs it makes good sense to use those that have been most thoroughly tried and tested over the longest possible period of time, before using a newer and less tested drug, because side-effects may be discovered only after some time

## TRICYCLIC ANTI-DEPRESSANTS

Most successful drugs have many varieties (when it is possible to vary the chemical structure without altering the therapeutic effect) and many trade names. The list (below) provides a guide to tricyclic and tetracyclic anti-depressants and their respective trade names. If you are already on an anti-depressant and the trade name is not on the list, ask your doctor the proper name of the drug. (See also the list of "MAOIs" on page 181.)

| Drug | Trade examples | Drug | Trade examples |
|------|----------------|------|----------------|
| amitriptyline | Domical<br>Elavil<br>Lentizol<br>Limbitrol*<br>Saroten<br>Triptafen**<br>Tryptizol | lofepramine | Gamanil |
| | | nortriptyline | Allegron<br>Aventyl<br>Motipress***<br>Motival*** |
| butriptyline | Evadyne | protriptyline | Concordin |
| clomipramine | Anafranil | tofenacin | Elamol |
| desipramine | Pertofran | trimipramine | Surmontil |
| dothiepin | Prothiaden | | |

### TETRACYCLIC ANTI-DEPRESSANTS

| Drug | Trade examples |
|------|----------------|
| doxepin | Sinequan |
| maprotiline | Ludiomil |
| imipramine | Tofranil |
| iprindole | Prondol |
| mianserin | Bolvidon<br>Norval |

*Amitriptyline is combined with an anti-anxiety drug, chlordiazepoxide

**Amitriptyline is combined with an anti-psychotic drug, perphenazine

***Nortriptyline is combined with an anti-psychotic drug, fluphenazine

177

(as with the terrible effects of thalidomide), and long-term side-effects may occur only after years. On the other hand, some newer drugs may have an advantage which makes the small risk worth taking. Since no tricyclic or tetracyclic has been proven to have a greater anti-depressant effect than any other, the choice depends on the side-effects, which do vary, and on the safety record.

The best-tried drugs are amitriptyline and imipramine, and therefore the drugs of first choice. Amitriptyline is especially useful if you are anxious and have difficulty in sleeping as it has quite a strong sedative effect. Unfortunately, it also has quite a strong side-effect (**A**), which bothers some more than others. Your mouth can get very dry. Sedation and side-effect (**A**) start after a few hours of taking the drug, but the anti-depressant effect, as with all the tricyclics, takes 10 to 14 days. Imipramine has less sedative effect and fewer side-effects (**A**). Mianserin is relatively new but has the least side-effect (**A**), little side-effect (**C**) and can be taken if you have glaucoma. Protriptyline is the least sedative of the tricyclics, and is useful for those who are already "sedated" by their depression. Doxepin and Maprotilene have little cardiotoxic effect – side-effect (**C**) – and therefore are drugs of choice if you have any heart disease that makes your heart more likely to beat out of rhythm.

**Dosage**   Since all the suggested drugs stay in the body for a long time, they need only be taken once a day, usually at night once it is established that the drug is effective.

Effective doses vary for different people, and generally are lower in the elderly, who have less efficient mechanisms for excreting the drug from their bodies.

The ideal way to start is on a fairly low divided dose of amitriptyline or imipramine, 50-75 mg per day in two or three doses, and then to increase the dose by 25 mg each day, till 150 mg per day is reached, or until there are annoying side-effects. If there are no untoward reactions, then the whole 150 mg can be taken at bedtime. This dosage is continued until the 14th day, when an evaluation can be made of the anti-depressant effect. If the drug is still not beneficial, gradual increases can be made up to 300 mg per night, or the maximum tolerated dose. If it is still not effective, another tricyclic may be tried instead. If 150 mg per night is helping, this dose may be continued until three or four months after the depression has stopped, after which it can be cut down gradually. Several studies have shown that the incidence of relapse is considerably reduced by maintaining tricyclic anti-depressants for a few months after the depressive episode.

## TRICYCLICS AND TETRACYCLICS – DOSAGE RANGES

| Drug | Dosage range |
|------|--------------|
| amitriptyline | 75-300 mg before going to bed |
| imipramine | 75-300 mg before going to bed |
| mianserin | 30-150 mg before going to bed |
| protriptyline | 15 - 60 mg before going to bed |
| doxepin | 75-300 mg before going to bed |
| maprotiline | 75-300 mg before going to bed |

Whichever drug you are taking, it is a good idea not to rely upon it wholly, but to take active steps to find out why you are depressed, to do everything you can to reach the basic energies of your body, mind, feelings, and spirit, and later, to find ways of preventing another episode. The more you rely on yourself the better you will be able to deal with possible further bouts of depression (see *Self-help*, page 121, and *Keeping depression out of your life*, page 188).

# MONOAMINE OXIDASE INHIBITORS

Known as MAOIs, these drugs are also anti-depressants, but are used less frequently than tricyclics because they are generally less effective, have potentially worse side-effects and are more dangerous.

A comparison of 13 studies showed MAOIs to be more effective than placebo in eight. They are reckoned to come somewhere between placebo and tricyclic anti-depressants in terms of effectiveness, though they may be more effective in particular kinds of depression.

**How they work** The drugs inhibit the enzyme that destroys monoamines, thereby increasing the effective level of monoamine neuro-transmitters and counteracting the possible depletion of monoamine transmitters due to depression (see *Chemical theories on depression*, page 104).

**Who are they suitable for?** MAOI drugs are generally not drugs of first choice and are not frequently prescribed. They are used when tricyclic anti-depressants do not work, or cannot be used because of particular side-effects. They can also be helpful in particular types of depression where there is considerable anxiety, phobia (fear of particular things or situations), over-sleeping and/or more grey rather than black symptoms.

## FOODS TO AVOID

The following foods should be avoided while taking MAOIs and for a further two weeks after the last dose of an MAOI.

The reason for these restrictions is that these foods and drinks contain tyramine and the body can no longer metabolize tyramine (a monoamine) because the enzyme that deals with amines has been inhibited by the MAOI. The effective overdosage of tyramine can suddenly elevate the blood pressure so that a blood vessel bursts – this is rare even with eating such foods, but not worth risking.

- Meat extracts, for example, Bovril, Oxo or marinated meat
- Broad bean pods
- Cheese
- Yeast extracts, for example, Marmite
- Pickled herrings and other pickles
- Flavoured, textured vegetable proteins
- Hung game
- Chicken livers
- Chocolate
- Alcohol intake must be severely restricted and Chianti wine must be completely avoided.

**Side-effects**

● *Common ones* are: dizziness and fainting on rising suddenly, because of low blood pressure; dry mouth; nausea; swelling of the ankles; "night shocks" (starts and flashes of sensation as you go to sleep); weakness; tiredness in the first few days of taking the drug.

● *Less common ones* are: headache; crises of high blood pressure with headaches and palpitations of the heart; difficulty in sleeping; impotence; muscle twitching; sweating; euphoria; blurred vision; rashes; constipation; difficulty in passing urine; jaundice.

Most of these side-effects are unlikely to occur, however, and quite often symptoms arising for other reasons are ascribed to a current drug. The main danger of MAOIs is in their interactions with other drugs and with various foods.

**Drug interactions**

Severe and dangerous reactions may occur with: amphetamines and diet pills, methylphenidate, fenfluramine, ephedrine, adrenaline, atropine, phenylpropanolamine, chloroquine, tricyclic anti-depressants, cocaine, pethidine, morphine, heroin, some drugs used for high blood pressure, drugs for Parkinson's disease, some cold cures, nose drops for congestion and some cough mixtures. Ask your pharmacist for advice when buying home remedies over the counter. The effects of the following drugs may be potentiated: sleeping pills, drugs used for diabetes, alcohol, anti-histamines, pain killers and anaesthetics.

**Contra-indications and precautions**

MAOIs should be avoided if you have liver disease, heart failure, disease of the cerebral arteries, phaeochromocytoma (tumour of the centre of the adrenal gland) or epilepsy. They should not be used during pregnancy and lactation, and only with great care in the elderly.

## MAOIs — WHICH TO TAKE

Don't take any MAOIs unless you need to and tricyclic anti-depressants have not been effective. Phenelzine is probably the safest of the four. If you are concerned about possible side-effects or have any questions about possible diet or drug interactions while you are taking MAOIs, consult your doctor.

| Drug | Trade examples |
| --- | --- |
| isocarboxazid | Marplan |
| iproniazid | Marsilid |
| phenelzine | Nardil |
| tranylcypromine | Parnate/Parstelin |

**Dosage**

Phenelzine comes in 15 mg tablets; 75 mg per day is usually an effective dose and should be taken in divided doses as the drug is excreted from the body relatively quickly. However, as with the tricyclics, it is best to start with smaller doses and gradually build up to 75 mg per day. It may take two to three weeks before there is a therapeutic effect.

# LITHIUM

Lithium is a simple salt. As with many medicines, no-one really knows how it works. There are conflicting theories about its effects on brain amines.

Lithium has mostly been used as a prophylactic drug, protecting against recurrent mania, manic depression, and, to a lesser extent, recurrent depression. For some manic depressives, it has completely changed their lives, providing sustained relief from periodic suffering.

There is a famous case of a man who had a regular 48-hour cycle of mania/depression/mania/depression and so on. He was given lithium, and for two and a half years had no further manic or depressive episodes. At the end of two and a half years, without him knowing it, a placebo drug was exchanged for the lithium, and his 48-hour cycle resumed.

**Who is it suitable for?**

Lithium is used to treat those in a manic episode, usually in combination with other drugs. It is often highly effective in preventing recurrent mania, and the depressive and manic phases of manic depression. Although lithium has been phenomenally successful, it should be used only if the episodes of mania and depression are definitely recurrent. Lithium can have many side-effects, and sometimes mania and depression occur only once in a lifetime.

Lithium is also used to prevent recurrent black or white depression, although there are conflicting views as to whether it is a better preventive than continued use of tricyclic anti-depressants, which are safer.

**Side-effects**    There is only a small gap between the dose of the salt that is effective and the dose which is toxic.

### Minor side-effects

- Increased thirst and urination.
- Loss of appetite, initially.
- A fine tremor in the fingers, which sometimes gets worse on drinking alcohol.
- Headache.
- Weight gain.
- Nausea, loose stools.

### Side-effects which are a warning sign of impending toxicity

If you have any of these, and more especially, a combination, you should stop the next dose of lithium and see your doctor who will do a blood test to ascertain the lithium level:

- Severe thirst and excessive urination.
- Vomiting and diarrhoea.
- A pronounced tremor of the hands, lack of coordination, slurred speech, slight drowsiness.

### Signs of overdose and severe toxicity

See your doctor or go to hospital immediately if you have any of the following:

- Generalized trembling, spasms and twitches (which may lead on to epilepsy).
- Ringing in the ears and blurred vision.
- Severe drowsiness (leading to coma).

### General risks

- Lithium may cause temporary hypothyroidism (see *Specific illnesses* page 109, and *Hormones*, page 171), which can be treated with thyroxine.
- Overdosage may cause kidney damage.
- The rhythm of the heart may be affected, which can be a danger if there is already heart disease.

**Drug interactions**    Diuretics, appetite suppressants and steroids may affect the excretion of lithium and therefore the lithium blood level. Generally, they should not be taken together.

**Contra-indications and precautions**
- Hypothyroidism. Thyroid function should be monitored before starting on lithium therapy, and checked with a once-yearly blood test.
- Malfunctioning kidneys. Kidney function should be tested and found normal before starting lithium therapy.
- Heart problems.
- Any severe unstable physical illness precludes treatment with lithium.
- The drug should be stopped during pregnancy, unless it is essential for the mother's survival. Women of child-bearing

age on the drug should therefore use a contraceptive until they stop taking it. Although it is probably not dangerous in breast milk, mothers are advised to bottle feed their babies.
● Changes in fluid intake, very hot weather, and infectious diseases may affect blood lithium levels, which should therefore be measured in case a dose adjustment is necessary.

**Dosage** This is usually between 800-1600 mg of lithium carbonate per day. Dosage depends on estimation of blood levels of lithium, which should ideally be maintained between 0.6-0.8 millimol per litre (0.6-1.2 milli-mol per litre may be acceptable). This means having a blood test every week until the lithium level is stabilized, after which the tests can gradually be more and more spread out, but should not be carried out less frequently than every three months. The blood tests should be done roughly 12 hours after you have taken a tablet. A blood test should always be taken if side-effects begin to appear while you are being treated with lithium.

---

## LITHIUM – WHICH TO TAKE

As sustained release drugs are taken into the bloodstream more gradually, they can produce a more consistent blood level with less frequent doses. Priadel or Phasal can be used once a day for long-term prevention. The tablets should not be crushed or taken with hot liquids. If you are concerned about possible side-effects, check with your doctor.

| Drug | Trade examples |
| --- | --- |
| lithium carbonate | Camolit, Liskonium |
| lithium carbonate sustained release tablets | Phasal, Priadel |
| lithium citrate sustained release tablets | Litarex |

---

# ADMISSION TO HOSPITAL

Hospital may be advised or needed in cases of black or white depression. If you or a friend are likely to be admitted, it is worthwhile considering the advantages and disadvantages.

**Advantages** Hospital provides a refuge, a place of asylum. Although the concept of asylum has had rather a bad press in recent years, for someone who is desperate, a period of rest can be a life-saver. Hospital provides a break from all the pressure of the outside world and a place where most basic needs are taken care of. For someone in the very depths of hopelessness, a period of asylum can break the vicious circle of trying to perform, failing, feeling worse, feeling the pressure mount higher, trying again with even less hope, failing, and so on. Asylum does not necessarily need to be a hospital, but the reality is that there are few places that are willing or able to deal with very severely depressed people.

Your family or friends may look after you for some time if you are not capable of looking after yourself. However, it can be extremely difficult and exasperating to care for someone who is severely depressed. When these feelings are apparent in those who are looking after you, you are likely to feel even more guilty and may be relieved to have previously unknown professionals taking care of you.

Sometimes, it may be easier and safer to administer treatment in hospital, particularly ECT or the beginning of lithium therapy. Some treatments cannot be done on an out-patient basis (for instance, combined tricyclic and MAOI anti-depressants) because they need the careful monitoring available in hospital.

Admission to hospital will be necessary if you are a danger to yourself or others. Although it is very rare for a depressed person to be dangerous to others, it can occur in white depression when you believe you are doing loved ones a favour by helping them out of this world. Every year there are tragedies of psychotically depressed mothers killing their children. Much more commonly, you may be a danger to yourself and the hospital may provide some protection against suicide. It is not the answer for most suicidal people, who need guidance and counselling, but may provide interim protection for some.

Some psychiatric hospitals have a "therapeutic community" in which selected patients are encouraged to work together and help each other. This can provide useful feedback from people not (initially) emotionally involved with you, and a chance to be useful and regain some feeling of self-worth. Group psychotherapy (see page 165) is used to facilitate these processes.

**Disadvantages**    The drawback of hospitals, apart from their enormous expense, is that they tend to encourage abdication of responsibility. There are times when this is appropriate and useful (for instance, in white depression), but for some the possibility of being looked after encourages passivity. Since publicity about the effects of institutionalization, hospitals have in general tried to provide an atmosphere in which patients have more of a sense of individuality (for instance, wearing their own night-clothes and having their personal possessions around them). Hospitals have also tried to encourage more self-reliance, by offering half-way houses between the hospital and the outside world, and by encouraging earlier discharge and more day-patient and out-patient care.

The problem is that however much the hospital offers and provides in terms of promoting more patient responsibility, it is still the hospital that is doing the encouraging. There is a temptation, however well the hospital is run, to use it as an easy escape route. A patient who said she saw an elephant sitting on a lamp post later told her psychiatrist that she just wanted to get back to hospital again – she had had enough. When I worked in psychiatric hospitals, I was saddened to see how many people would get better temporarily and then be readmitted. For some people, part of this was due to the fact that they very clearly did not want to look at why they had become ill or at the ways in which they might have some responsibility for their condition; nor did they want to think about ways in which they might improve themselves or their situations so that a recurrence was less likely. Instead, their basic attitude was to seek the pills or treatment for their condition in such a passive way that it seemed that their condition had nothing to do with them. They would then go back to exactly the same situation, which might well precipitate another crisis. Sometimes it was hard to know how much this passivity created depressive episodes and how much the passivity was part of the depressive process. Either way, the hospital has the very difficult task of being required to look after those who have become incapable, and yet at the same time to try to encourage more self-reliance.

# ELECTRO-CONVULSIVE THERAPY

Electro-convulsive therapy (ECT) is like banging a TV set when it does not work. However, the crudity of whamming a 100-volt electric shock through someone's brain does not take away the fact that this technique has saved people's lives when all else has failed. As with every new and seemingly successful physical treatment of mental ailments, such as tranquillizers and anti-depressants, ECT has a history of gross overuse. It has also been misused in some institutions as a form of control or punishment.

ECT produces a temporary epilepsy. It was started on the theory (later found to be untrue) that epilepsy and schizophrenia never co-exist. It was therefore used to treat schizophrenia but with no success beyond a significant placebo effect. However, the technique was also used on people in severe depressive states with incredible results. In a few weeks people who were expected to remain in hospital for months or even years were recovering from the blackest and whitest of depressions.

**How it works**  The technique involves passing a 100-volt electric shock between two electrodes placed on either side of the head. Before receiving this shock, which causes a temporary epileptic fit, you are anaesthetized with an injection and then given a short-acting muscle relaxant so that the body movements resulting from the epileptic fit are minimized. All that is usually visible of the fit is a jerky twitching of the toes and fingers. After a few minutes you wake up, sometimes with a headache – or else you fall into a natural sleep. There are a number of theories as to why it all works:

● The procedure becomes an expiation of guilt.

● Such a complicated manoeuvre involving loss of consciousness has a strong placebo effect.

● Monoamine levels in the brain are raised, giving an anti-depressive effect.

● Circular, self-reinforcing, depressive/negative circuits in the brain are broken apart by the shock, which has an enormous voltage compared to the tiny electric currents within the normal brian.

The placebo effect cannot be the only reason for success, as people given mock ECT – the whole procedure without the shock – do not do so well.

**Who is it suitable for?**  ECT should be used only for those in black or white depression who do not respond to anti-depressants or in whom a delay in treatment (anti-depressants usually take two weeks to be effective) might be dangerous. ECT is the most effective known treatment for black or white depression. However, because of its mode of action and side-effects, it should be used only when absolutely necessary. I would not like to have it done to me unless I was really desperate and every other treatment had failed.

**Side-effects and risks**  ● *Temporary confusion, loss of inhibition of feelings and loss of memory.* For six to seven weeks after ECT the brain waves measured on an electro-encephalogram (which records electrical brain waves with electrodes placed on the scalp) are abnormal. During this period you may be less inhibited than usual, you may get confused (for example, about dates), and your memory may be worse, especially about the few weeks or months preceding the ECT treatment. All these effects improve, with the exception of permanent loss of particular memories before the ECT, though not the loss of the capacity to memorize. However, with many repeated courses of ECT there is some, though conflicting, evidence of permanent loss of capacity to memorize and loss of sharpness of intellectual function. Confusion and memory disturbance are lessened by the use of unilateral ECT, that is, a shock through one side of the brain only, though this may reduce the effectiveness.

● *Headache, temporary muscle aches.* (Before the days of muscle relaxants, the epileptic seizure sometimes used to fracture bones by the sheer power of the muscle contraction.)

● *Risks.* The anaesthetic risk, as in any minor operation; a temporary rise in blood pressure which can be dangerous to those prone to stroke; temporary effects on the rhythm of the heart which may be dangerous to those with heart conditions.

**Drug interactions**

Chlorpromazine and drugs used to lower blood pressure may be dangerous because of a temporary lowering of blood pressure (before the temporary rise) due to the ECT.

**Contra-indications and precautions**

● Heart conditions, especially after a heart attack.
● Recent stroke.
● Recent bone fracture or weakened bones.
● Thrombosis in the legs, because the seizure may cause a clot of blood to break off and get stuck in the lungs.
● Peptic ulcer – tendency to bleed may be increased.
● Acute respiratory infection – increases the anaesthetic risk.

**Dosage**

Usually a course of five or six electro-convulsive shocks is given, two a week, for three weeks. Although the treatment can be given on an out-patient basis, it generally necessitates admission to hospital.

# NEUROSURGERY

Brain surgery is not recommended as a first-line treatment for depression. Although I cannot conceive or imagine being in a state so terrible that I would want or agree to have my brain cut, there are people walking around today thankful for their operation. Brain surgery for depression is usually carried out only when all the following conditions are evident: you have been ill for at least 10 years; your life is intolerable, you are totally incapacitated, and have a high risk of suicide or death; and you have not responded to all other treatments.

Some intolerable, chronic, untreatable severe depressions have improved enormously, with a "stereotactic limbic leucotomy", which breaks some of the pathways in the limbic tracts (pathways in the brain related to emotion). Accompanying changes in personality (for instance, increased impulsivity) are much smaller since the advent of more refined techniques of operation which are made on far more restricted sections of the brain.

# Part 4

# KEEPING DEPRESSION OUT OF YOUR LIFE

# Introduction

If you are prone to depression, it is very worthwhile learning to recognize its earliest signs, before the "barrier of will" (see *Different levels of liveliness*, page 16) dampens the enterprise which you will need to stop yourself going down further. You need to reverse the process while you still have the powers of decisiveness, concentration and vitality. The point of the list (below) is to help you be aware of something being wrong at the earliest opportunity. However, I don't wish to be alarmist about these signs. You may well feel unsatisfied or tired for very good reasons, quite apart from depression. You may well notice some of the signs during a temporary and insignificant moment of the blues. If you are concerned about any of the warning signs, go through the charts at the beginning of Part 2 to find a possible cause and try some of the suggestions in *Self-help*, page 121, particularly *Changing the symptoms*, page 136.

**PREVENTIVE DRUGS**

If you are prone to recurring bouts of severe depression (dark grey, black or white) and you have chosen and been prescribed a preventive course of medication with either lithium or tricyclic anti-depressants, it is important to be conscientious with your tablet-taking. If you find yourself forgetting or stopping because you resist being on the tablets in the first place, you are probably in need of clarification. It is a good idea to discuss with your doctor the risks of not taking the medication compared to the nuisance and/or side-effects of taking it, and then to make your own decision. That way there is no outsider to resist and it really is up to you which way you choose.

---

## WARNING SIGNS

■ Losing a little confidence, trusting yourself less and depending on others more
■ Having less power of concentration than you usually have
■ Being more indecisive than usual
■ Having less initiative than usual; having more difficulty in getting started at anything
■ Not having as much pleasure as usual, either at home or at work
■ Undervaluing yourself
■ Being more self-critical than usual
■ Feeling a bit tired, listless, and slower
■ Having less energy than usual
■ Feeling disinterested, bored or unsatisfied
■ Experiencing sensations less intensely than you usually do

■ Feeling more distant from other people, especially those normally close to you
■ Losing interest in sex
■ Feeling a loss of purpose in life
■ Having thoughts of suicide, for example, imagining yourself driving the car into a tree
■ Feeling you are not worthwhile inside
■ Feeling gloomy and pessimistic, or guilty
■ Not caring about how you look
■ Feeling unattractive
■ Sleeping poorly
■ Gaining or losing weight
■ Drinking more alcohol
■ Getting more irritable
■ Feeling unreal, as if there is more distance between you and the environment around you

---

**KEEPING YOUR ENERGY MOVING**

For those with a tendency to less severe depression (loss of sparkle to light grey), by far the best preventive measure is to keep your energy level up. Energy and vitality are the very opposite of depression. Some levels of energy in some people can be easily changed (for instance, emotional energy can sometimes be dramatically increased by releasing formerly inhibited feelings), while some levels of energy seem to have a "natural" level particular to a person (for instance, emotional energy may be limited by a seemingly natural calmness or coolness). What is difficult to know is how much of your own balance of energy is dictated by unconscious allegiances, and how much it is truly an expression of who you are.

**UNCONSCIOUS ALLEGIANCES**

Since most learning about deployment of tension, feelings and energy in general is carried out by unconscious imitation (see *Learning by copying*, page 91), most of us are at least partially allied to others' ways of thinking, feeling and being, without fully realizing the extent of the allegiances. Usually a man is not aware that he moves his hand in the same way, speaks with the same tonal modulations and has the same difficulty with expressing feelings as his father, and a woman does not realize that her possible difficulty with being assertive is related to her parents, her class, her country or expected female behaviour. Because so many of the people in their families or immediate environment have learned exactly the same things, their gestures, mannerisms and attitudes all appear, to them, both unremarkable and natural.

By the time you are adult you have been programmed in all kinds of ways. Some programmes are useful for increasing efficiency, enabling tasks to be done automatically and with ease. But to the extent that you are pre-programmed, you lack the adaptability to deal with new situations. Creativity and sparkle depend on being able to choose when to use a pre-set programme and when to look afresh. The choice is clearer if you recognize the programmes, discover the unconscious allegiances, and question them openly.

The courage and intelligence to question openly creates both uncertainty and excitement. Excitement is the antithesis of depression. The questions that run through the rest of Part 4 are: How effectively do you employ your energy? What aspects of yourself do you use or not use? Are you using your most profitable talents and energies? And, finally, is the balance of energy and activity that you choose a productive balance for you?

There are no general answers to these questions as everyone is different. The following sections are designed to stimulate thought, rather than to provide specific directions.

# YOUR ENERGY PROFILE

To obtain a profile of which aspects of your total energy you tend to use more or less, circle the appropriate symbols and then refer to *How to score* at the end of the questionnaire.

The energy profile is not and cannot be objective, so please take it lightly. The aim is to stimulate your awareness and questioning of which aspects of yourself you prefer and use.

**A** PHYSICAL ENERGY

| | YES | NO |
|---|---|---|
| **1** Do you play sport less than once a fortnight on average? | ● | ■ |
| **2** Do you play sport at least once a week on average, or does your work involve manual labour? | ■ | ● |
| **3** Do you play sport at least twice a week on average, or is your work mostly manual labour? | ■ | ● |
| **4** Do you often exercise enough to get out of breath? | ■ | ● |
| **5** Do you do aerobics or some other form of exercise twice a week or more? | ■ | ● |
| **6** Do you lack stamina to keep going physically during a long busy day? | ● | ■ |
| **7** Do you avoid physical effort when you can? | ● | ■ |
| **8** Can you feel all parts of your body from inside, when your body is still and relaxed? (If you do not understand this question, answer *no*.) | ■ | ● |
| **9** Do you often get tired during the day? | ● | ■ |
| **10** After a day at work do you usually collapse, lose your energy, or go to sleep in a chair? | ● | ■ |

**B** MENTAL ENERGY

| | YES | NO |
|---|---|---|
| **1** When you read, do you create counter-arguments, illustrations or examples in your mind? | ■ | ● |
| **2** Are you studying something new, or a different approach to an old problem? | ■ | ● |
| **3** Do you usually dislike games or activities that invoke thought, for example, chess, bridge, crossword puzzles? | ● | ■ |
| **4** Do you tend to question what others say? | ■ | ● |
| **5** Do you think a lot? | ■ | ● |
| **6** Do you think you think too much? | ■ | ● |
| **7** Do you find it difficult to concentrate on ideas? | ● | ■ |
| **8** Do you enjoy solving problems? | ■ | ● |
| **9** Do you dislike intellectual debate or dialogue? | ● | ■ |
| **10** Do you become so absorbed in a hobby or study that you do not hear what is going on around you and lose your sense of time? | ■ | ● |

**C** EMOTIONAL ENERGY

| | YES | NO |
|---|---|---|
| **1** Will you answer back if someone criticizes you? | ■ | ● |
| **2** Do you ever cry by yourself? | ■ | ● |
| **3** Is it difficult for you to cry with somebody else? | ● | ■ |
| **4** Is it difficult for you to express anger? | ● | ■ |
| **5** Is it difficult for you to express tenderness? | ● | ■ |
| **6** Is it difficult for you to touch or hold someone else who is crying? (This does not include crying children.) | ● | ■ |
| **7** Do you sometimes feel overwhelmed with emotion? | ■ | ● |
| **8** Do you sometimes feel you can't control your feelings? | ■ | ● |
| **9** Is it easy for you to laugh and let your hair down? | ■ | ● |
| **10** Do you make friends with ease? | ■ | ● |

**D** SEXUAL AND SENSUAL ENERGY

| | YES | NO |
|---|---|---|
| **1** Are you physically demonstrative with people that you like of either sex? | ■ | ● |
| **2** Do you hug or kiss to show affection? | ■ | ● |
| **3** When you have an orgasm, do you feel it in your genitals alone? | ● | ■ |
| **4** When you have an orgasm, do you feel it in your genitals and in nearby areas of your body (e.g. thighs, belly)? | ■ | ● |

**5** When you have an orgasm, do you sometimes feel it in your genitals and most of the rest of your body?  YES ■  NO ●

**6** During orgasm do you find that you usually control your pelvic movements?  YES ●  NO ■

**7** Do you feel uncomfortable or shy with different sexual positions?  YES ●  NO ■

**8** Can you lust so much that you feel out of control?  YES ■  NO ●

**9** Are there some areas of your body that you can hardly bear to have touched?  YES ●  NO ■

**10** Are you comfortable with sex being either gentle or aggressive?  YES ■  NO ●

---

**E  SPIRITUAL ENERGY**

**1** Do you believe in God or a force beyond you which inspires humility?  ■ ●

**2** Do you think that "spirit" has a symbolic meaning but not an actual existence in reality?  ● ■

**3** Are you sometimes deeply moved by music or works of art or moments of creativity?  ■ ●

**4** Do you ever feel a kind of inner connection with other living creatures?  YES ■  NO ●

**5** Can a vase of flowers change your perception of a day?  YES ■  NO ●

**6** Can a look on an unknown persons' face change your perception of a day?  YES ■  NO ●

**7** Do you feel that this questionnaire on spiritual aspects is inadequate because it ignores the question of depth?  YES ■  NO ●

**8** In spiritual matters, is depth more important than content?  YES ■  NO ●

**9** In spiritual matters, is depth infinitely more important than content?  YES ■  NO ●

**10** Is it possible to have no understanding of questions 7, 8 and 9 and yet to be spiritually aware?  YES ■  NO ●

### How to score

Add up your score for each category scoring 1 point for each ■, zero for each ●. Now take the five total scores and enter them on the blank profile by drawing a cross on the appropriate number of the appropriate energy. Then connect the ten crosses (five are already marked) with straight lines.

## THE SHAPE OF YOUR STAR

Unless you are exactly equal in all your five energies your profile will be a rather lop-sided star, the length of each arm of the star indicating the amount of the relevant energy. Take your star as a question on potential, not as anything definitively accurate.

Having looked at the lengths of the arms of your star, you have the choice of whether to try to develop your "short arms" or else to concentrate on what you are already good at and develop the "long arms" further. Again, the answer is different for different people. Some people try to develop all possible aspects of themselves, whereas others focus with narrowed concentration on one particular aspect. Some find that developing other aspects of themselves broadens their "long arms" – for instance, developing your feeling and body energy can increase both your creativity and depth of thought; developing your powers of curiosity and questioning may free inhibitions resulting in greater physical, emotional and sexual energy. Others develop a "long arm" to

such an extreme it "breaks through" to another field of energy – for instance, enormous mental energy put into mathematics of the universe has, by a kind of exhaustive logic, led some people to greater spiritual awareness. There are no rights or wrongs in the length of the five "arms". Longer "arms" may seem more desirable, but many people become less productive overall if they think too much, or are over-emotional, or develop a spirituality which is separated from the physical body. A balance of energy is required; this balance is different for every person and changes in the different phases of a person's lifetime.

The next four sections on keeping your body, mind, feeling and spirit in trim provide brief suggestions on developing your energy in different ways. Not all of them will appeal to you, but if reading through them stimulates you to reassess some of your priorities on how you use your total energy, that may be useful. Being energetic, in your own particular way, can keep depression out of your life.

# ENERGY PROFILE STARS

### Sample profile
As an example, if someone scored 4 on physical energy, 7 on mental energy, 3 on emotional energy, 3 on sexual energy and 5 on spiritual energy, their star would look like this.

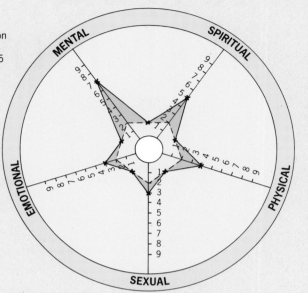

### Your profile
When you have drawn your own star, read *The shape of your star* (see opposite) and then decide which sections in part 4 warrant more of your attention.

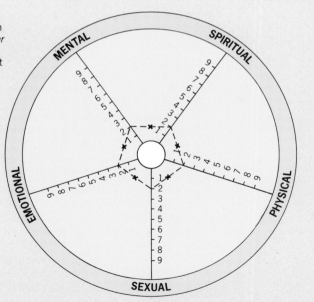

193

# Keeping your
# body in trim

Your body is the base from which feeling and thought can arise. The quality of this base, the housing of your mind and spirit, affects the quality of your feeling and thought. Your mind cannot be at its best if the body is neglected. Taking exercise, eating a varied, stimulating and healthy diet, and finding your own positive balance between work and leisure are all ways to look after the body. A healthy, fit body is more resistant to all kinds of stress, and feeling in tune with your body gives you a sense of freedom of action, thought and feeling – the very opposite of depression.

## SPORTS

My own experience of sport is of being pushed into doing it as a child and resenting it. It was only in my adult life that I had a second chance to discover that sports could be enjoyable when I played them out of choice and if I could focus on the pleasure of the movement or the pleasure of the competition, rather than on a comparison of my performance with others. Without this second chance I may never have played. Unfortunately this experience of sport in childhood is very common. A teaching attitude of ridiculing incapacity puts many people off sports for good. While boys tend to be taught to focus too heavily on performance rather than pleasure, girls are often given no encouragement at all and therefore gain little confidence in their ability. I have seen many women who have initially believed themselves to be unco-ordinated and hopeless at sports but who have, later in their lives, challenged this attitude and found to their delight that they were in fact well co-ordinated and could play with confidence and pleasure.

Not everyone will enjoy sport and you may simply not want to put your energy into it. But for most people there is a sport that they could derive a great deal of fun and pleasure from. When you are very busy, it is easy to undervalue recreation, and it is easy to forget that a moment's break from work with a sport that you enjoy may make you more creative and productive overall, despite losing an hour or so of working time.

The sport that suits you best may not necessarily be one that you learned as a child or that you have practised. There may be sporting activities that you had not really considered seriously which may fit your particular personality. If you are uncertain about what your body can take, check with your doctor. If you start playing an energetic sport, do warm-up exercises before you begin and take it slowly at first. Sports can provide you with many or all of the following:

- **Fun**
- **Exercise** The movement of muscles, and the stretching of ligaments, reduces tension and tones up the body. After a game of squash, for example, it is common to feel initially tired but then exhilarated and peaceful.
- **Aggression and competition** Sport is a socially acceptable way of working out your aggression. All the frustrations of the day can be put into one well-timed smash of a ball. At the same time, the aggression is controlled so that other people are not hurt, and the art of the balance between feeling and control has its own pleasure.
- **Challenge** Most sports provide a challenge of skill and application. Some sports (for example, deep-sea diving, hunting, mountaineering, rock climbing) provide a life and death challenge which can test your limits, and reaffirm your will to live. Other sports, such as marathon running or long-distance swimming, challenge your endurance. Every challenge can be a source of energy and exhilaration.
- **A kind of meditation** Total involvement in sport, as in any activity, can be a kind of meditation. All your energy is focused to such a degree that the mind is emptied of other thoughts and pre-occupations. The worries of the week can be forgotten if you are totally absorbed in doing a single activity as well as you can. Afterwards problems and concerns are often placed in a better perspective, and you can feel quite rejuvenated by having focused on something different. A long walk in the country or a horse ride, for example, may help you see things in another light.
- **Friendship** Since most sports involve participating with somebody else, they provide a very good opportunity for meeting others and for communicating without words. Striving for excellence together, mutual competition, expressing your personality through your sport – these are all experiences that are shared and that can go towards creating and deepening friendships. This can be especially important for men, who often find it harder than women to talk about themselves and their feelings.

# KEEPING YOUR BODY LOOSE

Any worry that you have increases your level of muscular tension. Any specific feelings that you inhibit are likely to be related to specific areas of muscular tension – for instance, if you inhibit aggression you may feel tension in your limbs. If you inhibit the voicing of a feeling, you will automatically find a physical way of stopping the process of sound production at some point between your lungs and your lips. You may:

- Temporarily stop breathing or else breathe more shallowly.
- Constrict the muscles of your neck. (When such tension is held for a long period it can lead to a headache at the back, top and/or front of your head.)
- Tighten the muscles of your jaw. (Jaw tension can lead to a headache on the sides of your head around your temples.)
- Tense your tongue and stiffen or purse your lips.

If you try doing all these things at once, you will get a feeling of the "stopping of something coming out of you". Usually, such tensions go unnoticed unless they lead to headaches or other physical symptoms. Unfortunately, tension held in the muscles limits receptivity to the feelings of others as well as to your own feelings and inner processes; whereas the more relaxed and flexible you are physically, the more you can allow feelings and vitality to flow through your body. It is worthwhile learning the difference between tension and relaxation. The ability to perceive when you are tense at an early stage gives you a useful warning system because muscle tension may be an indication that something in your life needs looking at or changing. You can learn to realize your own level of muscle tension by practising tensing and relaxing your muscles, as follows: lie down; tense the muscles in your legs, buttocks, belly, chest, arms, neck, jaw and face as tightly as possible; stay tense for about 30 seconds and then release the tension as you breathe out with a sigh. To learn to notice tension in specific areas of the body, practise tensing and relaxing each area separately.

**SPEAKING YOUR MIND**  If you are tense, try speaking your mind – when you have said what you really wanted to say to somebody, or when you allow yourself to feel the feelings that are inside you, you may relax with relief. (See also *Creative expression*, page 207.)

**HEAT**  Any form of pleasant heat tends to relax muscles. A hot bath or a shower after a day of tension can change a potentially depressing evening full of preoccupations with the day's events into an evening when you are more open to something or somebody else. Sometimes the relaxation of muscles in the bath allows feelings to arise which were previously blocked. You may, for instance, find it easier to cry in the bath. Outside the home, going to a Turkish bath or sauna can be a relaxing and invigorating experience.

**YOGA** This ancient system of stretching and breathing may bring about all the effects common to the stretch exercises described below. In addition, yoga may be more like a form of meditation, focusing on the control of muscles, breathing and feeling, leading to the possibility of greater calm and clarity. The stretch exercises on pages 200 and 201 are yoga based, but if you want to learn more about yoga contact one of the organizations listed at the back of the book (see *Useful addresses*, page 218), or join a local class.

**STRETCHING EXERCISES** There are many forms of exercise which gently stretch your muscles. After such exercises it is quite common to experience yourself as emotionally open, a natural result of loosening muscular tension and increasing the depth of breathing. The more open you are emotionally, the more pain, laughter and sparkle are possible to you.

The exercise programme described on page 200 may help you relax, get rid of negative feelings, remove muscular tension, and feel more energetic. Try doing the programme regularly, perhaps every evening in order to relieve tensions that may have built up over the day. It is designed to both prevent and relieve depression. It should also help to correct any postural faults that are symptoms of depression.

**MASSAGE** Getting a friend or your partner to massage any tense area of your body can relieve tension as well as give you a feeling of pleasant contact with the other person. If you feel uncomfortable with such a personal approach you will find that it will make you more tense. You may prefer to go to a masseur for a more extensive and professional approach.

With practice you can learn the art of giving a massage; the important thing to remember is to keep your hands in contact with your partner's body and to maintain a regular rhythm – if you stop and start, you may disturb the relaxing effect. On page 202 there is an illustrated guide to the best-known massage techniques. This guide may inspire you to read a more detailed book, or attend a massage course (for details see *Useful addresses*, page 218).

Once you become familiar with the techniques try developing your own feel for what is most relaxing. You will have your own natural rhythm which, within the guidelines suggested here, you can trust. At the same time, if you are giving a massage, be aware of signals, both verbal and non-verbal, from your partner. If you feel a muscle tense beneath your fingers, you may need to be more gentle or to apply pressure from a different direction. The adjustment of your touch according to your awareness of your partner can make the process of massage a pleasant form of communication.

**MEDITATION AND SELF-HYPNOSIS**

There are many ways to meditate or induce hypnosis, so it's best to find one that suits you or appeals to you. The aim is to discipline your mind to concentrate on one thing only, to the exclusion of everything else: this can be a phrase or word which you repeat; an object; your own breathing; a peaceful picture developed in your own mind; or a feeling or sensation in part of your body. A suggested method of relaxing through self-hypnosis/meditation, which you can try yourself, is included below. Such an exercise can be practised for about 15 minutes, once a day. The more you practise, the less you will find your mind wandering or yourself falling asleep. (You can also use this method to help yourself get to sleep by doing steps two, three and four lying down. After making some positive suggestions to yourself about the next day, say to yourself something like "My breathing is getting slower and deeper as in a normal sleep", "My body is becoming more and more relaxed", "My body is getting heavier and heavier", or "I am sinking deeper and deeper".)

---

## HOW TO MEDITATE

**1** Sit down in a comfortable, preferably straight-backed, chair in a quiet room free from all distractions.

**2** Breathe slowly and deeply. Say to yourself (not aloud) the following, using all your imaginative powers in order to envisage the words taking effect:

■ "My legs are feeling heavier"; then imagine them feeling heavier and heavier on the floor.

■ "My body is feeling heavier"; then imagine your body sinking into the chair.

■ "My shoulders are feeling heavier"; then imagine them dropping downwards.

■ "My head is feeling heavier" and imagine your head sinking downwards with its weight, as if your neck was shortening.

**3** Now focus on a small spot in front of you, perhaps a mark on the wall, and look at it intensely for 30 seconds. Then count slowly from 1 to 10, at each count closing and opening your eyes, still focusing on the spot when your eyes are open. As you count each number imagine your eyelids getting heavier and heavier so when you reach ten you can hardly open them. At ten close your eyes and imagine that your eyelids are so heavy that they are pressing your eyes inwards.

**4** In this focused and relaxed state, you will be more receptive to messages and suggestions that you make to yourself. These might be, for example, "I will feel relaxed today", "I will feel more energetic", "I will act with confidence", "I can feel warmth in my heart", "I can feel the warmth in my body moving down into my legs". You will find yourself in a curious double state in which you can consciously make suggestions to yourself, and unconsciously, be more open to take the suggestions seriously.

**5** To bring yourself out of this relaxed state slowly count down from 5 to 1, imagining yourself coming back to your usual, alert frame of mind on the count of 1.

**CARING ABOUT YOUR PHYSICAL APPEARANCE**

Though vanity tends to be maligned, it is, in a certain proportion, a human essential. I assume this because I have never yet met anyone without vanity, either open or disguised. How you look does not only affect the impression made on other people, it affects how you feel about yourself, and it can be a form of expression of your inner self or of how you hope to feel. I have met several people who could not change their low opinion of themselves with extensive psychotherapy until they had first worked on changing their appearance so that they felt good about how they looked.

Changing the outside can affect the inside as much as changing the inside can affect the outside, so long as your main motivation is to feel good about yourself, as opposed to obeying regulations and unconscious allegiances about how you *ought* to look. For ideas about altering your appearance, see the suggestions in *Changing the symptoms*, page 136.

**EXPANDING THE CAPACITY OF YOUR BODY**

Nearly everybody has some negative feelings about some part of their body – you may feel your chest is too big or too small, your legs are too thin or too fat, your breasts are too small or your nose is too long. Quite often a general feeling of inadequacy is focused on the particular part of the body that is felt to be underdeveloped or somehow unacceptable. The realization of this may reduce the worry and it sometimes helps to see that everybody else feels the same way about some part of their body. You may on the other hand decide to change part of your body by exercise and/or diet. This is not very effective on noses, but for body and limbs significant changes can be made with good advice and hard work. The effort that goes into this and the satisfaction that comes from effecting a change that seemed impossible, as well as the result itself, can all change your feeling about yourself.

Developing your body by increasing your stamina and fitness can also have a profound effect on your inner belief about yourself. One of the most positive changes in one man who I was seeing for psychotherapy came when he started running marathons, after which he became more confident and self-assured. Sometimes expanding the stamina of your body actually increases your stamina for feeling. People with very tight constricted bodies often have a very low tolerance for feeling: they just cannot take too much and are forced to cut off from too much feeling in themselves or in their environment. In these people, sometimes, developing themselves physically increases their tolerance for emotion. Any of the forms of exercise and relaxation mentioned in this chapter may help you expand the capacity of your body, or you may try another method such as weight training.

# STRETCH EXERCISE PROGRAMME

Always start your programme standing up straight, with your weight evenly distributed on both feet. Relax your shoulders and try to stretch up through your spine. Return to this position at the end of each exercise, except where specified. In all the exercises, hold the final position for a few seconds initially, building up gradually to the time recommended. Begin each movement as you breathe out and then breathe normally; don't hold your breath during an exercise as this causes tension. As you come out of a stretch breathe in.

## EXERCISE TWO

1 Move your feet about 1m (3ft) apart. Keep your knees straight and stretch your arms out to your sides at shoulder height.

2 Turn your right foot in slightly, and your left foot out, lining up your left heel with the arch of your right foot. Gently bend sideways, not forwards, keeping your spine extended and chest open so you can breathe in deeply. Go as far as you can and hold the position for up to 30 seconds. With practice you will be able to reach your ankle. Repeat the stretch on the other side.

## EXERCISE ONE

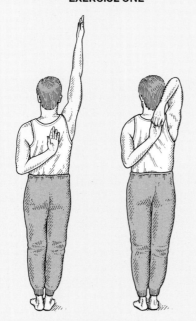

1 Keeping your feet together, stretch your arms out to your sides. Then place your left hand behind your back, bending your elbow so that your hand is palm out, resting on your spine. Breathing in, raise your right arm above your head.

2 Breathing out, bend your right elbow behind your head and "catch" your hands. Hold for five seconds and then repeat with your hands the other way round. Do the exercise at least twice on each side alternating the role of each arm.

## EXERCISE THREE

**1** Move your feet about 1.3m (4½ft) apart, with knees straight and arms outstretched strongly sideways. Turn your head to the left and focus beyond your fingertips. Turn your right foot in slightly, and your left foot out, lining up your left heel with the arch of your right foot.

**2** Breathe in. Then, as you exhale, bend your left knee and drop your hips down gently, so that your left thigh is parallel to the ground. Hold the position for up to 30 seconds, then repeat the stretch on the other side.

## EXERCISE FOUR

**1** Put a strong chair against a wall so that it cannot slip, and stand up straight, facing the chair.

**2** Place your right foot on the chair seat, with your raised thigh parallel to the floor. Put your right hand at the base of your spine and left hand against your right knee. Twist to the right, stretching up as you do so, looking back over your right shoulder. Keep your shoulders relaxed and chest open. Hold the position for up to 30 seconds, relax, and repeat twist to the left.

## EXERCISE FIVE

**1** With the chair against the wall, as in exercise four, kneel on the floor with your hands by your side, and your back to the chair.

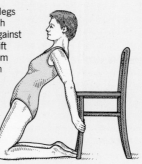

**2** Grip the chair legs firmly with both hands and push against them so that you lift your hips away from your heels; stretch your thighs as far forwards as possible. Hold the position for a few seconds, relax, and then repeat the stretch.

## EXERCISE SIX

Relax for five minutes after the exercises. Lie on your back with your trunk raised on a low table, or across a low single bed, and your head and shoulders resting on a cushion on the floor. If you use a table, it should be covered with a folded blanket. Keep your feet flat on the floor with your knees bent. Keep your eyes open. Before you stand up again, slide on to the floor and rest.

# MASSAGE TECHNIQUES

A massage should be given in a warm, softly lit room. Ask your partner to lie face down on a blanket or towel, on a large table or the floor, either naked or wearing only underwear. Do not use a bed, as the mattress would absorb most of the pressure. Using a lubricant, such as body cream or baby oil, which can be spread over the body by the long strokes at the beginning of a massage, helps make the movements smoother. The following four techniques can be used as a basis for your own massage programme. You may find that one particular technique helps relieve tension in a specific area of the body.

## Stroking (right)
Start a massage with large, circular stroking movements, with your thumbs on either side of your partner's spine, moving your palms upwards and outwards. Apply firm pressure as you move upwards, and gentler pressure on the downward strokes. Rhythmical stroking movements, either deep or light, can be made on any area of the body.

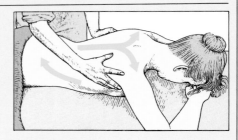

## Kneading (left)
Rolling, pressing and squeezing movements, like those used when kneading bread dough, can be made on any of the fleshier areas of the body, particularly the buttocks, sides, hips, thighs, calves and – lightly – the stomach. Lift up and squeeze bunches of flesh, alternately releasing the hold of one hand as the other takes up another handful.

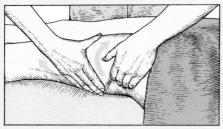

## Friction (right)
Small, firm, circular pressure movements using the thumbs can be made to apply "friction" at the base of the skull, and then to the spine, moving your thumbs down the back, with one just to each side of the spine. Slightly wider circular pressure movements made with the thumbs can also be used on the soles of the feet.

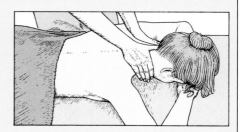

## Hacking (left)
Fleshy areas like the buttocks and thighs can be stimulated with fast, hacking movements made with the sides of the hands, applying first one hand and then the other. These should not hurt, so make fairly light bouncing movements. Similar movements can also be used to pummel the fleshier areas of the body, only using the fleshy sides of loosely clenched fists.

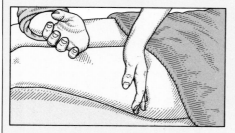

# Keeping your mind in trim

It is a fairly common belief that most brains are considerably underused. Various theories have arisen as to what percentage of the brain is used; some neurologists believe only a tiny percentage is used effectively. Whatever the percentage, it is certainly true that many people avoid thinking when they can. This makes a lot of sense: thinking afresh is very hard work – it is so much easier to follow what somebody else has said, to obey the rules, to disobey the rules, or to find some way of depending on the thoughts of another. In many areas (for example, learning the law or medicine) this is a necessary and efficient thing to do. The danger comes when all areas of your life are pervaded by the thoughts and hidden dictates of others, so that you are no longer free to be individual, creative and sparkling. Keeping your mind alive is a constant and changing challenge. If you are to do so, you may need to maintain your interest and curiosity, accept that change is necessary, and be challenged mentally.

## INTEREST AND CURIOSITY

One of the delightful, sometimes exasperating, things about children is the constant questioning, "Why? . . . Yes, but why?" At times, if you are open to it, it can really make you reconsider why you do in fact do a certain thing in the way in which you do it. If the child is not asking you "Why?" in order to avoid doing what you asked him or her to do, but is genuinely asking out of curiosity, it may make you reflect on where your own curiosity has disappeared to. Curiosity is one of the greatest marks of intelligence and a lively curiosity which will not accept "Well, that's the way it's done" can always find new answers and new depths. "Why? . . . Yes, but why?" can lead to surprising answers.

To be genuinely curious requires the humility to admit you do not know and the courage to be led in a direction you cannot totally control.

# THE NECESSITY OF CHANGE

There are times in your life when it is tempting to think "Ah! that's it, I've got it now – all I have to do is carry on like this and I'll be OK". Unfortunately it never works like that because life changes, and you change, and what is appropriate for you now may be completely inappropriate in a year or two's time. Keeping abreast of what is right for you at a certain moment involves nothing more than the whole art of living – and that involves the development of an inner sensitivity to your own person and an outer sensitivity to others, your environment and the trends of the world.

Change is also necessary because some things simply get boring. On the other hand every pattern you develop has its own comfortable feeling of security. You need the wisdom to judge which patterns are boring and deaden your vitality and which patterns are usefully continued so that necessary programmes can be repeated quickly and efficiently, leaving more time for the development of more creative pursuits. You also need to ask yourself which patterns give you real pleasure from a kind of ritual, and which patterns only provide security against novelty.

There is a great deal of cultural pressure which tends to put you in a particular role or stream of activity. When I took nine months off from medicine I was told by many people, both within and without the profession, that it would ruin my career, and that it would be difficult for me to get another job, or at least a good one. When I applied for my next job, I had no difficulty whatsoever and realized that all the good intentions and advice that I had received were based on the fear that doing something different, for whatever motive, would be judged as unacceptable. Sometimes colleagues, friends and family will try to stop you because a change may threaten their ideas. At other times you find it hard to change your role because any new role is unknown and cannot be realised without anxiety. Because of these pressures and fears, many people stick at something they do not really enjoy or that they have grown out of. How easy it is to dream of wonderful possibilities while you slavishly follow your old depressing pattern and comfortable ways.

For a life lived more in the "gold", you may find that different times in your life require different kinds of work, different kinds of experience and different kinds of friendships. On the other hand, some constant developing friendships, some constant patterns and the constant development of one line of work may be productive and exciting for you. The question and the art is which and when.

# MENTAL CHALLENGES

For the development of your mind's potential you need to be intellectually challenged, both at work and at leisure. Being fully involved, interested and challenged by your work is a wonderful bonus. It has to be admitted that almost every kind of work involves some laborious repetition and times of tedium, but if it is at least punctuated by times of interest and the challenge of an uncertainty dependent on your own efforts, so much the better – at least for some people. Others may develop a different style of involvement which is less related to challenge or uncertainty, and more related to an aim towards perfection or a kind of meditation. The most mundane and repetitious job can be carried out with a pleasure in excellence.

Leisure may be time off from any kind of involvement: sometimes it feels good and is useful to do absolutely nothing. At other times, especially for those who find they can relax only through activity, it is necessary to get thoroughly involved in something other than work. It may be a crossword puzzle, a game, a sport, an interesting conversation – the art is to find the right thing for the right time. Also consider doing something different – perhaps learning about a new subject at evening classes or doing something with friends outside your usual sphere of activity.

**Conversation**

Since conversation is so important in living a full life, and since loneliness and depression are so closely connected, the art of conversation is well worth developing. To make a conversation more interesting, you are required to take the risk of opening up subjects which are on the edge of acceptability, to transcend small talk for more intimate, challenging conversation. It may be worthwhile bearing in mind a few thought-provoking points:
- If you are bored by somebody, it is more profitable to find out why he is interested in the subject he is talking about than to pass silent judgement. Be curious.
- Give, rather than expect to receive.
- Laugh at yourself and look for the humour in situations.
- Self-consciousness is selfish. Lose it very simply by directing yourself to what the other person is interested in. Turn yourself outwards by cultivating friendliness and by imagining yourself in another's place.
- If you find yourself holding back, take that as a sign that it is time to talk.
- Feeling inferior or superior is a conversation-stopper.
- Treat others as interesting and often they will become so.

# Keeping your feelings in trim

Since happiness, contentment, satisfaction, fulfilment and fun are kinds of feelings, it makes sense to develop the quality of your feeling life. Feelings are very often not acceptable for cultural or personal reasons, and repression of unacceptable feelings can have a depressive effect. Some people remain generally inhibited and somewhat depressed (at least, lacking in sparkle) for their whole lives. Others get caught in the process of "bottle or explode"; feelings are held down to such an extent that, when they do come out, they tend to be explosive or negative. Both bottling and explosion of feeling tend to create distance from other people, rather than communication. What is required for higher standards of communication is the development of expression of feeling with such creativity that on the one hand your own feelings are not held back, and on the other hand, other people are not pushed or blasted into defensiveness.

## FEAR OF "ANIMAL" INSTINCTS

One of the fears that people have of expressing feelings is that the brutish animal within will be released with damaging results. Animal feelings are not, in fact, essentially destructive. If you look at a bird flying at a cat to protect its babies or a hungry lion stalking its prey, you see raw aggression. Such aggression is nearly always used to protect the young, or search for food. More limited or ritualized aggression is usually used to fight for a mate or for supremacy in the social hierarchy. The socially evolved mammals, such as the apes, have highly developed caring instincts. We human beings are the most destructive species and also the species that most represses animal instincts.

The problem with repression is that it creates the need for more repression. If you trap a bear within a cage, the bear naturally gets angry, but when the anger is of no avail it may become twisted into vengeful nastiness directed at anybody unfortunate to come within range. Meeting the bear for the first time, it is easy to think that its nature is inherently nasty and to forget that the nastiness was first created by the cage. This is an allegory of human repression of feeling. In general, repressed feeling tends to become twisted. When natural reaction is held back for a long time, the human warmth of the reaction becomes replaced by coldness. Anger turns to hate and spite. But the witheld feeling does not disappear, it lurks in the background, making the odd appearance by twisting its way through chinks in the armour. Hate becomes a needle of witty sarcasm. Spite takes hidden pleasure in another's pain. It is so easy to construe this as evidence of innate nastiness and then to build stronger barriers of repression, not realizing that there may also be positive feelings trapped within.

Anger can be loving, hateful or defensive. It can be a way of penetrating or confronting another person in order to make warm contact. It can be a way of trampling on another with the intent of hurting. It can be a defensive camouflage to avoid softer feelings, intimacy or fear. Repression is necessary for those who cannot or do not wish to get through to inner levels of positive feeling. Some people do not have enough hope to believe that they can be positive inside. To some extent the degree of repression that you require is related to your inner wisdom. Some people do best by following a line of duty, while others can learn to trust and follow the goodness of their own hearts.

# CREATIVE EXPRESSION

For most people, however, repression is less necessary than is often taught. It is nearly always possible to find ways of expressing feelings which can create more contact and understanding, or which at least are not destructive. Some of these ways are mentioned in the self-help section (see *Express the feeling,* page 122). The following section explores the area between holding back entirely which is likely to make you depressed, and letting go indiscriminately which is likely to have repercussions beyond your desired result.

**Containing feelings**  Expression or repression are not the only two alternatives. It is also possible to *contain* feeling so that it is not expressed, yet not avoided, but remains simmering below the surface. Repression involves making the feeling unconscious by a process of diminishing body energy and feeling, whereas containment involves no deadening of feeling but a "movement" of feeling within. Containment is not related to depression.

**Directing feelings**   Find a way of expressing your feeling and thought that takes the other person into account, not so that you lose your integrity, but so that your expression can also get through to the other person. This is an art, which may take you years to develop with finesse. Yet paradoxically, you cannot afford to be too careful – sometimes you need to "explode" and sometimes only an extreme reaction will get through to another. The care must be in *directing* the feeling effectively, not in stopping it out of too much consideration.

Expression of feeling, even violence, can be directed positively. When Mrs. B threw the plates to miss her husband (see *Life events*, page 56), her anger was clearly not indiscriminate. First of all, she waited for the right moment by containing the feeling without killing it. Secondly, the anger was specifically directed not to hurt her husband but to make her point with a little emphasis. The final result was more, rather than less, contact and the glimmer of a possibility of revitalizing a dead marriage. But before you pick up a pile of plates, every person, situation, moment and appropriate expression is different. Perhaps the most important thing about Mrs. B was that her underlying intent was loving rather than hurtful (though her husband might have found this difficult to realize with a plate flying towards him). She protected herself from depression and spite, and she tried to protect her marriage from distance, coldness and hate.

However, directing the expression of feelings in the most positive direction takes practice, experience, and wisdom. If you really *cannot* direct it, you may be better to wait. On the other hand, practice will be effective only if you are prepared to make a fool of yourself and make mistakes. Sometimes holding back is wise – but depression is usually worse than making a mistake.

**Friendly and "political" situations**   Make a division between a friendly and a "political" situation. With a good friend with whom your main motive is to make good contact, you can go too far, make a mistake and look a fool without losing your friendship. In a political situation (for instance, in most situations at work) your motives for expression of yourself are often to create an efficient effect. If you are to avoid the loss of sparkle that follows depressing your response, you will require creativity to maintain your position and at the same time keep your spirit alive. A woman was in a situation at work where her own excellent and new ideas had been taken over and used by a colleague without acknowledgment. She could:
**A** Do nothing and feel bad.
**B** Throw a tantrum.

**C** Tell her colleague that she wished her idea to be acknowledged (and to say this with some aggressive force in her eyes, posture, tone of voice and choice of words).

She chose **C** but her colleague side-stepped the issue by saying "Of course I will tell them it was your idea if they ask me." In this statement he affected innocence and threw a disguised punch at the same time. He would tell them "It was your idea", as if such a concern with whose idea it was was really beneath a "better" person's consideration. Her answer to this dilemma was to enter the room at the time when her colleague was demonstrating the idea to his superiors, and to say: "Oh, you used my suggestion – it's worked out very well!" Thus she kept her position and her spirit, and rightfully won the battle.

**Avoiding blame**    Creative expression excludes blame. Self-blame is inverted pride and twists emotional communication. Blame of the other simply makes the other defensive, according to the dictum: *If you attack you provoke defensiveness; if you defend you provoke attack.* A battle of attack and defend then takes over from communication.

**Bridging distance**    When you feel negative about, distant from, or angry with somebody, do not start by assuming that you do not like him, thereby giving yourself a reason to sever contact or keep your distance. Begin by asking yourself about your own intent and your part in the distance or the bad feeling. Answer yourself as honestly as you can. Here are some possibilities:

● Your friend has done something that you are annoyed about and you have failed to tell him. As soon as you do say something about it the barrier between you usually goes, and you realize that there has been no intentional wrong.

● You are jealous of your friend who has a quality, a possession or a relationship which you do not have. Because you judge your own jealousy as bad, you do not say anything and the distance grows. Many friendships get broken in this way. The problem is not the jealousy, but the judgement that jealousy is bad. Jealousy (like practically everything else) can be used positively or negatively. The negative side is to plot to destroy the success of another, to say in effect: "If I don't have it, you won't either." The positive side is to achieve your own success in your own way, to say in effect: "Well, if you have that, I am going to make sure I have something good for myself too." Jealousy spoken positively is nothing more than a compliment: "I really envy your family (friends, success etc.)." The honesty to admit you are jealous can give a relationship a little more depth and trust.

● Seeing your friend using his talents fully reminds you that you are not doing what you are capable of. Since you may not want to be reminded of this, an easy answer is to have contact only with people who make the same or less use of their talents than you.

● You have done something to your friend which you feel bad about and you are reluctant to face your own guilt. However, the guilt will never go without action. It is a long-term emotional economy to admit your mistake, apologize or take action to reverse your error, which is nearly always worth the short-term cost in pride.

● Your friend has an aspect of his character that you find off-putting, because it reminds you of a characteristic in yourself. It is often difficult to be aware of this and somehow so much easier to see the faults or strengths of another and to remain ignorant of our own. If you realize that you have the same characteristic as your friend your negative feeling towards him may suddenly drop into perspective.

● You are to some extent paranoid. Paranoia in the extreme sense of believing people are plotting against you or pumping poisonous gas through your floorboards is uncommon. Common everyday paranoia is a particular flavour of egotism which assumes that other people are more concerned about what you are doing than they actually are. Perhaps you walk into a room full of people who are busy. "Hello," you say cheerfully. No-one is very interested in your entry and all you receive is a couple of low-energy grunts of acknowledgment. It is easy to start thinking in this situation: "Have I done something wrong?" This thought may be quickly overtaken by the rationalization: "Oh, they must be busy", but somehow the doubts linger in the background of your mind. The logical presumption in these fleeting suspicions is that the primary reason for something going on (or not going on) between you and others must be related to *you* rather than the others. Paranoia often creates its own self-fulfilling prophecy. Once you are suspicious of other people's motives or feelings for you, your distance and your own aggrieved feeling will be perceived (more or less consciously) by those others, who will naturally react by being wary of you or more distant from you. On perceiving their distance, you can then say to yourself "Ah, I was right to be suspicious of them," and so the distance grows.

**Reducing paranoia** There are a number of practical steps you can take to reduce the distance of paranoia:

● Make the wilful decision to assume that others are acting out of the best intentions. Even if you are wrong (in other words your paranoid suspicions were right), your assumption of the best in others will often bring out the best in them.

● Check it out. If you think someone doesn't like you, ask. Since this can be rather embarrassing as a bald question, a bit of humour may help. You walk into the room of busy people and get no reaction; so you say with humour "What's wrong, don't you like me any more?" If they say absolutely nothing your paranoia was probably accurate. More than likely, though, someone will say "Of course we like you, but we're busy, you dummy!" In seconds, your suspicions have evaporated: paranoia disappears with human contact.

● Check it out indirectly by making contact (rather than maintaining the distance). Instead of saying nothing and feeling bad talk to the person you are suspicious of. Find any way to remake contact, and imaginary suspicions will fade in the light of reality.

After questioning yourself or having more awareness of yourself, you still may, after all, not like somebody. You may be right not to trust somebody and keeping your distance may be the most positive thing you can do.

**Dealing with the past**

If negative feelings keep arising with particular kinds of people, by the statistics of chance the problem is more likely to be yours than theirs. There may be reasons from your past experiences which are interfering with the present. If such unsatisfactory "repeats" keep occurring in your life, consider exploring the reasons (see *Psychotherapy*, page 145).

**Finding your own balance**

Many of the above points about creative expression do not apply to the psychopath who seeks power at all costs or to those whose main problem is with controlling anti-social behaviour. In the end, there are no absolute rules. It is up to each person to find his or her own balance.

# SEX AND SENSUALITY

Your sexual energy declines when you are depressed, and conversely, those who limit their sexual energy tend to limit the sparkle available to them. Although some people choose to put their sexual drive into other energies and pursuits, the commonest limitations are unconscious.

**UNCONSCIOUS LIMITATIONS**

Deep allegiances are often very powerful in the sexual field. Your parents may never have made or expressed a single judgement on sex but you will inevitably have picked up a sense of what was permissible and what was not by their attitudes to their own bodies and their possible difficulties, embarrassment or silence on the subject of sex.

The effect of centuries of sexual inhibition and a judgemental attitude to the animal energy that is part of us has been to separate sexual energy from mental, physical, emotional and spiritual energy. Sexual energy, sometimes coupled with aggressive energy, has been seen as the "dark side" – an unfortunate devilish need which taints the purity of mental and spiritual pursuits. Today it is common to think that such an attitude disappeared at least a generation ago; however, while the attitude has become less prevalent, it still has less obvious effects. There are many people who can let go sexually only with someone they do not care about, such as a prostitute, because sexuality and care are divorced from each other. More generally, the huge cultural reaction to sexual inhibition (that is, greater sexual freedom) has sometimes served to continue the split between sexual and other energies. Focusing on techniques, on greater sexual exploration within couples, on the possibilities of different "styles" of sex (aggressive; gentle; romantic; "pornographic") has provided more sexual freedom for many people. On the other hand sexuality has sometimes become over-geared to technique, conquest and performance, and has sometimes become separated from the rest of our human responses and energies.

If your sexuality feels low or empty, consider the chance of more depth of feeling by rejoining it to the following:

● **Physical energy** Just as muscular tension reduces other feelings, so an over-tense body limits its capacity to let go and experience sexuality. This is specifically true of tension in the muscles connected to the pelvic bones. You can learn to loosen your pelvic muscles with exercise and relaxation by doing the exercise below, perhaps every other day, and possibly in conjunction with the stretch exercises on page 200.

## LOOSENING AND RELEASING TENSION FROM THE PELVIC MUSCLES

■ Stand with your legs 0.5 m (1½ ft) apart, your knees very slightly bent, and your hands on your hips. Relax your shoulders.

■ In this position, breathe deeply, as far down into your abdomen as possible. (If you find this difficult, try practising with one hand on your stomach; as you breathe in, your hand should be pushed out.) When you have taken a full breath exhale quickly, but without actually pushing the air out.

■ After three or four breaths like this, rotate your pelvis forwards as far as you can and hold it there for 12 seconds. Then, very slowly, rotate your pelvis backwards as far as you can and hold it there for 12 seconds. Repeat this four or five times.

■ Begin to rotate your pelvis backwards and forwards very slowly without holding it in either position. Your hands should rotate a little with your hips, but they should not move backwards and forwards with your pelvis. Do this for about two minutes. If the muscles in your legs or pelvis tremble a little, don't stop as this is usually a sign of releasing muscular tension.

● **Sensuality** Many people, especially men, find it hard to enjoy the experience and emotional contact that comes from touching sensually, because the touching too easily becomes a technique that leads towards sex and orgasm. Greater sensual enjoyment is something that you can learn with practice (see *Express the feeling*, page 122).

● **Mental energy** Mental energy is often seen as being contrary to sexual energy because of centuries of mental judgements on sex, and because it is so easy to think too much during sex, and lose the feeling. But mental excitement can also be a prelude to good sex.

● **Emotional energy** Sex may become stereotyped – for instance, it may always be softly romantic or it may always be forcefully aggressive. You may find that it initially makes you feel anxious to have sex with a different feeling. Being willing to share feelings, concerns or desires can add a new dimension to the intimacy possible between two people. Laughter often becomes inhibited in the "serious" business of sex – but what a relief when you can laugh at your own difficulties or laugh with the fun of the playfulness of sex.

● **Spiritual energy** The basic animal in us is as much an expression of the spirit as any heavenward look. Sex contains the potential for a particular depth of intimacy with yourself or with another.

● **Each other** Depersonalized sex may be what you both feel like sometimes – just sex for sex's sake, with minimum personal contact. But at other times you may long for intimacy. Intimacy is completely unrelated to performance: it is related, more than anything else, to personal honesty. The awkwardness of admitting "I don't know what to do" may create a moment of intimate contact, whereas trying to cover up your uncertainty creates greater distance. It is sometimes difficult though, when you feel as vulnerable as you are during sex, to avoid getting prickly or blaming rather than facing your own awkwardness. When sex goes wrong, the slightest hint of blame of the other provokes a defence based on pride, or a counter-attack.

Someone who is frightened of wild passion might say, for instance: "You always move around too much". Such an accusation encourages distance between partners or puts the accused on the defensive. To say, on the other hand, "Sometimes I get a bit scared when it gets wild or passionate", would be more honest, would not threaten, and would foster closer contact. Sensitivity to your own limits and sensitivity to the limits of your partner reduces the pressure to perform and creates room for your own personal intimacy, which is quite unrelated to what anybody else does.

# Keeping your spirit in trim

This is a very personal and private matter, and everyone has their own way of following their own path. Some of the most spiritual people would never talk about "spirit" or even necessarily understand intellectualization about the spirit (see the limited questionnaire on spiritual energy, page 192). Some people who would consider themselves very religious are obedient to the external authority of a church, but miss the essence of the spirit, while others use their religion as a form through which a certain kind of spiritual contact can be made. By "spirit" I do not mean anything hushed or holy, I mean the power of life, the life-force. The spirit is earthed to the mundane, for as the Chinese proverb says: "Man with head in clouds cannot have feet on ground unless very big man." You can feel your spirit on a mountain, in a movement of music, doing exercises, having sex, preparing a meal, when you are alone, or in a moment of human contact. There is no prescribed road to the spirit.

**INNER PROCESSES**
When I learned medicine I was taught to take the pulse accurately, noting the speed, the strength, the regularity and the shape of the pulse wave. From this information certain conditions of the blood circulatory system could be deduced, and it made complete sense to my logical mind.

When I learned a little about acupuncture, I was expected to be able to feel the "energy" of six different pulses on the one pulsing radial artery at the wrist which was supposed to provide information on "energy balance", as well as specific information about parts of the body which had no obvious relationship with the blood circulatory system.

Although I tried very hard to keep an open mind, it was easier to be sceptical than to appreciate my own ineptitude and my own ignorance of a whole facet of human energy. It was not long after this that my wife saw an acupuncturist for the first time. Before he had taken any medical history or examined her in any other way, he felt her pulses and told her she had had an operation 16 years ago, what the operation was for, what had been done and the outcome: all the information was correct.

The mechanisms through which he obtained his information are not important for my purpose in this section. The point is that there are processes within, which are not always logically deducible nor mechanically obvious. Such processes can become out of balance, which can make you more susceptible to all kinds of ailments, including depression. There are many possible ways to redress the balance: you can change the balance of the energies that you use; you can change your diet; you can change the people you spend most of your time with; you can change your goals; you can avoid substances or situations that put you out of balance; or you can go to a professional who specializes in energy balance (an acupuncturist or an osteopath for example).

**MOMENTS OF QUIET**

Most people experience from time to time moments of quiet and repose when a seemingly stronger, calmer, more confident presence within allows them to make decisions with clarity and pleasure. Although such times can, practically, save hours of confused thinking or discussion, it is easy to forget to provide the time necessary for quiet. It is so easy for life to become a sort of continuous sub-panic of non-stop activity, where you hardly dare stop. It is almost as if you lose faith in life continuing if you don't keep on and on making things happen.

To stop outside activity, to relax, to drop inside yourself, to have a moment of quiet and deeper reflection, can rekindle your own hope and sense of inner worth. It can provide peace, a different perspective, clearer thinking, more focused feeling and a sense of connection with your own self or with the outside world. Different people achieve this feeling in different ways; here are a few suggestions on how to do so:

● Yoga or other forms of relaxation exercises (see page 197).

● Meditation or self-hypnosis (see page 198).

● Learning an art of Zen. You do not necessarily need to learn anything about Zen Buddhism; you may gain moments of peace from total concentration and absorption in something you love – which could be anything from arranging the pictures in a room to maintaining a motorbike. Total focus on a sport, a garden or cleaning a room you love can be a kind of meditation which clears the dust from the mind.

● Writing down your thoughts on paper. This can help to clarify your ideas. A particularly useful approach is to create a dialogue between yourself and a real or fictitious person.

● Listening to music. It's easy to forget to listen to music, especially when you don't feel very cheerful. Music can alter the way you feel and change your day. Of course it is important to choose music that moves you rather than music that you think you ought to listen to.

● Your own way that you have discovered – you may, for instance, find a kind of peace when you are on a boat or when you walk to a particular place that has meaning for you.

**FRIENDSHIP**  Good friendship feeds the spirit and is probably one of the greatest pleasures a person can have. Many people are lonely because they don't have sufficiently strong friendships and miss something of the richness that can come from depth of contact. Many people also miss a sense of community or a wider family feeling that comes from belonging and being accepted despite foibles and eccentricities. A lack of lively interaction with others can create loss of sparkle and a loss of sense of purpose.

However, good friendship can be hard work and has its cost. It takes an effort to really hear what others are trying to say and to be willing to feel their sorrow as well as their joy. Reacting to others and caring for others can be inconvenient and uncomfortable; sharing feelings can be painful. It is partly because of these costs that many people avoid a deeper quality of friendship.

For improving contact with others, the sections on *Changing the life non-event* (see page 125), and *Creative expression* (see page 207), may be helpful. But more important is your own capacity and willingness to give, since the best way to make friends is to offer friendship rather than to ask for it.

# SELF-MANAGEMENT

Part 4 covers a diverse range of ideas, some of which may appeal to you. If you can use any of these ideas to develop a more productive use of your energy and talents, you are more likely to prevent depression. However, staying productive and finding the right balance between work and leisure requires effective management of yourself. This means taking account of your own energy and personal preferences and arranging your life so that you can express who and what you are – in other words, deciding for yourself how to organize things so that there is time for different parts of yourself – for instance, time for sport, quietness, friendship, vanity, laughter, hard work and so on. You need to learn to be sensitive to your own needs. You also need to learn to take an objective overview so that you can ask yourself the question "What do I need for myself in my life now?"

**Planning your daily life**

One aspect of self-management that you can easily arrange is the planning of your daily life so that each day you have something to look forward to. If you have a game, a drink with a friend, a dinner, or anything else that you enjoy, arranged for the evening, you will probably feel differently about the whole day. Similarly, if you arrange something that gives you pleasure at the weekend, it can change the feeling of the whole week. It takes practice to organize yourself enough so that there are things to look forward to, but not to such an extent that the activities become a scheduling pressure.

Another aspect of self-management is to give yourself the things that you find "feed" you. It may be sipping freshly squeezed orange juice at the beginning of the day, it may be buying something for yourself that makes you feel good, or listening to a piece of music you love. A good party, a challenging sport, a moment of quiet meditation or an intimate talk with a friend, may all, at different times, fill the spirit. It is often such things that make life worth living.

**Accepting change**

Good self-management requires the ability to discriminate between the times when it is wise to make a stand and the times when change is appropriate. If your attitudes tend to remain more or less permanently fixed then you are bound to fight the constantly changing flow of life. This involves stopping your own changing inner feelings, which is a depressive process. Those who think in stasis rather than flux think too much of future results and see the present process as transient and unimportant. If you can enjoy the process of change rather than focus on future results, you cannot be depressed. Perhaps this is why young children hardly ever get depressed.

**Keeping your inner vitality**

To maintain an energetic life without loss of sparkle, you may need to question some of your personal priorities. For instance, do you run your work or does your work run you? If you feel you are run by life's pressures, then your own life-force is depressed.

Keeping your spirit alive and maintaining a life of enjoyable productivity requires a degree of hard work: it takes both effort and creativity to keep your body in trim, your mind active, and your feelings moving, and it is sometimes difficult to persevere when there are no clear routes and no guarantees. However, if you are willing to look at and experiment with your choices, you can discover the pleasure of your own inimitable and vital style. When you are enjoyably productive you can give from the heart, and the more you give from the heart, the more energy you can feel within. This vital energy cannot be depressed by any outward circumstance.

# Useful addresses

## EMERGENCIES

**Samaritans**
39 Walbrook
London EC4
01 283 3400/626 9000
*(offers advice to anyone in
distress)*

*For local branches see the tele-
phone directory, either on the
emergency numbers page inside
the front cover or in the
alphabetical listings.*

## GENERAL

**Fellowship of Depressives
Anonymous**
36 Chestnut Avenue
Beverley
Humberside HU17 9QU
*(provides access to a network of
local branches)*

## THERAPIES

*The following organizations
should supply information
about particular therapies and
approaches. Some may also
provide a guarantee of a standard of training, but none can
offer any guarantee as to the
quality and suitability of the
people who practise under their
aegis. If you decide a therapy
might be suitable for you, then
the organization listed may
help you get in touch with relevant practitioners. You
should then interview your
potential practitioner and decide for yourself on his or her
personal ability and integrity.*

**Association for
Humanistic Psychology
in Britain**
62 Southwark Bridge Road
London SE1 0AU
01 928 8254
*(provides a list of therapists,
and information)*

**British Association of Art
Therapists**
13c Northwood Road
London N6 5LT
*(provides an annual register of
qualified members and publishes information)*

**British Association of
Psychotherapists**
121 Hendon Lane
London N3 3PR
01 346 1741
*(provides training in
psychotherapy and has a register of trained and approved
psychotherapists)*

**British Psychoanalytical
Society**
63 New Cavendish Street
London W1
01 580 4952
*(runs training courses for
therapists)*

**Holwell Centre for
Psychodrama**
East Down
Shirwell
Nr. Barnstaple
Devon EX31 4NZ
027182 597
*(the centre runs training
courses and provides
treatment)*

**Human Potential
Research Project**
Adult Education Department
University of Surrey
Guildford
Surrey
0483 571281
*(organizes courses and work-
shops for those interested in exploring their potential for
development)*

**In Search of Gold**
17 Wigmore Street
London W1H 9LA
*(provides psychotherapy for
those with loss of sparkle looking for a better quality of life)*

**Institute of Group Analysis**
1 Daleham Gardens
Swiss cottage
London NW3 5BY
01 435 7696
*(runs training courses and
workshops)*

**Institute of Transactional
Analysis**
BM Box 4104
London WC1 3XX
01 405 0463
*(runs training courses and
workshops)*

**National Register of
Hypnotherapists and
Psychotherapists**
National College of Hypnot-
ists and Psychotherapists
25 Market Square
Nelson
Lancs
0282 699378
*(offers training and keeps a reg-
ister of practitioners)*

## GENERAL HEALTH

### Health Education Council
78 New Oxford Street
London WC1A 1AH
01 637 1881
*(publishes information)*

### Scottish Health Education Group
Woodburn House
Canaan Lane
Edinburgh EG10 4SG
031 447 8044
*(publishes information leaflets)*

### Age Concern
Bernard Sunley House
60 Pitcairn Road
Mitcham, Surrey
01 640 5431
*(national centre for 950 independent groups serving the needs of elderly people)*

## COMPLEMENTARY MEDICINE

### British Acupuncture Association and Register
34 Alderney Street
London SW1 4EV
01 834 1012
*(publishes information and a list of practitioner members)*

### British Holistic Medical Association
179 Gloucester Place
London NW1
01 262 5299
*(publishes information)*

### British Wheel of Yoga
General Secretary
Grafton Grange
Grafton
York YO5 9QQ
090 12 3386
*(provides a list of all qualified yoga teachers in the UK)*

### Clare Maxwell-Hudson
87 Dartmouth Road
London NW2 4ER
01 450 6494
*(for information on massage courses)*

### General Council and Register of Osteopaths
21 Suffolk Street
London SW1 4HG
01 839 2060
*(provides a list of qualified practitioners)*

### Institute for Complementary Medicine
21 Portland Place
London W1N 3AS
01 636 9543
*(publishes information)*

### Transcendental Meditation Centre
Mentmore Towers
Leighton Buzzard
Beds LU7 0QH
0296 661881
*(publishes information)*

## CHILDBIRTH

### National Childbirth Trust
9 Queensborough Terrace
London W2
01 221 3833
*(provides ante-natal classes, counselling and support)*

## RELATIONSHIP AND FAMILY PROBLEMS

### National Marriage Guidance Council
Herbert Gray College
Little Church Street
Rugby, Warwicks
(0788) 73241
*(for access to a network of local counselling and advice centres)*

## ALCOHOLISM

### Alcoholics Anonymous
11 Redcliffe Gardens
London SW10 9BQ
01 352 9779
*(offers advice and support to alcoholics)*

### Al-Anon
61 Great Dover Street
London SE1
01 403 0888
*(offers advice and support to the families of alcoholics)*

## DRUG ADDICTION

### Narcotics Anonymous
PO Box 246
London SW10
01 351 6794
*(for advice, information and counselling on drug addiction)*

## KEEPING-FIT

### Sports Council (England)
16 Upper Woburn Place
London WC1H 0QP
01 388 1277

### Scottish Sports Council
1 St. Colme Street
Edinburgh
031 225 8411

### Sports Council for Wales
National Sports Centre
Sophia Gardens
Cardiff CF1 9SW
0222 397571

*(Sports Councils have lists of sports centres in England, Wales and Scotland and publish brochures about courses)*

# Index

# Acknowledgments

**Author's acknowledgments**
Thank you to Christine Halpin, Jenny Pulsford and Debbie Richardson who typed the manuscript. I am grateful to the staff at Dorling Kindersley who made this book possible and who worked very hard to create the book in this form.

Thank you to Kathryn for her positive criticism in my early, and later, draughts and for her loving support during some challenging times.

Nothing I have written is wholly new and I am indebted to many diverse influences: to clients who have taught me to understand and to friends, authors and colleagues whose ideas I have used or been inspired by. Thank you to Dr. Charles Vank, Caroline Tanner, Dr. Andy French, Philip Portal and Jody Jakob for suggestions and comments, and thank you to Mark Scott and Frank van Lerven for ideas and support. Richard Bach, Joan Grant and E. A. Jensen have all written books which I have found positive and useful. I am indebted to A. T. Beck and M. Hamilton who created the Beck Depression Inventory and the Hamilton Rating Scale from which I have drawn material freely for my "Are you depressed?" questionnaire.

Thank you, especially, to Nadine Scott who is an outstanding example to me of living life to the full and who inspired me with a discriminating belief in my own, and others', resources.

**Dorling Kindersley** would like to thank: Sue Wason for editorial help; Diana Burns for proof-reading; and Richard and Hilary Bird for the index.

**Illustrators**
Line and Line, and John Woodcock

**Sources**
☐ p.11 Graph adapted from C. A. H. Watts, Depressive Disorders In The Community (John Wright, 1966)
☐ p.35 Nasrudin anecdote: from Idries Shah, The Exploits Of The Incomparable Mulla Nasrudin (Octagon Press, 1983)
☐ p.60 and p.106 Graphs adapted from Katharina Dalton, Depression After Childbirth (Oxford University Press, 1980)
☐ p.84 Obedience study: from Stanley Milgram, Behavioural Study Of Obedience (Journal Of Abnormal And Social Psychology, volume 4, 1963)
☐ p.159 Case history 1: first appeared in the British Journal Of Psychiatry (volume 148, January 1986)

**Typesetting**
SX Composing Ltd
Airedale Graphics

**Reproduction**
Reprocolor Llovet Barcelona SA